INTEGRATED PEASANT ECONOMY IN CENTRAL AND EASTERN EUROPE

RURAL HISTORY IN EUROPE

VOLUME 18

Integrated Peasant Economy in Central and Eastern Europe

A Comparative Approach

Edited by

ALEKSANDER PANJEK

BREPOLS

THE SERIES RURAL HISTORY IN EUROPE

The countryside forms a complex and evolving universe. Clearly, it exhibits both inertia and ruptures, but it would be an illusion to contrast a contemporary rural world in rapid transformation with a traditional rural world of frozen landscapes, petrified societies, immobile economies and lethargic political contexts. Even if rural societies have been overthrown, rural landscapes have been profoundly transformed and the intervention of the State has considerably strengthened the regulation of production and trade, history must of necessity be considered as the main explanatory factor for our time.

The rural world can also only be fully understood if it is viewed in a manner which transcends national boundaries and if the discrepancies which can best be observed by adopting a broad view are taken into account. The aim must be to create a dialogue between researchers which goes beyond national frontiers, crosses chronological barriers and breaks disciplinary boundaries.

The main objective of the 'Rural History in Europe' collection is thus to provide keys to unlock the changes experienced by present-day European rural societies in the light of their historical experience. It will produce the necessary historical knowledge to make it possible for all to conceptualise the future of European country-dwellers as they face problems of the kind historians have always grappled with in examining societies of the past. How can the changes taking place in present-day Europe be understood without taking into account a past which is still very present, and which determines both structures and behaviour?

The volumes will be published after a peer-review process for each paper, supported by the editorial board, the authors and the editors of each book. In order to ask the relevant questions about the future of the peasantries and rural spaces in transformation, the volumes of this collection will deal with the longue durée and will present either research in progress or a synthesis on a regional or national scale. The outcome of this procedure will be a series giving a detailed overview of historical developments in Europe as a whole.

This publication is a result of the project 'Concepts of peasant economy: a theoretical and empirical comparative approach (15th-20th c.)' financed by ARIS – Slovenian Research and Innovation Agency (J6-1799).

We are grateful to Susan Deborah Cook who revised and harmonized the English language of the chapters.

Cover illustration: Cesta [Road] (1923), painting by Veno Pilon (1896-1970). Oil on canvas. Collection of the Pilonova galerija Ajdovščina – The Pilon Gallery, n. 210/S. Photo: Primož Brecelj.

D/2024/0095/284
ISBN 978-2-503-59004-2
eISBN 978-2-503-59005-9
DOI 10.1484/M.RURHE-EB.5.120623
ISSN 2032-6084
eISSN 2566-0063

Printed in the EU on acid-free paper.

Contents

List of Illustrations

Aleksander Panjek

Piotr Guzowski and Radosław Poniat

Josef Grulich

Ines Beguš & Aleksander Panjek

Miloš Ivanović

Philippe Gelez

Volodymyr Kulikov

Lev Centrih and Polona Sitar

ALEKSANDER PANJEK

1. Results of a Comparative Approach

This book addresses two relevant themes in European rural history: How to grasp and understand the peasant economy in its diverse variations through space and time on the one hand, and on the other, how to tackle the underrepresentation of the eastern part of the continent as well as its simplified picture in international scholarly literature. In doing so, its goal is to test the applicability of the 'integrated peasant economy' model by adopting its inherent research method, based on a comparative approach through regional case studies. The integrated peasant economy is a rather recent concept, first developed on the empirical evidence of the peasant economy in the southern Alpine area (Slovenia and Italy) and then successfully tested on Slovenia, the Italian Alps and Scandinavia (Panjek-Larsson-Mocarelli, 2017), as well as more extensively on Slovenia from the late Middle Ages to the twentieth century (Panjek-Lazarević, 2018), along with other regional examples at several conference panels and project workshops. In recent years, many colleagues have contributed to the development of the integrated peasant economy concept with their support, discussion, criticism, and empirical confirmation. In this collection of case studies, six actual countries of central and eastern Europe have been observed: Poland, the Czech Republic, Slovenia, Bosnia and Herzegovina, Serbia and Ukraine.[1] Among them Poland, and lately Bohemia as well, are undoubtedly the ones that are better represented in western historical literature.

This volume represents a result of the project *Concepts of peasant economy: a theoretical and empirical comparative approach (15th-20th c.)*, financed by the Slovenian Research and Innovation Agency. It represents the outcome of a project workshop and of a panel at the Rural History conference in Uppsala in 2022. Two of the project's objectives are tackled

1 I wish to thank Aleksej Kalc, Žarko Lazarević, Luca Mocarelli, Jesper Larsson, Mats Morell (†), Alessio Fornasin, Renato Sansa, Paolo Tedeschi, Satoshi Murayama, Anne-Lise Head-König, Sandro Guzzi-Heeb, and all the contributors to the first books, as well as to the present one.

Integrated Peasant Economy in Central and Eastern Europe, ed. by Aleksander Panjek, Rural History in Europe, 18 (Turnhout: Brepols, 2024), pp. 11–28
BREPOLS PUBLISHERS 10.1484/M.RURHE-EB.5.142462

in this volume. The first is to deepen the comparison between the integrated peasant economy and other concepts in order to obtain a better theoretical refinement. The second is to expand the empirical comparative approach with case studies from regions and periods which previously have not been included, in particular central, south-eastern and eastern Europe, as well as socialist Slovenia. In south-eastern Europe the *zadruga* family model was identified as a particular challenge, as was the socialist system.[2] Comparability is enhanced and made easier by an integrated peasant economy checklist that serves as a comparative tool.

The integrated peasant economy may be defined as a holistic approach to the peasant economy. In this sense it somewhat echoes Chayanov's approach, but its focal points more directly descend from and combine elements of concepts such as proto-industry, pluri-activity, and (economic) agency. The engagement of peasants in non-agrarian sectors and off-farm activities is one of the most prominent features in the history of the European countryside. Until not long ago and still partly nowadays, the prevailing thesis seems to be the social and economic passivity of the peasant, which emphasizes the survival tendency, while at the same time listing a multitude of activities outside the narrow scope of farm management. Such contradiction can be overcome by a new paradigm that considers the peasant economy as a comprehensive system of agrarian and non-agrarian, on- and off-farm activities, combined based on the available resources, technology, and knowledge. This renewed perspective reveals a system, defined as the integrated peasant economy, which comprises activities pertaining to all three economic sectors (primary, secondary, tertiary) as equivalent components of the whole. The integrated peasant economy questions the prevailing assumption that peasants strove exclusively for survival and discloses how they demonstrate agency and the capacity to pursue a better standard of living and the ability to enhance the productivity of their work and time, as well as raise the carrying capacity of the environment they live in and, not least, to actively contribute to growth and development. This does not exclude the occurrence of misery and want, nor the existence of hindrances posed by the social and institutional framework in which peasants acted. The integrated peasant economy is not rosy – bread mostly remained pretty hard. Another rooted trait in international historiography is the tendency to perceive the East-Central and Eastern European peasants' social and economic status as fundamentally different and opposed to the Western one; the latter is seen as enjoying a significantly larger degree of freedom and a wider range of possibilities to enact his agency and choice-making ability. Thus, by testing the

---

2 As results of the project, two books are already published, namely on the whole of Slovenia between the sixteenth and eighteenth centuries (Panjek, 2023) and a monograph on socialist Slovenia (Centrih and Sitar, 2022).

applicability of the integrated peasant economy model to our case-study regions, we also question the assumption that Central and Eastern rural Europe were 'different'.

Before that, there is a path that has to be traversed, one that leads through theories and interpretations of income integration within the peasant economy in historical research. This is the topic of the second chapter. It goes without saying that it is not possible to mention every theory in agrarian and rural history, anthropology and sociology. Proto-industry, pluri-activity, Coppola's Alpine integrated economy, Chayanov's peasant family economy, de Vries' industriousness, and mountain peasant's migration-linked economy are addressed. Attention is then devoted to the supposed fundamental discrepancy of second-serfdom-shaped Eastern Europe and to the degrees of agency recognized to peasants in different parts of Europe by historical research. In fact, a wide range of historical evidence testifies that income integration was very widespread throughout Europe. It represented an integral part of the peasant economy, as the second chapter as well as the single contributions to this volume confirm. The final part of the second chapter presents an updated explanation and definition of the integrated peasant economy both as a concept and as a phenomenon.

Among the central and eastern Europeans, Polish economic historians were the ones that, during the socialist period, probably kept the most intense scientific contacts with their western colleagues, as is testified by the fact that authors such as Kula and Topolski may undoubtedly be listed among the big names in early modern European economic and rural history. Widely known themes in Polish economic history are the 'second serfdom' and the specialization in cereals, which were largely exported westwards. Without entering into the debate on the extent of the 'second serfdom' and the interpretation of increased cereal production, Piotr Guzowski and Radosław Poniat choose an ingenuous approach to overcome the lack of information due to the fact that the prevailing literature and knowledge regard the agrarian aspects of Polish rural economic history. In order to tackle the question of whether peasant income integration practices were present in a seemingly unsuitable socioeconomic environment – if we rely on the still prevailing picture about early modern Poland – they use a book in manorial economics written by a Polish nobleman as well as tax records, both from the sixteenth century. The first source is narrative and written based on a micro level experience, corresponding to the manors owned by its author, but intended to treat issues of general interest. The second source is at a macro level and is characterized by some of the typical shortcomings of the fiscal sources, such as the reliability of data based on taxpayer declarations. Nevertheless, it can be used at least as a proxy for the identification and quantification of peasant off-farm activities. In fact, the taxes under scrutiny were based on land possession and on professional profiles. In both cases Guyowski and Poniat conclude that the Polish noble elite in the sixteenth century considered cultivation as the basis of the peasant economy, but at the same time were well aware of the fact that the combination of on-farm with off-farm activities was widespread, that the latter belonged to the primary, secondary, and tertiary sector and were quite diversified, as well as that there was a variable, but far from irrelevant, share of villagers who possessed very little or no land and lived on income integration. Based on their results, Guzowski and Poniat were able to detect a fairly wide range of activities in their integrated peasant economy checklist for Poland in the sixteenth century (see table 1 below and chapter 3).

The Bohemian or Czech lands are known as one of the core areas of European 'proto-industry' as well as of modern industrialization, a trait that stands out even more within the narrower frame of central and eastern Europe. At the same time, evidence from its economic and social history contributed to undermine the assumption that the entrepreneurial-led putting-out system was not compatible with the feudal 'second serfdom' system. In fact, German-speaking historiography proposed the term *Wirtschaftsherrschaft* to define the intertwining between late feudal mechanisms and entrepreneurial initiatives by manorial landlords in northern Austrian and Bohemian lands. Besides pushing in the direction of 'second serfdom', they established manufactures based on their subjects' work. This is the reality that Josef Grulich outlines as a context to his original insight into a region which does not belong to known Czech 'proto-industrial' areas, namely South Bohemia. By relying on the 1654 'Berni rula' tax cadaster and on the early eighteenth century 'Theresian tax cadaster', he shows how peasant income integration practices were present also in this region, among both the land-poor strata of the rural population and the more well-off ones. On the one hand, Grulich identifies poor environmental conditions for agriculture in hilly areas and the single-heir inheritance system as factors creating a segment of the population who had to look for their living without reliable agricultural incomes. On the other hand, he argues that the involvement of rural people of different social strata in non-agricultural activities was not merely the result of social, economic, demographic, or environmental compulsions, but rather the result of their choice. Even those working in their landlords' manufactures and putting-out networks were not forced to be employed there. The variety of activity profiles that Grulich detects in South Bohemia is quite wide. He identifies the mid-seventeenth century as the time when the phenomenon of income integration practices spread in Bohemia in the form of cottage industries, the putting-out system, and tertiary sector activities. One might wonder whether this chronology depends on existing research and analysed sources or if the well-known early seventeenth century economic and demographic catastrophe in the land represents a milestone in this field, as well. However, based on his results, Grulich detects a wide range of activities in the integrated peasant economy checklist concerning Southern Bohemia between the mid-sixteenth and the mid-eighteenth centuries (see table 1 below and chapter 4).

Although their research mostly took place away from the eyes of international historiography, already in the past century Slovenian historians realized that the early modern peasants' engagement in non-agrarian activities was an extremely widespread phenomenon and dedicated perhaps more attention to this aspect of the countryside than to agrarian history proper. A large part of the research concentrated on the outstanding diffusion of phenomena that were put under the large umbrella of 'peasant trade', which included commercial and transport activities, overshadowing the engagement in cottage, domestic, and putting-out forms of industry. This is the environment where the concept of the integrated peasant economy was first developed. Based on a wide range of historical literature and adding the results of recent research, Ines Beguš and Aleksander Panjek present the peasant economy and in particular the income integration practices in early modern central and western Slovenia in two steps. The first part of their chapter is dedicated to presenting the conceptual tools and the quantifications of non-agricultural peasant activities in older Slovenian historiography, then focusing on the process of farm fragmentation and on the diffusion of manorial dues payed in money, which are used as proxy indicators of the extent to which the peasant population engaged in market-related activities in different parts of the region. The second part of the chapter consists in an overview of the great variety of ways in which peasants in Slovenia combined on-farm self-sustenance agriculture with off-farm activities and more generally with involvement in the market. In doing this, Beguš and Panjek distinguish between three environmental and agrarian situations, namely the Alpine area, the karstic highlands, and Lower Carniola. The resulting picture shows that peasant income integration was present everywhere, that peasants ingenuously used local opportunities (natural assets, climatic conditions, transport routes, etc.), as well as extra-regional demand to their own advantage, that engagement in the market was present in all social strata of peasant society (well-off peasants, smallholders, cottagers, lodgers) and that, far from being a mere makeshift in the survival struggle, it was clearly an act of voluntary agency to improve their standard of living. This is reflected in the integrated peasant economy checklist, where nearly all the listed activities in the primary, secondary, and tertiary sectors are recorded in central and western Slovenia between the sixteenth and the eighteenth century (see table 1 below and chapter 5).

Research attempting to detect, qualify and even more so, quantify, multiprofessionality and income integration in a feudally organized medieval countryside, may resemble pursuing elusive shadows, because the great majority of sources stem from landlords and rulers, and are primarily preoccupied with the control of agricultural production or with legally fixing social and economic relations. For this reason, most of the information to our theme may be gained only indirectly, although this is at least partially true also for the early modern period. Miloš Ivanović tackles this task by combining pieces of information from different kinds of sources into a compelling overall picture on late medieval Serbia. He uses the charters of subsequent Serbian rulers to extract their instructions regarding feudal dues, in particular in the case of single monasteries. This allows him to present the social structure and stratification of the rural population, characterized by the coexistence of quite numerous different social statuses with specific economic and professional profiles. In addition, he includes interpretations and examples from scholarly literature, which mainly consist in small segments on our theme of interest. To round up the image, Ivanović relies on information from the Adriatic city of Dubrovnik (Ragusa) and from the early Ottoman era, just after they conquered the region. After presenting the economic activities of the different strata of the peasant population, which allows the presence of marketing practices to be traced, he assesses the impact that the development of urban centres had on the peasant economy, primarily by offering the opportunity to sell their produce, and of employment in nearby mines. Peasant commercial activity may be detected also at village fairs. There are two rather peculiar aspects highlighted by Ivanović. One is the special social status of the Vlachs, which, besides animal husbandry, also allowed them to engage in transport and trade as far as the Adriatic coast, with cases in which individuals founded commercial enterprises with city merchants. The second is the significant role played by military activity as a source of peasant income, from employment as soldiers to banditry and looting. In conclusion, although 'trade was a secondary activity for the peasants in the Balkans', as he states, his integrated peasant economy checklist for late medieval Serbia reflects a reality in which market-related activities, although generally of minor relevance at the level of most household budgets, are fairly well represented (see table 1 below and chapter 6).

In the proposal of the project *Concepts of peasant economy*, we identified the large autarkic family form known as *zadruga* as one of the challenges to the integrated peasant economy that we aimed to face. It is fortunate that Philippe Gelez agreed to tackle it. But as his chapter reveals, the challenges he faced were more numerous and trickier than the *zadruga*. That is because in the historical literature on Bosnia and Herzegovina there are many works on agriculture, but those mentioning peasant income integration are sporadic, while the archival sources of the Ottoman period are silent about our topic of interest, not least due to the fact that the taxation system was based on agricultural produce. Moreover, in the whole addressed period from the sixteenth to the nineteenth century the economy of the region was 'entirely dominated by agriculture and pastoralism', as he writes. In order to cope with these problems, Gelez adopted a research path that starts from the macro level and gradually moves to focusing on more micro levels. First, he reconstructs the trajectories and commodities in foreign trade, then he moves to internal trade and then to the taxation system. In all cases, agricultural and livestock produce largely prevail. In the next step he distinguishes among areas, concluding that in the eastern and northern parts of Bosnia the traces of peasant marketing activities are very scarce, while in the karstic areas of western Bosnia and of Herzegovina income integration practices are present, even in the form of temporary and seasonal migration. Very interestingly, Gelez puts forward the interpretation that it was not the Bosnian *zadruga* family (which contrary to the myth was not very large) but the village that was autarkic. The branch that was most market oriented and mostly contributed to income integration was animal husbandry, in particular transhumant, connected to the port towns on the Adriatic coast of Dalmatia, which was in the hands of the Vlachs. But it may well be simplistic and the information we have is not sufficient for any firm conclusion. In any case, the resulting picture is that of a region where the integrated peasant economy, as a phenomenon and as a concept, seems to be only partially detectable and applicable, which is reflected in the lowest score in the checklist among all the case studies in this book (see table 1 below and chapter 7).

The next chapter takes us into a different dimension, because it relies on the enviably rich and detailed data contained in the statistical surveys of imperial Russia between the last decades of the nineteenth and the first of the twentieth centuries. The available empirical information and scholarly tradition allow Volodymyr Kulikov to formulate difficult questions and reach complex answers through original analyses and interpretations. At the centre of his attention is peasant agency, and he begins by presenting some microeconomic theories on peasant decision-making. Coherently with his stance that context matters, Kulikov continues with an interesting and colourful presentation, which also relies on narrative sources, of how the labour market functioned, with particular attention to seasonal and temporary employments. Among the peasants, misinformation about job opportunities prevailed; in the labour market there was high uncertainty and weak regulation. The central part of the chapter is dedicated to the analysis of a fairly large number of peasant household budgets in three southwestern areas of the Russian empire in the decades between the late nineteenth and early twentieth centuries, coinciding with present-day eastern Ukraine. In his analysis of the budgets, Kulikov distinguishes households by categories of wealth based on the quantity of their agricultural land. Off-farm work was very common in all categories, although with important differences between the wealthy and the poor as far as, among others, the type of jobs, the wages and the degree of choice are concerned. Kulikov also offers an interesting insight into the implementation of aspirations by girls and boys, which did not necessarily take place in such an idyllic manner as described, for example, by de Vries. At least three important points are made in this chapter. In evaluating peasant agency concerning off-farm employments, it is on the one hand necessary to also consider single family members and the possibility of conflicting aspirations, meaning that the peasant household should not be understood as a granitic whole, while on the other hand non-negligible differences in the logic, scope of choice and, consequently, economic agency between poor and wealthy households must be taken into account, since the wealthy could choose rather freely, while the range of choice of the poor was narrowed by need. The third is that cultural values also count, and not only strictly economic considerations. As far as the range of income integration activities detected in the Ukrainian provinces of late imperial Russia is concerned, it is among the highest scored among our case studies (see table 1 below and chapter 8).

A common trait between the last chapter and the previous one lies in the very good data on off-farm activities and incomes it can rely upon. In their case study, Lev Centrih and Polona Sitar tackle another specific challenge to the integrated peasant economy that was pointed out in the research project from which this book stems. Let us put it straightforwardly: was it feasible for peasants to enact income integration, which entails market involvement, in a system that in principle negated the market economy and in practice constrained its functioning? Their approach to this theme is interdisciplinary and rather original. They use existing Slovenian and international historiography and present scholarly discussions and interpretations regarding socialist agricultural policies and the social and economic reality of farming households. They use contemporary economic and sociological studies in Slovenia as a source, too, along with census data. Last but not least, they rely on a series of original interviews with men and women belonging to two generations who lived through the period of socialist economic and agricultural policies in Slovenia. The chapter offers an overview on the Yugoslavian and Slovenian socialist political and legislative attitude towards farmers and agriculture in general. On the one side, the attitude was influenced by the state's industrialization policy and on the other by an agricultural policy that underwent rapid transformations, progressively shifting from coercion to liberalization. As census and research figures reveal, the final effect was that private farms and integration with off-farm employments, mostly in the quickly developing industries, prevailed in socialist Slovenia. It is therefore far from incidental that at the time, a series of appellatives was coined to define this amphibious household economy: 'semi-proletarian', 'part-time farmer', 'worker-peasant', or 'peasant-worker'. Lev Centrih and Polona Sitar reconstruct a reality in which most of the farming households engaged in off-farm activities, the major part of their income derived from off-farm employments, and the living standard was highest in the households that engaged in them. Last but not least, it was mostly men who got employed in off-farm jobs, leaving room for women to gain a relevant role in the management of the farm, even getting to drive tractors, for example. All of this is clearly reflected by the fact that nearly all of the activities in the peasant income integration checklist were detected in socialist Slovenia (see table 1 below and chapter 9).

The integrated peasant economy comparative checklist consists in a scheme including the activities, grouped in wider sets, that brought a differentiation and increase in income, in relation to agricultural production for self-consumption. The initial list was constructed by summing up the activities referred to by Coppola (1991) in the southern Alps and by de Vries in western Europe (2008, 71-121, 169). The activities are grouped by economic sector (primary, secondary, and tertiary), in order to highlight the presence of work in different sectors, which is at the base of the term 'integrated economy'. The checklist gives a graphic and immediately visible picture of the presence of income integration practices, therefore allowing for an easy and apparent comparison between different places and regions, as well as between different periods in the same area. The first version of the checklist was applied to preindustrial western Slovenia and showed how a vast majority of different activities registered in the Southern Alps and in Western Europe was present. This means that their diversity, diffusion, and density were very high. Since then, some areas of activity have been added to the checklist, based on evidence from different case studies, with which the applicability of the integrated peasant economy concept was successfully tested on Italy, Scandinavia, and Japan. This is the case of works of trust and fishery (Morell, 2017; Westin et al., 2017; Päiviö, 2017; Murayama et al., 2017), and tourism (Kavrečič, 2017). The new applicability test on central and eastern Europe, carried out in this volume, suggested adding military service (see Grulich on Bohemia, chapter 4), warfare and looting (see Ivanović on Serbia, chapter 6), along with organized forms of banditry, as activities pertaining to the integrated peasant economy. Credit was also added (see chapter 2). The scholars who authored the chapters in this volume were given the previous version of the checklist and were invited to test it and upgrade it, if necessary.

The comparative checklist reveals the presence of a wide variety of activities involving increases and differentiations of incomes from production, labour, and services directed to and originating from the market, in regions of central and eastern Europe with different social and institutional systems throughout the long time span from the late Middle Ages to the second half of the twentieth century. The fields that show the most generalized diffusion are: specialization and intensification of cultivation, quarries, and fishing in the primary sector; the transformation of primary goods, rural crafts, and migrant handicraft in the secondary sector; and transport, trading with own goods, and trade-related services in the tertiary sector. Our case studies do not show any clear difference, neither between regions in the north and south or in the east and west, nor between earlier and later centuries. Slovenia stands out as the region with the highest diversity of income integration activities both in the early modern and in the socialist periods, while most of the other regions reveal a fairly similar density, apart from Bosnia and Herzegovina. If we exclude the latter from the comparison for a moment, a slight quantitative difference appears between earlier cases, such as late medieval Serbia and sixteenth century Poland, and later ones, namely south Bohemia in the sixteenth and eighteenth centuries and the south-western Russian empire in the late nineteenth and early twentieth centuries.

It is, however, necessary to make some clarifications. This comparison includes cases dating back to different historical periods and of different duration, while the opportunities to engage in market activities may vary with changes in the general economic climate. In fact, the integrated peasant economy can experience fluctuations and reorientations. Secondly, the results of this comparative study do not only depend on the factual diffusion of market-related and off-farm employments, but also on the different degree to which historical research has addressed income integration by the peasant population in single countries. This can have a non-negligible impact on the overall image of a given region in the comparative checklist.

In this regard, it is worth highlighting the case of Bosnia and Herzegovina (chapter 7) in particular. Although some of the typical conditions that favour combining on- and off-farm activities are met, such as the presence of extensive hilly areas and of trade routes between the inland of the Balkans and the Adriatic Sea in particular, the relative scarcity of income integration calls for an interpretation. One of the explanations might be sought in the peculiar societal organization in the Balkans, as is apparent both from the late medieval Serbian and the early modern Bosnian case. Some of the most profitable activities, potentially generating non-strictly agrarian income, such as animal husbandry through sale, transport and trade, were *de jure* or *de facto* mostly in the hands of the Vlachs (a name that could designate an ethnic group, a social-professional group, or both at the same time, Mirdita 2009). This system of labour division based on the social status left ordinary peasants deprived of some marketing opportunities. It goes without saying that this is only a preliminary hypothesis, since literature on the topic appears rather scarce and more targeted research would be necessary to reach steadier conclusions.

As a whole, the chapters in this volume demonstrate that the integrated peasant economy approach is applicable to the regions of central and eastern Europe and several authors explicitly confirm this, too. They confirm that peasant income integration was a widespread phenomenon and testify to the fact that economic agency was not only possible, but largely enacted in the countryside of this part of Europe like in the western part of the continent. Finally, they show how landless and landed villagers and everyone in between would engage in combining on- with off-farm and market-related activities, signalling that their motives went beyond sheer need, want, and survival, and were the expression of choices deriving from the desire and will to improve their living standard. Along with previous examples (Panjek, Larsson and Mocarelli 2017), the case studies in this volume reveal how the integrated peasant economy was capable of arising in very different economic systems, such as (late) manorialism, early and industrial capitalism and even socialism. This widespread form of peasant economy was not simply a response to exogenous influence and coercion, either economic, institutional or deriving from livelihood needs, but was itself capable of conditioning the functioning of the economic systems in which it operated, as well as to use and create, within those systems, opportunities to its own advantage. It turns out that the peasant economy and society was a historical actor well worth considering.

Table 1. Integrated peasant economy in Central and Eastern Europe compared

Activity	Chapter 3 Poland 16th c.	Chapter 4 South Bohemia – Czechia (Habsburg) 17th-18th c.	Chapter 5 C.-W. Slovenia (Habsburg) 16th-18th c.	Chapter 6 Serbia 13th-15th c.	Chapter 7 Bosnia & Herzeg. (Ottoman)* 15th - 19th c.	Chapter 8 East Ukraine (Russia)* 19th-20th c.	Chapter 9 Slovenia (socialist Yugoslavia) 20th c.	Total (out of 7)
Primary sector								
Agricultural specialization	x	x	x	x	x	x	x	7
Intensification of cultivation (no fallow, mixed-cropping, etc.)		x	x	x		x	x	6
Wage day-labour in agriculture and longer-term farmhands on larger farms	x	x	x			x	x	5
Extension/ intensification of animal husbandry	x	x	x	x	x	x	x	7

Activity	Chapter 3 Poland 16th c.	Chapter 4 South Bohemia – Czechia (Habsburg) 17th-18th c.	Chapter 5 C.-W. Slovenia (Habsburg) 16th-18th c.	Chapter 6 Serbia 13th-15th c.	Chapter 7 Bosnia & Herzeg. (Ottoman)* 15th - 19th c.	Chapter 8 East Ukraine (Russia)* 19th-20th c.	Chapter 9 Slovenia (socialist Yugoslavia) 20th c.	Total (out of 7)
Intensification of forest exploitation (through primary sector activities, but also secondary and tertiary)	x	x	x	x			x	5
Extension of cultivated land (reclamation of commons and woods)		x	x			x	x	4
Quarries	x	x	x		x	x	x	6
Fishing	x	x	x	x		x	x	6
Secondary sector								
Transformation of primary	x	x	x	x	x	x	x	7

Activity	Chapter 3 Poland 16th c.	Chapter 4 South Bohemia – Czechia (Habsburg) 17th-18th c.	Chapter 5 C.-W. Slovenia (Habsburg) 16th-18th c.	Chapter 6 Serbia 13th-15th c.	Chapter 7 Bosnia & Herzeg. (Ottoman)* 15th - 19th c.	Chapter 8 East Ukraine (Russia)* 19th-20th c.	Chapter 9 Slovenia (socialist Yugoslavia) 20th c.	Total (out of 7)
resources/ products (e.g. wine, cheese, meat products; charcoal, lime)								
Rural crafts	x	x	x	x		x	x	6
Domestic, putting-out system (proto-industry)	x	x	x	x		x		5
Work in 'centralized' industries and plants (manufactures, mining, etc.)		x	x	x		x	x	5

Activity	Chapter 3 Poland 16th c.	Chapter 4 South Bohemia – Czechia (Habsburg) 17th-18th c.	Chapter 5 C.-W. Slovenia (Habsburg) 16th-18th c.	Chapter 6 Serbia 13th-15th c.	Chapter 7 Bosnia & Herzeg. (Ottoman)* 15th - 19th c.	Chapter 8 East Ukraine (Russia)* 19th-20th c.	Chapter 9 Slovenia (socialist Yugoslavia) 20th c.	Total (out of 7)
Migrant/mobile craftsmen (e.g. bricklayers)	x	x		x	x	x	x	6
Wage labour in the industrial sector			x			x	x	3
Tertiary sector								
Services in the field of long and medium distance trade (draft animal lease, fodder, lodging and food – inns, etc.)	x	x	x	x		x	x	6
Transport of other people's products	x	x	x	x	x	x	x	7

Activity	Chapter 3 Poland 16th c.	Chapter 4 South Bohemia – Czechia (Habsburg) 17th-18th c.	Chapter 5 C.-W. Slovenia (Habsburg) 16th-18th c.	Chapter 6 Serbia 13th-15th c.	Chapter 7 Bosnia & Herzeg. (Ottoman)* 15th - 19th c.	Chapter 8 East Ukraine (Russia)* 19th-20th c.	Chapter 9 Slovenia (socialist Yugoslavia) 20th c.	Total (out of 7)
and goods over short to medium distances								
Trading with own products and goods over short to medium distances	x	x	x	x	x	x	x	7
Peddling		x	x	x			x	4
Smuggling	x		x		x		x	4
Migrant/mobile workers (dock-workers, etc.)	x		x		x	x	x	5
Works of trust (offices in local institutions, estimation of			x				x	2

Activity	Chapter 3 Poland 16th c.	Chapter 4 South Bohemia – Czechia (Habsburg) 17th-18th c.	Chapter 5 C.-W. Slovenia (Habsburg) 16th-18th c.	Chapter 6 Serbia 13th-15th c.	Chapter 7 Bosnia & Herzeg. (Ottoman)* 15th - 19th c.	Chapter 8 East Ukraine (Russia)* 19th-20th c.	Chapter 9 Slovenia (socialist Yugoslavia) 20th c.	Total (out of 7)
land, testimonies, etc.)								
Tourism			x				x	2
Military service, warfare, looting, banditism		x		x				**
Credit (access to loans and leases, money-lending on interest)								**
Total (out of 22)	15	17	21	15	9	17	21	

*Evidences for Bosnia and Ukraine have been simplified to a yes/no level here; for more detailed descriptions see the tables in the respective chapters.

**Military service etc. and credit were added after the single chapters were finished, so most of the authors were not invited to express judgements about them. For this reason, they are also not included in the calculation.

Bibliography

Centrih, L., and Sitar, P. (2022). *Pol kmet, pol proletarec. Integrirana kmečka ekonomija v socialistični Sloveniji, 1945-1991*, Koper.

Coppola, G. (1991), 'Equilibri economici e trasformazioni nell'area alpina in età moderna: scarsità di risorse ed economia integrata', Coppola, G. and Schiera, P. (eds), *Lo spazio alpino: area di civiltà, regione cerniera*, Napoli-Pisa, pp. 203-222.

Kavrečič, P. (2017), 'Tourism as a Source of Non-Agricultural Rural Income: The Case of The Karst (16th–19th Centuries)', Panjek, A., Larsson, J. and Mocarelli L. (eds), *Integrated Peasant Economy in a Comparative Perspective: Alps, Scandinavia and Beyond*, Koper, pp. 259-281.

Mirdita, Z. (2009), *Vlasi: starobalkanski narod (od povijesne pojave do danas)*, Zagreb.

Morell, M. (2017), 'Pluriactivity, Proto-industrialisation or Integrated Peasant Economy? Scandinavia in the 18th-20th Centuries', Panjek, A., Larsson, J. and Mocarelli L. (eds), *Integrated Peasant Economy in a Comparative Perspective: Alps, Scandinavia and Beyond*, Koper, pp. 395-414.

Murayama, S., Nakamura, H., Higashi, N., Aoki, T. (2017), 'Disaster Management and Integrated Economy in Early Modern Japan Amakusa in the 19th Century', Panjek, A., Larsson, J. and Mocarelli L. (eds), *Integrated Peasant Economy in a Comparative Perspective: Alps, Scandinavia and Beyond*, Koper, pp. 283-308.

Päiviö, E. L. (2017), 'Livelihood Diversification in Early Modern Sami Households in Northern Sweden', Panjek, A., Larsson, J. and Mocarelli L. (eds), *Integrated Peasant Economy in a Comparative Perspective: Alps, Scandinavia and Beyond*, Koper, pp. 137-159.

Panjek, A. ed. (2023), *Integrirana kmečka ekonomija. Koncept in dejstva.* Založba Univerze na Primorskem, Koper.

———, and Lazarević, Ž. eds (2018), *Preživetje in podjetnost. Integrirana kmečka ekonomija na Slovenskem od srednjega veka do danes*, Koper.

———, Larsson J. and Mocarelli L. eds (2017), *Integrated Peasant Economy in a Comparative Perspective: Alps, Scandinavia and Beyond*, Koper.

Vries, J. De (2008), *The industrious revolution: consumer behavior and the household economy, 1650 to the present*, New York.

Westin, A., Isacson, M., and Lennartsson, T. (2017), 'Land and Labour as Resources of an Integrated Peasant Economy in a Swedish Mining District During the 1860s Great Famine', Panjek, A., Larsson, J. and Mocarelli L. (eds), *Integrated Peasant Economy in a Comparative Perspective: Alps, Scandinavia and Beyond*, Koper, pp. 309-332.

ALEKSANDER PANJEK

2. Concepts of Income Integration and the Integrated Peasant Economy

Western and Eastern Europe Reconsidered

I. Peasant income integration in historical research

I.1. Proto-Industry: The peasant will never be the same again

The concept that brought pan-European attention to non-agricultural activities among the peasantry, setting in motion a large wave of historical research, was Mendels' 'proto-industry' (1972). His original model defined proto-industry both in economic and social-demographic terms. Peasants would partly engage in production in the secondary sector, forming a pattern of diffused small-scale producers working in their homes, connected into a network by merchant-entrepreneurs who managed the working capital, collection, and marketing of the products (putting-out system). Besides this basic form of production organization, from the economic point of view there were two characterizing assumptions: the production was export-oriented and the system represented the phase leading to the modern industrialization process. From a social point of view, the key assumption was that the actors of proto-industry were poor peasant families who more effectively used labour-free time caused by seasonal fluctuations in agriculture to engage in industrial work. Some areas specialized in (proto)industrial production, and therefore developed a demand for food, giving other areas the opportunity to specialize in 'commercial agriculture'. A relevant trait of the proto-industry concept from its very beginning was its presence 'in many regions of Europe'. Mendels mentioned the Northern Low Countries as well as Saxony, Lusatia, and Northern Bohemia in the sixteenth and seventeenth centuries (Mendels, 1972: 241, 248). Proto-industry was widespread and stimulated specialization.

In the Flemish countryside, where Mendels detected a proto-industrial development, 'linen industry was only a by-occupation', a 'subsidiary income for an essentially agricultural population' (Mendels, 1975: 203). Peasants who engaged in it 'in most cases [...] were at the bottom of the social scale and remained there. They were those who had not enough land

Integrated Peasant Economy in Central and Eastern Europe, ed. by Aleksander Panjek, Rural History in Europe, 18 (Turnhout: Brepols, 2024), pp. 29–66
BREPOLS PUBLISHERS 10.1484/M.RURHE-EB.5.142463

to make out a living for their family after rent and taxes were deducted from gross output' (Mendels, 1972: 242-243).

Truth be told, he pointed to the fact that proto-industry was not the first instance of 'rural industry'. Rural industry is 'the activity of households engaged in both industry and agriculture, partly for the market, partly for home consumption'. It was present in many regions between the sixteenth-eighteenth centuries and 'profoundly transformed the relationships between people and the land, even in traditional "pre-industrial" Europe', since land was no longer necessary for a living (Mendels, 1972: 247, 250, 258). Proto-industry differed from such 'part-time industry' because it tended to specialization at the level of households and geographic areas, became more labour-intensive, produced for an external market and was connected with merchant-entrepreneurs.

Another important distinguishing character in Mendels' view was represented by the demography of proto-industry. The relation was twofold. Proto-industry allowed peasants to 'multiply' their numbers without an increase of arable land. At the same time, in some areas its diffusion was also a 'response to population growth'. For this reason, 'there was a mutual and continuing interaction between industrial and demographic growth' and in proto-industrial regions population growth was 'the most rapid'. Increasing numbers of proto-industrial peasants meant that this development path did not lead to 'sustained increases in the standard of living'. As he concluded his essay on Flanders, its role 'was therefore perverse in the sense that it perpetuated the dismal pressures that had first induced its penetration into the countryside' (Mendels, 1975: 203, 252).

Soon thereafter, Kriedte, Medick, and Schlumbohm published their own version of the concept (1977, in English 1981). Their work evolved proto-industry into a more abstracted model, that among other things strongly relied on the peasant family economy borrowed from Chayanov. Kriedte stressed how the viability of a proto-industrial activation by peasants was determined not only by the intensity and length of agricultural work in different agrarian systems, but on the property relations upon the land, too. In his view, small and poor peasant owners were the primary candidates for proto-industrial work, while in the east-of-Elbe German and Slavic Europe the free time and energies of peasants were consumed by landlords in the form of coerced labour within the 'second serfdom' system, unless converted into a money payment. In the latter case, proto-industry was possible. In the view of Kriedte, Medick, and Schlumbohm, proto-industrialization represents not the first, as in Mendels, but the second phase of the transition to modern industrialization, the first being a loosening of feudal pressure (which would not have occurred in the East). It was a form of rural development in which the peasant population lived (largely, completely) on industrial production for external markets organized in two (chronologically subsequent) ways: earlier in the form of the *Kaufsystem* (domestic system), in which the means of production belong to the producers and marketing is in the hands of merchants, and later in the *Verlagssystem* (putting-out system). In their view, proto-industry was most likely to be found in mountain regions deprived of favourable conditions for agriculture (Kriedte-Medick-Schlumbohm, 1981).

In a decade, proto-industry conquered Europe. Numerous researches were carried out, re-reading historical realities, verifying the presence of proto-industry throughout the continent, as well as testing its prediction that it represented the main road to modern industrialization. Besides the widespread enthusiasm, proto-industry also encountered some early criticism. Pollard declared that the concept 'fails to deal with what ought to be one of the most fundamental aims of enquiry: the way in which some of the regions affected were able to convert into full industrialization, while others de-industrialized' (Pollard, 1981: 76). Coleman (1983) argued that proto-industry was 'a concept too many', showing how it did not fit the characters in the first European country to experience modern industrialization: England. Poni pointed to cases in which proto-industrial regions did not develop into modern industrial areas, and advanced the idea that proto-industry should include centralized manufactures and 'urban proto-industry'. He even asked whether rural proto-industry was, in fact, merely 'a reformulation of the concept of the "Verlag system"' (Poni, 1983 and 1985). In the early eighties, many if, not most, of the basic features of proto-industry were the subject of criticism: its role in preparing modern industrialization, the fact that it neglected other forms of industrial production, that it was not applicable in most of Europe outside the north-west, and its demographic dimension. 'Not all proto-industrial regions had greater population density, faster demographic growth, lower ages of marriage, higher fertility rates, larger households or a breakdown in the family and gender division of labour.' On the contrary, all of this could also be found in areas, and at times, of intensifying and expanding agricultural production (Ogilvie-Cerman, 1996: 8-9).

The criticisms based on contrary empirical evidence did not bring proto-industry to a dead end. By the end of the seventies, proto-industry 'had proliferated into a family of different theories, which adopted rather different definitions' (Ogilvie-Cerman 1996: 5). As suggested by Isaacson and Magnusson, an important turn in determining the long life of 'proto-industrialisation' against all odds, may be the realization that the development of modern industry did not necessarily occur through 'big spurts', but was based on small-scale units of production, and continued throughout the nineteenth century. Proto-industry could be adapted to fit this new picture of development. It was not necessary anymore to confront the results of proto-industrial forms of production with the appearance of centralized plants and at the same time it was possible to extend their duration throughout the industrialization process. But to do so, most of the theoretical rigidities of Mendel's model had to be abandoned, and the concept had to become more flexible (Isaacson-Magnusson, 1987: 2-17).

Along with the differing theorizations, through this acquired flexibility the concept of proto-industry got a life of its own, progressively discarding many of its theoretical features as unnecessary constraints. It was no longer necessary for proto-industry to lead to modern industrialization, to be based on export-oriented production, to be rooted in nuclear families with early marriages and numerous offspring, to be a form of dispersed production, and not even to be located in rural areas. In the end, proto-industry seems to have become a synonym for pre-industrial forms of industry *tout-court*. On the other hand, a more "orthodox" reading keeps considering proto-industry as a term to be used for the dispersed forms of industrial production in rural areas, possibly coordinated by a merchant-employer and export-oriented.

Yet, considering the topic of this book, it makes sense to stress at least three positive aspects. Firstly, the wide scholarly literature on proto-industry across Europe has collected substantial evidence testifying that peasant income integration through activities pertaining to the secondary sector was a widespread phenomenon over the continent in pre-industrial times as well as during industrialization.

Secondly, with the introduction of the proto-industry concept the relations between agriculture and industry would (and should) never be the same again, as signalled by Poni: while earlier historians considered agriculture as having a subordinate role to industrialization (allowing capital 'draining', foodstuffs, cheap labour force, and a market for industrial products), the proto-industrial model uncovered a 'countryside and agrarian regions producing industrial goods for the world market'. It is a novel 'epistemological change', in which rural areas and agriculture are no longer an 'external' sector to industrial development (Poni, 1983: 8). In his 'balance sheet' Schlumbohm also identified this as one of its main aims – 'to introduce into economic and social history a new approach' (Schlumbohm, 1996: 12-13).

Thirdly, it is relevant that Mendels included in the proto-industrial model the combination of peasant work and income from industrial activities with that from self-production and wage work in agriculture. In doing so, he established a systemic connection between the agricultural and industrial dimensions of the peasant economy, which turns out to be a system composed of different activities and labour forms pertaining to the primary and secondary sector. Moreover, he recognised that 'rural industries' freed the peasants from dependence on the available arable land and were widespread in Europe, even if they did not fit into his proto-industrial theory.

Still, proto-industry is not the most useful conceptual tool to disentangle the peasant economy, since it focuses on one economic sector, the secondary. In spite of possible semblance, its interest in the peasantry was indeed instrumental. Even if a myriad of peasants throughout Europe were its working force, proto-industry was named after industry, while its two organizational variants were named after the buyer (*Kaufsystem*) and the supplier (*Verlagssystem*), that is, the merchant and entrepreneur.

I.2. Pluri-activity: Peasants between sickles and hammers

The promoters of a new concept, 'pluri-activity', criticized proto-industry precisely because it does not encompass all of the peasant economy. Pluri-activity originated in France at a conference in 1981 (Hubscher, 1988: 9, 16). The starting point of the participating economic historians, sociologists, and anthropologists was, interestingly and meaningfully, the acknowledgment that pluri-activity was a phenomenon present in 'contemporary' farms and at the same time 'deeply anchored' in history (Pingaud, 1981: 113). As Hubscher put it, 'largely inscribed in the rural space, pluri-activity is a permanent and structural fact in the French countryside' (1988: 8).

Hubscher contributed greatly to elaborating the definition of pluri-activity. The concept was programmatically born wider than proto-industry, with a polemic note to older rural historians: 'Work at home, in the workshop or in the factory, the household head alternating between the agricultural sector and the secondary or tertiary sectors, family helpers exercising a valuable auxiliary activity [...]. Nevertheless, pluri-activity has not constituted a specific field of study for historians'. Pluri-activity posed itself from the beginning as an alternative approach to proto-industry, concentrating on rural society and economy instead of industrial and development history. For Hubscher it was necessary to go beyond occupations in industry and to enlarge the interpretation in three directions:

1. in space: including local rural industries but also long-distance and often multi-month migrations;
2. in sectors: given the tertiary activities in which peasant families engaged;
3. in time: since pluri-activity exceeds the chronological limits of proto-industry.

The fundamental characters of Hubscher's understanding of pluri-activity may be synthetized as follows:

1. pluri-activity investigates the integration of the 'rural world' into industrial society;
2. pluri-activity offers the peasant room for manoeuvre between agricultural and non-agricultural income sources;
3. proto-industry is one of the possible forms of pluri-activity;

4 the agricultural component must be studied in detail to understand the modes of combination with the second, non-agrarian activity;
5 pluri-activity proves plasticity, flexibility, and the ability to adapt to different situations, which explain its maintenance over centuries;
6 pluri-activity does not have a preordained outcome in terms of resilience of the peasant economy and society *vis-a-vis* change (Hubscher, 1988: 9-11).

Hubsher and the French school considered that pluri-activity existed only in the case where the first occupation was in agriculture and it was combined with another activity in the industrial or tertiary sector. Work in agriculture was excluded, whether carried out on-farm, even when the activity was market-oriented, or off-farm, even when exercised 'out of the region' (Rinaudo, 1987: 284; Garrier-Goujon-Rinaudo, 1988: 233-234). Pluri-activity therefore existed only beyond agriculture. In this sense it was even more rigid than Mendels, who considered wage work in agriculture as a common ingredient of the proto-industrial peasant household's economy.

Pluri-activity is understood as the way peasants 'adapt to or resist the encompassing society' (Hubscher, 1988: 10). French scholars studied pluri-activity as a means of the peasants' adaptation and involvement in industrialization and modernization processes. In the proposed periodization, the 'first phase' begins in 1850 (Garrier-Goujon-Rinaudo, 1988: 235).

Rinaudo and colleagues distinguished between an open and closed version. 'Closed pluri-activity' designated the combining of activities and professions within the single village, aimed at covering the community's life-necessities and contributing to its 'collective autarchy'. 'Open pluri-activity' was projected outside the village and commercially oriented, it was 'extroverted' and had an 'openly commercial vocation', participating 'fully in a market economy' and involving cash payments. At the level of activities, it required some specialization and was 'linked to forms of proto-industrialisation', evolving through time and modernizing 'if necessary' (Garrier-Goujon-Rinaudo, 1988: 234; Rinaudo, 1987: 284). What interested was the opening-up that pluri-activity brought by exposing the peasant economy to the market, to 'national if not international economic impulses which the countless peasant weavers, metallurgists or miners cannot escape' (Hubscher, 1988: 9). But still, peasants 'cannot escape' – their position vis-à-vis market influences is perceived as a rather passive one, inducing adaptation at best, while the idea persists that in modern times a 'closed' and 'autarchic' village economy could have existed.

Another important question was the social and economic goals of the pluri-active peasant. Besides 'penury or subsistence pluri-activity', there were other possible destinations of the capital earned through pluri-activity, which pointed in the direction of social mobility (Hubscher, 1988: 9). This opinion resisted further research tests in France. A decade later

Mayaud stressed that 'peasant pluri-activity is not only a pluri-activity out of necessity'. From the point of view of 'the poorest wanting to rise, the recourse to pluri-activity appears a possible, if not a necessary route to the maintenance and improvement of the small peasant farms' (Mayaud, 1999: 233-235).

A theoretical debate arose between French and Italian scholars. Italian historians, besides a convinced acceptance of pluri-activity, expressed criticism towards the rigidity of the French interpretation, preferring a more "inclusive" approach. There was also a basic difference between the two. While the French concentrated on the industrialization period (nineteenth and twentieth centuries) and were interested in the role played by peasant pluri-activity in the inclusion of rural society in modernization processes, Italians stretched the discourse back to preindustrial times, mostly the eighteenth century. The perspectives and questions on the Italian side were wider than just 'peasants facing industrialization', although they agreed in overcoming the proto-industrial approach. Research on pluri-activity had a wider viewpoint, beyond industrialization; its goal was 'understanding the ways of survival and the opportunities of inclusion of the agrarian family units facing social change' (Cafagna, 1989: 79).

Cafagna pointed out how the 'rigorous' French definition of pluri-activity as 'a second, necessarily extra-agricultural activity' was unable to include the 'multi-professionality or the precariousness of labour' in rural Italy. Peasant 'integration choices' included primary sector activities, for example those related to silk production. To exclude them would be 'pedantic' (Cafagna, 1989: 80-81). Federico stressed that 'the family's working power is in principle undividable based on the kind of occupation. That's why – contrary to the definition of pluri-activity by Hubscher – it includes agricultural work (both from pure wage and from owned capital)' (Federico, 1989: 90). Italian historians considered employment in the agricultural sector (mostly seasonal), along with wine or oil manufacturing and silk- related activities, as part of the concept, as was the case in reality. The inclusion of primary sector activities remained a characteristic of Italian-school pluri-activity. Its main considerations in upgrading the French concept may be synthetized as follows:

1 Work outside the farm is not necessarily an activity for idle times of agriculture, but may become more remunerative than agriculture itself.
2 Pluri-activity includes agricultural work (both on-farm and off-own-farm wage-work).
3 Pluri-activity is not caused by exceeding manpower on the farm, but depends on the choices, the tactics, of the family; appropriate changes are possible to adjust labour demand and offer. The persistence of a long-term disproportion is therefore the result of economic choices determined by market conditions and the availability of alternative employment opportunities (Federico, 1989: 90-91).

Besides the notable basic divergences, there was a large common ground. An important feature recognized by both schools is that pluri-activity should not be seen only as a defensive survival strategy. The 'subjective aims, the inspirative strategies' of pluri-activity may be twofold: 'defensive necessities' (granting survival or living standard) or 'aspirations of change/improvement'. In fact, the peasant decision to combine income sources may well take place in a 'strategic perspective of acquiring property [...], a pluri-activity choice for "independence", as Hubscher would say' (Cafagna, 1989: 79, 81). Pluri-activity gives the peasants recognition of their ability to aspire to a better living standard and larger income, as well as to actively pursue this goal by enlarging the spectra of income sources. This is an important conceptual move.

The pluri-activity approach disclosed many examples of peasants combining agricultural and non-agricultural income sources. Less than a decade after its launch, Mayaud could state that in France between the late nineteenth and twentieth centuries, pluri-activity was a 'way of life' and 'structurally linked to the peasant farm'. Practised in idle times or within forms of labour division in the families, it was 'extremely flexible and adaptable in both the short and the long term'. In France, 'the list of examples of pluri-activity, in the last century' had no limits and did not 'spare any rural area' (Mayaud, 1999: 233-237).

Three traits most characterize the approach in pluri-activity research: great attention is given to the agricultural system and to the kind of activities in which peasants were involved, while the third is the issue of development-related change. The type of cultivations and their demands in terms of work intensity and seasonality, the form of land ownership, the dimension of holdings and the environmental conditions are considered when analysing how the combining of agricultural and non-agricultural work is possible and what are its features. Mirrored in this is the attention dedicated to the specific characteristics of various market-related activities in terms of the necessary raw materials, technology, technics and skills, products, forms of production and organization of labour, as well as the market and demand. Consequently, attention is paid to specific combinations between the agrarian system and the integrative activities, determined by circumstances at the local level (a province, a valley). Uniting the two focuses leads to the identification of 'typologies', that is patterns of integration between agricultural and non-agricultural activities. This way, dual combinations emerge: the peasant-weaver, peasant-miner, peasant-quarryman, peasant-pedlar, peasant-seasonal migrant, peasant-watchmaker, peasant-metallurgical worker, etc. The third common element is the diachronic perspective, through which the influencing factors, variables, and challenges are addressed. These are often exogenous (institutional and land reforms, development or stagnation, industrialization and competitors, shifts in the demand and in labour markets). Pluri-activity research understands the peasant economy mostly as an open economy, in which change is frequently a response to exogenous factors.

Although the scholars who originally theorized pluri-activity stressed how it was a structural character of the rural economy and society in the long run, research focused on the modern period because of the prevailing interest in the mechanisms of "change" and development. Besides a better understanding of the processes in the countryside at the turn of the eighteenth and nineteenth centuries in particular, this focus succeeded in demonstrating how peasant income integration practices reach deep into the twentieth century. By concentrating on the phenomenological aspects of combining activities in specific rural areas, research on pluri-activity has yielded a rich array of examples of peasant income integration, further demonstrating that it was a diffuse reality.

I.3. The Alpine integrated economy: Coppola's step towards a system

Despite the solid, though disputed, theoretical foundations with detailed definitions, pluri-activity was not developed into a model, since its focus is more on the varied local phenomenology of income integration practices. It is probably no coincidence that a first move towards the detection of a "system" of peasant income integration has been made through a holistic perspective that looked within a rural society such as the Alpine one, where local economies were characterized by a high degree of non-agricultural market-oriented activities. Adopting this perspective enabled Coppola to see that peasant income integration practices in the Italian Alps were more than a variegated phenomenology of combinations, but rather different expressions of something more comprehensive. In a theoretical article based on empirical examples he used the term 'integrated economy', referring to the income integration practices and strategies enacted by peasants (Coppola, 1991).

In a nutshell, Coppola named the 'overall characteristics of the early modern Alpine economy' as an 'integrated economy'. Characterized by the 'scarcity of resources', such economy was also able to keep the 'economic equilibrium' when facing 'transformations', even enacting them when confronted with change. His basic premise is that, due to the environmental conditions and type of agriculture, 'at a macro level, related to the total number of the population', the Alpine area suffered from a 'chronic alimentary deficit, especially of grain'. If such a 'system stands', that is, if the population increases, if there is no massive definitive emigration, if peasant proletarianization is not detected in significant measure, and the economy 'appears perhaps poor but not miserable', Coppola suggests, 'it means that the income integrations from other activities and sectors are of much greater importance than the cultivation of the fields alone' (Coppola,

1991: 203, 213-214). That is, in the Alpine and Subalpine peasant economy, agriculture is not the main, nor even necessarily the basic, activity.

In such an economy, income integration acquires 'primary support functions, granting the solidity of the context'. There is an 'organic complementarity' between production sectors and a 'complex balance' between single activities. The intensity of the presence of single activities may vary in space and time. The existing resources are cautiously safeguarded and systematically integrated. When one or more parts composing the system become 'fragile and weakened', reactions and countermeasures are enacted in the form of 'processes of substitution'. As a result, the Alpine integrated economy is 'a system able to ensure proportionate processes of income formation' and to make 'adjustments to the changes in market conditions' (Coppola, 1991: 221-222).

The attention to transformation and the flexibility of income source combination are a clear influence of the pluri-activity approach. But in this case, we have a 'system'. An important stress in Coppola is that the Alpine integrated economy could maintain a higher level of population than would have been possible with the local grain production, doing so by keeping a balance between many different income sources. Such balance was flexible enough to adjust to changes in market conditions and in the ratio between population and income sources. Activities could be adopted or abandoned, increased or decreased; their share in the peasant household's income structure could consequently change over time. In any case, 'the income integrations from other activities and sectors' maintained a fundamental role in the system.

II. Peasant economy between subsistence and consumption

II.1. An early holistic approach to the peasant economy: Chayanov was not Chayanovian

Chayanov is the author of an early economic theorization on peasant economy, developed in the 1920s, but gaining international attention only in the 1960s. He worked on the rich Russian statistical data from the second half of the nineteenth and early decades of the twentieth century. His approach is mainly that of an agrarian economist and was particularly influential in rural sociology (Ploeg, 2013) and economic anthropology (Sahlins, 1972). Kriedte, too, largely based his explanation of the proto-industrial family on Chayanov's family economy. Interpretations soon suffered from simplification and misunderstandings (Tannenbaum, 1984; Shanin, 1986). An extreme synthesis of the simplified reception of Chayanov's model could sound as follows: the aim of the peasant family economy is not profit or well-being, but reproduction, both in physical terms and of its means of production. To this end, the peasant family does not use wage labour but only the work of its family members, it lives on self-consumption, is autarkic and avoids the market and working beyond the necessities of survival. But Chayanov himself explicitly stated: 'In view of the numerous misunderstandings that largely obscure the essence of the matter, we ought to stress with particular insistence that by the product of peasant labour, peasant farm income, and so on we always understand the joint income of the peasant family both from agriculture and from crafts and trades' (Chayanov, 1986b: 70).

In order to understand the misunderstanding, it is useful to consider that part of Chayanov's work is theoretical while the other part is based on empirical data, and the theoretical part is somehow brought to its logical extreme consequences, including some exaggeration (Shanin 1986). From a historian's point of view, this distinction applies to his theorizing the 'natural farm': as Chayanov warned, the absence of the market is a pure theoretical assumption (Chayanov, 1986a: 11).

In his view, the internal logic and structure of this theoretical 'natural farm' are 'the same as those of farms with commodity exchange', with two main differences. Firstly is the absence of the economic 'factor of market location', secondly, a 'less important, yet essential, social factor is the traditional standard of living, laid down by custom and habit, which determines the extent of consumption claims, and, thus, the exertion of labor power'. He considered that 'natural farms' were a form of 'family economy' found, for example, in the 'feudal system'. This must be understood as a mere 'theoretical analysis' (Chayanov, 1986a: 12, 17, 25). At best it is a hypothesis, not based on historical evidence – yet it represents the most influential part of Chayanov's work, which was taken for granted and labelled as 'Chayanov's peasant economy'.

Chayanov's work and interpretations based on empirical evidence are more relevant. In late nineteenth and early twentieth century Russia, the prevailing 'peasant family labour farm' conducted a 'commodity economy' with connections to the market of varying intensity (Chayanov, 1986a: 17-25). Chayanov's insistence in denying the possibility of using capitalistic concepts (e.g. 'profit') to explain the peasant family farm economy which does not employ wage labourers, does not imply that in such a system the aspiration for better well-being was absent.

Often historians mention how Chayanov's peasants avoided "drudgery" to underline the fact that traditional peasants would not work more than the minimum necessary, but his argumentation is more complex. Chayanov stated that the peasant family economy is based on a 'peculiar equilibrium between family demand satisfaction and the drudgery of labor itself'. In his view, based on empirical evidence from late nineteenth and early twentieth century Russia, peasants worked longer and harder when the family's 'standard of living' was 'threatened by increasing demand', that is, when there was an increased number of family members unable to work. Although 'the volume of the family's activity depends entirely on the number of consumers', such exclusive influence of consumption demand only takes place when other factors stay the same. When the conditions offered 'the opportunity to increase their output considerably', and the workers/consumers ratio remained unchanged, this immediately 'brought about an increase in family and consumer well-being'. Chayanov's peasants did not avoid the chance to make a better living. If the peasant increases his productivity, he 'satisfies his family's demands more completely with less expenditure of labor'. Peasant families may even buy expensive land and borrow money at high interest rates if such investment 'promises to achieve' an 'increase in prosperity' through improved labour productivity or expanded cultivated area (Chayanov, 1986a: 8, 10). The 'colossal stimulus to accumulation and to acquisition [...] characteristic of the majority of the European peasantry, sometimes overcoming consumer demands', was found also 'in many strata of the Russian peasantry'. Perhaps the best synthesis is the following: 'The family labor farm has to make use of the market situation and natural conditions in a way that enables it to provide an internal equilibrium for the family, together with the highest possible standard of well-being' (Chayanov, 1986a: 7; 1986b: 76-81, 89).

What Chayanov says is that the peasant family's agency is not unlimited and infinite. When the family sees that the obtainable improvements in living standard do not justify longer and harder working, it relents, meaning the balance between the drudgery of labour and satisfaction of consumption needs is met. In the other direction, Chayanov's peasants were ready to work longer and harder as well as to pay high interest on loans to ensure an acceptable living standard and even improve it, but only up to the point when the "drudgery" no longer paid off, since it is itself an element that lowers well-being. So, on the one hand, 'the harder the labor is, compared with its pay, the lower the level of well-being at which the peasant family ceases to work', while on the other, 'the annual intensity of labor declines under the influence of better pay' (Chayanov, 1986b: 80-81).

Peasants directed their improved consumption possibilities towards goods such as 'clothing and other items in the personal budget'. The diversity and luxury of consumption depended not 'only on increased incomes', but 'also on an expansion of the demands themselves due to the elements of higher urban culture that penetrate into the countryside'. The level of consumption also grows in relation to the budget structure, as a consequence of 'an increase in the extent to which the farm is money based, and having crafts and trades' (Chayanov, 1986b: 128-131). Income integration through market-related activities in the secondary and tertiary sectors represent a path to new desires and better well-being. All this means that consumption standards were neither fixed nor set at the level of survival. The latter was only the case 'in those areas and periods' when the low productivity of peasant labour granted incomes that barely met 'the physiological minimum for existence'. But in the case of improvement in labour productivity and market opportunities, 'the satisfaction of demands moves away from the physiological minimum' (Chayanov, 1986b: 105).

After making it clear that the drudgery/consumption balance did not mean a lack of interest nor an anthropological inability to aim for a better living standard and accumulation, it is pertinent to stress that it also did not mean peasants would not work much. While avoiding unnecessary drudgery, peasants remained on the far side of lazy. Adding eight hours of sleep at night to the data on use of time in the Vologda area, it is possible to calculate the average number and length of working days. There was only one day off a week and one more festivity every two weeks. Consequently, the average working week lasted five and a half days and nearly forty-eight hours (Chayanov, 1989b: p. 74).

Chayanov has a complex, though coherently holistic approach to the peasant economy, in which the on-farm and off-farm activities, as well as the marketing of produce, are inalienable components of the whole. The unit he observes is the family farm. The result of the family's year's work is 'an amount of produce which, after being exchanged on the market, forms the gross product' of the economic unit. In Chayanov the 'peasant farm income' is always 'the joint income [...] both from agriculture and from crafts and trades'. But he made a further conceptual step, stating that they form an intertwined system: 'Because the family's agricultural undertaking and crafts and trades activity are connected by a single system of the basic equilibrium of economic factors, they cannot be reviewed independently of one another'. Incomes from agriculture, crafts and trades give the 'single family labour income', together representing 'the elements of this system' (Chayanov, 1986a: 5; 1986b: 70, 90, 102-103).

Chayanov's late nineteenth and early twentieth century Russian peasant families lived, organized their farm, worked, and consumed in close connection to the market situation. In doing so, they combined self-consumption with commodity agriculture and integrated it with off-farm activities. Not least, they made decisions about all of this, taking into consideration the environmental and economic conditions, varying market opportunities and changes in size and composition of the family during its life cycle. They were willing and able to increase their well-being and consumption levels, and even to accumulate. Nowadays we would say they displayed economic agency, and perhaps even industriousness, but surely income integration.

II.2. Industrious peasants of north-western Europe

The 'industrious revolution' concept (de Vries 2008) has some relevant features in common with proto-industry, since both spring from the Dutch-speaking area of north-western Europe, partly seek origins of industrialization in rural areas and in doing so include the peasantry in the wider economic dynamics, lean on the European marriage pattern and, last but not least, tackle the question of development. The concept of 'industriousness' has developed through the decades. Yet, from the very beginning de Vries' central question was: 'What role did the peasant as a consumer play in European economic development?' (de Vries, 1975: 205).

In earlier works, de Vries directly addressed the rural economy and peasantry in Dutch development during the sixteenth and seventeenth centuries, elaborating the differences between types of peasant household economies in early modern Europe (1974; 1975). Originally, he outlined three:

1 'The self-sufficient household' in his words 'requires no explanation'. Yet notably, he stressed that 'non-agricultural production plays a very important role in such a household', hence, 'the peasant cannot be understood simply in the role of cultivator'.
2 'The self-sufficient household with marketed surplus' is also 'a basically self-contained production and consumption system'. Such a household 'enters the market' only 'to gain the means to pay taxes' and 'some monetary rents' along with 'the purchase of small amounts of such goods as salt'.
3 In the 'market-dependent peasant household [...] goods previously produced at home are now purchased; services provided for oneself are provided by specialists'. Typically, it specializes in 'food production at the expense of handicrafts and domestic maintenance activities'. This 'entails a complete reallocation of labor time [...] and a complete alteration in the demand pattern of the household' (de Vries, 1975: 206-207).

It is possible to understand that the 'self-sufficient household with marketed surplus' was widespread in Europe, since de Vries states that 'many peasant-based economies have developed regions of specialized production and interregional trade on the basis of such a marginal market involvement'. The problem is that although such 'surplus' goods may have been very important for governing classes, most of the produce did not enter the market and the large majority of peasants remained 'isolated from the market as consumers' (de Vries, 1975: 207-208). In this peasant economy model, holdings are tendentially self-sufficient. Population growth reaches or even surpasses the limits set by agricultural productivity and causes progressive fragmentation of the holdings that leads to growing differences in wealth among peasants. In such circumstances, the peasantry cannot improve their low living standard and the rural economy cannot support development.

What changes with the 'market-dependent peasant household' is that it reduces the time dedicated to non-agricultural activities aimed at self-sufficiency (food, fuel, clothing) and to producing working tools, as well as 'by-employments' in handicraft production, a necessary additional income for 'marginal farmers'. Working-time is redirected to specialized agricultural production for the market. Consequently, a large part of consumption needs is met by acquiring goods and services on the market; 'consumption habits' change because the 'new goods' that the market can offer lead to new desires. This specialization model is, in de Vries' view, the one that evolved in the rural areas of northern Netherlands. Here, peasants ('farmers') responded to demographic growth by specializing in better paid commodity production (dairy farming and industrial crops) for the urban and export markets. Peasants are no longer compelled to produce grains, because they are imported. On the other hand, they no longer engage in the production of non-agricultural goods, which is left to urban centres as well as to an increasing industrial sector within the rural population itself. Because of the incomes from the sale of commodities and of specialization, peasants become an important market for urban and rural industrial products, stimulating demand.

Later on, when presenting his new 'industrious revolution' concept, de Vries' reasoning became more inclusive, both geographically and socially. The 'combination of changes' in household behaviour that constituted the 'industrious revolution' of the mid-seventeenth-early nineteenth centuries, may be traced 'in England, but in fact through much of North-western Europe and Colonial America' where many households 'made decisions' that increased the demand and supply of commodities and labour on the market. On the social scale, these changes may be now seen not only in peasant households specializing in food production for the market, but also in cottagers' households where unused time is directed to proto-industrial work, as well as in the fact that women's and child labour is increasingly market-oriented and that work becomes in general more intensive. Another upgrading is 'the reduction of leisure time' (de Vries, 1994: 255, 257).

The theory was then further upgraded by including the urban population, adding more ways in which households became connected with the market: agricultural specialization, 'proto-industrial' production, wage labour, and commercial services. Moreover, families that engage, for example, in 'proto-industrial' work do not do so out of want, but as a deliberate choice (de Vries, 2008: 82, 92-106). For the rest, this latest version of the industrious revolution remains faithful to itself. The thesis is that between the mid-seventeenth and the mid-nineteenth centuries, households in north-western Europe (England, Low countries, parts of France and Germany) displayed a new pattern in their economic choices and activities by increasing the quantity of labour performed. This is achieved by activating a larger number of family members (women, youth) in working tasks for longer periods of time, which is possible because time dedicated to leisure is diminished. The goal of such increased efforts is to gain more income with which to reach a better living standard through a higher level of consumption. Consumption itself changes, because new and innovative types of objects are desired (clothing, personal objects, home decoration, furniture). Households tend to specialize in some activity and to sell their products and services on the market, consequently becoming a source of increasing demand for a larger range of goods they no longer produce themselves. This mechanism enacts a virtuous circle in which the increasing demand stimulates a growing offer on the market. The eastern and southern parts of Europe do not participate in such developments.

The industrious household is characterized by the nuclear family based on the European marriage pattern (EMP), with a later age at marriage and greater role of women than in the 'traditional paternalistic' family. The economy of such a household includes decisions about production and consumption. The EMP enables a smaller, more autonomous and flexible family, able to dynamically react to market challenges and opportunities, to more fully realize the consumption desires of its members. Last but not least, such a household is an active agent in history and in particular was the actor of the 'industrious revolution' in north-western Europe.

The industrious revolution encountered criticism, too. Béaur, for example, recently remarked how it is 'rather disconcerting to discover that there was nothing specifically Dutch [...] about this wave of change. The [...] remarkable increase in levels of consumption and the widening range of objects in peasant interiors is universally present' in France and Spain, as well. What makes the difference and enables peasants to evolve their consumption patterns is the existence of 'economic opportunities', which 'depended on contingences; they cropped up in particular periods and in places scattered across the map. When the time grew ripe, a whirlwind of exchanges, work and consumption spread out from them across Western Europe, reaching perhaps even the extreme limits of the entire continent' (Béaur 2017: XI, XVI–XVII). Further on we will encounter other critics of the north-western exceptionality.

In the end, although rural households play a decisive role within the industriousness theory, the same observation that the pioneers of pluriactivity made regarding proto-industry may be made: in industriousness as well, rural households are given attention only instrumentally. In this case, the motive of interest is functional to their contribution to the development path theorized by the industriousness concept. The objective is not to understand how they functioned, but rather to identify the foundations of the 'first modern economy' and for this reason industriousness needs to be an exclusive trait of north-western Europe.

III. Movement of the people: from push and pull to migration as an asset

The immobile peasant, rooted in the village where he was born, lived, and died, his world limited to the sphere of his parish at most, is not yet entirely extinct in historical literature. This common understanding fails to acknowledge the progress made in migration history in the last half century. Indeed, in earlier migration research the 'pre-industrial society was considered sedentary due to its dependence on land and entrapment in feudal structures', while 'migration was understood as a typical trait of modern society, linked to industrialization' and the parallel changes in society and the economy. More recent migration studies 'revealed that pre-modern society was far more mobile' and demonstrated that migrations at that time were a 'continuous phenomenon structurally built into everyday social, economic, and cultural organizational frames and dynamics' (Kalc, 2024: 25-26).

Most of the earliest studies in European migration history started to appear during the sixties and seventies, with an explosion of scholarly interest between the mid-eighties and early nineties of the twentieth century. Important drivers of the research on migration were the urbanization during industrialization and overseas migration. From its beginning, it was concerned with themes connected to labour and the search for better opportunities in richer or more urbanized areas. All of this is also mostly true for an early work such as Lucassen's, in which the wealthy and developed North Sea area is the region that attracts masses of people coming from poor rural areas in search of subsistence through additional income in seasonal work. The phenomenon is interesting to our theme since it reveals how income integration was also possible through mobility and that it was a widespread phenomenon in North-Western Europe from the seventeenth to the nineteenth century. On the other hand, supplementing household income is seen as an expedient of the poor. Again we meet the presumption of north-western European exclusivism, in the form that labour mobility was only possible in Western Europe and not east of the Elbe River, where serfdom prevailed. In other parts of western Europe, where opportunities in domestic industry and in seasonal farm work were still available, migration would not have been as important (Lucassen, 1987).

This (north-)western presumption is present in another milestone work in migration studies, that of Moch. In this case, besides 'the differences in development that moved from west to east', an important structural role was played by the western 'European family systems' which produced 'the high proportion of single people' who formed 'a large contingent that could move easily from one household to another', especially in early adulthood, engaging as farmhands and servants. On the other hand, although depicting the history of mobility as one of increasing intensity from the preindustrial to the industrial era, Moch steadily and definitively embeds mobility in European rural society at least since 1650. 'Moving about was an integral part of preindustrial routine, central to the rhythm of seasons, the life cycle, and family life [...], migration was embedded in the dynamics of decisions, family formation, and inheritance.' Nevertheless, the kinds of mobility she detected in preindustrial western Europe were mostly related to marriage, those of farmhands and servants, collective movements for seasonal wage workers in harvesting, temporary or definitive transfers to towns and cities, and migrating to proto-industrial rural areas. Until around 1750, such movements were mostly of a local scope (Moch, 1992: 6, 31-35, 40, 55, 62, 72).

Neither Lucassen nor Moch represent a decisive contribution to understanding the deep linkage between migration and peasant economy. It took the mountains to teach us that migrations were an economic asset for peasant populations. Truth be told, Moch addressed migrating mountain people, finding them 'in the Pyrenees, the Alps, the central highlands of France' and so on. In her view, they displayed a 'migration born of pressures on areas with a chronic lack of resources' and had 'particularly strong traditions of seasonal migration embedded in alpine climates, practices of livestock grazing, and trading needs'. Her interpretation is based on environmental limits and climatic constraints that pushed the mountaineers in search of additional income. 'What the mountains had to offer was the strong arms of their men' (Moch, 1992: 61-62, 76). This is simply wrong.

As early as 1964 Poitrineau showed how seasonal and temporary emigration from the mountains in central France was indeed much more complex than that. In the eighteenth century, migration was practised mostly by males, who could be counted in thousands and amounted to large parts of the population. 'It is women in majority who, in the mountains, work in the maintenance of the roads and even in the repairs or the construction of the small bridges.' He identified different 'regional specialization of temporary migrants [...] by village or parish' both in terms of destination (France and Spain) and profession. Some would take their young sons on the road as apprentices. Some would reach some affluence. Poitrineau pointed to the fact that while in the mountains emigration was 'a very important resource', it could also become a 'safety valve' in times of crisis. In the nearby plains 'nothing like this' could be found, even the 'miserable' there opted for 'sedentarity' (Poitrineau, 1964: 5-9, 17, 20, 30-31, 46-49).

In another pioneering study on immigration in Torino in the first half of the eighteenth century, Levi presented more examples of specialization. 'The flows are constantly repeated from certain rural municipalities [...] with a clear professional character.' His most striking example is the community of Viù: in 1700, 62.3 percent of the families practiced seasonal migration, involving 'virtually all males of working age'. In Levi's opinion, what distinguished the preindustrial population from the modern one was not a weaker mobility, but temporality and seasonality: 'return predominates' and there was a 'traditional link with the family and with the community of origin'. Mobility routes and practices were persistent, too. 'The population flows follow iterated rules, which are both the life of the city and life of the minor rural communities that provide the city with professions, people, services, seasonally but every year, following paths and traditions repeated a hundred times' (Levi, 1971, 533-535).

In fact, mobility was structural. This is clearly already revealed by Poitrineau, who noticed that births followed a seasonal pattern, mirrored in the returns home of the migrating men. As Fornasin stated, 'the form of general seasonality curves of weddings and baptisms highlights the rhythms of emigration'. The distribution of births, concentrating in a limited number of months, could vary depending on the activities. In various 'Alpine regions, where there was a strong seasonal emigration' the results were similar: in the Swiss Uri canton the concentration was between May and June, in the French Limousin it was June-August, in Auvergne in January-June and in Venetian Carnia in March-June (Fornasin, 1998: 20-21). If year after year and decade after decade births show a clear seasonally concentrated pattern, seasonal migration connected with mobile labour was a long-term structural character, far from being only makeshift. Migrations of mountain peasants encompassed both a variety of specialized professions as well as forms of unskilled labour. Allowing peasants to bring in ready money from a variety of jobs, it could become a safety valve in times of crisis, albeit this was not its primary function.

Nevertheless, for decades two misunderstandings obstructed the historians' path to interpreting temporary and seasonal peasant mobility. The first consists in that migration was caused by the lack of natural resources and by an unfavourable relation with population numbers in the home villages. The second was consequent, since rural migrants were understood as poor people moved by want (towards wealthier areas and cities in search of survival. Seasonal and temporary migration were therefore perceived as corresponding to a classic push and pull logic. When facing a phenomenon persisting through centuries, of a structural nature, displaying many examples of specialized professions, the logic of peasant seasonal and temporary migration may be understood only by focusing on the communities and families of origin.

A decisive step in this direction was made by Fontaine (1996, French original 1993). She addressed the communities from which migrants departed 'so as to understand the nature of the social organization which was the driving force behind migrations'. In her work mountain migration is central and presented as a specific system, different from lowland seasonal and temporary migration. In Fontaine's own words, 'from the Middle Ages in the Alps, mountain society developed around the concept of migration' (Fontaine, 1996: 95). What distinguished the mountain migration system in her view was that it was organized and coordinated by a network of merchants and entrepreneurs, who were itinerant or established in cities, but originated from mountain communities. Knowing the demand for seasonal work in different professions, it was they who directed the groups of mountaineers who seasonally migrated from villages and valleys. Central in this system was the credit network, which was closely related to land and allowed such 'enterprises' made of migrant networks to function, the workers to move and live, and linked the merchants with the seasonal migrants.

These important steps in understanding the logic of mountain migration, which overcome the paradigms of misery and overpopulation, were made possible by three basic 'methodological shifts':

1 'Refusal to [...] take for granted the social and economic marginalization' of the profession of pedlars.
2 To search for 'common typologies and links that bound individuals together' instead of describing 'pre-categorised groups' (defined by wealth, geographic area, urban or rural).
3 'Not to see mobility as a [...] passage between two states, but on the contrary [...] that it, like the sedentary way of life, could also be a way of existing and appropriating territory' (Fontaine, 1996: 203).

Later, Fontaine expressed a strong criticism of three assumptions in the approach to migration in 'traditional studies', which she sees as 'simplified dichotomies':

1 the push and pull factors,
2 the separation of two geographical points: place of departure and place of arrival,
3 the distinction between two moments in time: before and after migration (Fontaine, 1996).

The model detected by Fontaine, a seasonal migration from Alpine areas coordinated by merchants and entrepreneurs stemming from village elites, was demonstrated to be widely practiced (Fontaine 2005). Besides this methodological and substantive progress, there are two important interpretive turns made by Fontaine. Firstly, her 'analysis of the source communities teaches us that mobility can be a way of occupying an area, and that it can support society and, independently of agricultural resources, create a dense human population' (Fontaine 1996, 205). Secondly, she stated that for peasants, 'migration can be an economic strategy, a way of using space as a resource and thus widening the boundaries of the territory' (Fontaine, 2005: 28).

The idea of 'space as a resource' may be further elaborated. Looking at seasonal migration from Alpine and mountain areas from this perspective, it becomes clear that these rural populations created a new asset, based on a combination of space, time, skills, and mobility, which increased the capability of their economy to sustain larger numbers of people. In this sense, migration is to be regarded as an asset, like soil, woods, and pastures. In order to exploit the opportunities offered by mobility in an enlarged space, both traditional skills were put to good use and new ones were developed. In the end, it was not overpopulation that pushed mountain peasants to the lowlands. On the contrary, it was seasonal and temporary mobility that enabled larger populations to live on highlands, allowing a degree of welfare and even prosperity. Thus, mobility may be understood as a multiplying factor which led to optimizing and enhancing the available space, time, and skills, whose product was a new asset in the peasant economy in the form of seasonal and temporary migration.

In fact, contemporary migration studies tackle migrants 'as conscious actors' (Kalc, 2024: 26). Peasant seasonal and temporary migrants may be regarded not as passive objects at the mercy of push and pull factors, but as individuals who made conscious choices and enacted them. They had agency, and even created a new asset in their economy.

IV. Peasant economic agency East and West: overcoming dualism

Three pervasive interpretations of the peasant economy in Europe influence and obstruct its understanding. The first is linked to the idea that in traditional society peasants did not pursue improvement of their living standards because they had different cultural values and social priorities and thus were not really interested in implementing economic agency. The second regards the question whether peasants were capable of making economic decisions and enacting them, given the institutional and social restrictions they lived in (Ogilvie, 2014). The third obstacle is the assumption in European development history, claiming there was 'a general lack of freedom and bondage of villagers' in east-central and eastern Europe (Cerman, 2012). Even admitting agency was present in western Europe, there remains no room for it among peasants in eastern Europe.

IV.1. Peasant mentality versus agency

As a convinced advocate of peasant economic agency in the guise of industriousness, de Vries showed repeated awareness that his theory collided with a 'widely held view' of the traditional peasant, detecting it in a broad historiography comprising authors such as Braudel, Hobsbawm, Le Roi Ladurie, E. P. Thompson, and Pollard. In these views, pre-modern peasants were not sensitive to the market but rather to reciprocity, kin, and neighbours. They approached the market as little as possible. Their desires were traditional: if wealthier they would buy more land, build a larger house, hoard the money, or use it for gargantuan feasts. They were used to working for subsistence, not to improve their well-being; when their incomes increased they stopped working, unused to working regularly for longer periods of time. They were carried by their destiny, unable to influence it, imprisoned in immobile structural constraints. De Vries in particular is critical towards 'anthropological thinking about the nature of peasantry as a category of human civilization', because it leads to the opinion that 'preindustrial agriculture was a world of culturally different people subject to different economic rules'. In contrast, English and Dutch medieval and early modern 'new agrarian history rejects this celebration of the otherness of European cultivators; it explores systematically the possibilities of market-based explanations of rural phenomena and peasant behavior' (de Vries, 1999: 130). No closer inspection is needed to realize that the understanding of peasant economic agency supported by this 'new' English and Dutch agrarian history does not recognize the capability of individual acting in all early-modern rural Europeans, but only in those in north-western Europe.

Peasant mentality deserves a few more words than a rejection. One should not forget that anthropologically inspired microhistorical approaches were also able to uncover unexpected dimensions of individuality in pre-modern rural society (Ginzburg, 1980). On the other hand, any historian acquainted with early modern court trial sources would hardly oppose the fact that people showed patterns of behaviour and conduct that are not precisely those of a twentieth-century Westerner. Not even in contemporary Europe is profit the only driver of everyone's actions, thus there is no reason to expect that from people in preindustrial societies. Indeed, a whole set of cultural values and social rules was quite different and differing in space and time. Still, this does not mean that preindustrial peasants were unable to act with economic logic and to desire a better material life, enacting consequent decisions. An example of a combination of peculiar values and economic agency is another microhistorical work, Levi's *Inheriting Power* (1988).

IV.2. Peasant economic agency as a pan-European phenomenon

The question here regards the agency of peasants in economic matters, their capacity to enact choices about work and production, while acting within a time-and-place-specific institutional framework. The conceptual and interpretative obstacles to admitting peasants were capable of economic agency are listed by Ogilvie (2014), whose merit is not least the inclusion of western, central, and eastern Europe in her empirically based picture:

1 Peasant mentality
2 Exceptional societies
3 Manorial coercion
4 Force of necessity

In the first obstacle, the responsibility for the peasant mentality is attributed to Chayanov's followers. This is the same conceptual hindrance that de Vries attributed to anthropology. Because of their mentality and 'cultural norms', peasants did 'not make individual choices about labour, capital, farm size, technology, market participation, or consumption style'. Instead, they 'engage in self-exploitation', 'avoid debt and credit', 'retain the family farm at all costs', 'avoid markets' and 'consume only traditional goods'. In Ogilvie's opinion this view on the 'Chayanovian mentality of limited goals' may be found, for example, in Kriedte, Medick, and Schlumbohm as well as Rösener (Ogilvie 2014: 270).

The second obstacle to ascribing agency to peasants is represented by the view that 'choice-making behaviour' was present in 'exceptional enclaves within the prevailing regime of peasant culture. That is, [...] in some parts of Europe but not in others'. This was the case in England, later extended to the Netherlands to form a 'distinctive North Sea region, characterized by a culture in which individuals made their own choices' concerning land transactions, market and labour market participation by men and women, credit, marriage, marital property rights, and inheritance. Elsewhere in Europe 'individual choice in such matters was culturally inadmissible'. As advocates of such views, Ogilvie mentions Macfarlane, Landes, De Moor, and van Zanden. Similar exceptions have been identified in France and Germany (Ogilvie 2014: 271-272). We have seen that de Vries is not immune to this view. Cases in which peasants enacting individualistic choices are detected in other parts of Europe are regarded as the effect of western influences.

The third impediment to peasant choice is serfdom. Manorial lords hampered 'all individual agency among serfs. [...] True serfdom, it is assumed, stifled all peasant choice'. The fourth obstruction consists in a generalized and constant state of want, 'peasants were too poor to make choices, they merely responded to necessity'. In case peasants borrowed money, participated in the market, worked longer or increased farm productivity, it was 'because' they were threatened by starvation, or had to pay 'feudal dues in cash' and 'higher taxes', or because of 'rising food prices and falling real wages' (Ogilvie, 2014: 272-273). A list of historians sharing such views would be very long.

Contrary to all these views, there is a wide array of scholarly works presenting empirical evidence that peasant economic agency may be found all over Europe since the Middle Ages and throughout the early modern period (Ogilvie 2014). Two main spheres in which historians search for signs of peasant individual economic agency may be distinguished: market-oriented behaviour and family behaviour. Within market-oriented behaviour evidence of agency is detected in the domains of credit, land market, wage labour, and production for the market. The scope of choices under investigation within the family include decisions about marriage, inheritance, the role of women and their property rights. The allocation of labour time among family members, and their inclusion in market labour based on age and gender, is considered too, interlinking the spheres of market-oriented behaviour and family behaviour. Phenomena signalling economic agency are also geographical mobility (testifying to both freedom of movement and individual enterprise) and social mobility (showing disentanglement from a non-profit mentality). Comfort and luxury objects in probate inventories are regarded as material evidence of their owner's agency (consumption liberated from a survival-oriented mentality).

Such a varied array of signs and evidences is not easily measurable and consequently not easily comparable, on a quantitative base in particular. Nevertheless, while English and Dutch peasants do not seem to need confirmation, peasants all over Europe show economic agency, since one or more of the aforementioned indicators were detected in a long and most probably incomplete list of countries such as Italy, Portugal, Spain, Germany, France, Switzerland, Norway, Sweden, Austria, Slovenia, Poland, Bohemia, Hungary, and Russia (Blanchard, 1997; Sreenivasan, 2004; Ogilvie, 2014; Cerman, 2012; Béaur et al., 2013; Broad-Schuurman, 2014; Ebert-Troßbach, 2016; Panjek-Larsson-Mocarelli, 2017; Mocarelli-Ongaro, 2020).

The rejection of the possibility that peasants were able to enact any agency is particularly strong regarding the eastern part of Europe, given the 'second serfdom' regime. For this reason, Cerman's effort to dismantle this view relying on a wide foundation of older and recent historical literature is of particular relevance. He directed his criticism towards 'the notion of a fundamental "agrarian dualism" between ancient régime Western and Eastern Europe [...], in which the Western model came to represent liberal modernity and the Eastern re-feudalisation and authoritarianism' (Cerman, 2012: 1). Cerman argues that central-eastern and eastern Europe were characterized by a great variety in property and power relations between landlords and peasants, much the same as in western and southern Europe. The Elbe-divide in early-modern rural societies is a simplistic conception with no basis in historical evidence and, consequently, the 'dualistic' view on Europe it generated is simplistic as well. The agrarian and power relation system labelled as 'second serfdom' may be detected also to the west and to the north of the Elbe line, in Germany and southern Scandinavia, while in central-eastern and eastern Europe, in Cerman's view, real serfdom was the exception, not the rule. On these premises he proposed that the very term 'second serfdom' should be replaced by 'demesne lordship' (*Gutsherrschaft*) and that the peasants should not be defined as 'serfs' but rather as 'subjects', consistent with how they were mostly named in historical documents from that area. He concluded that 'dualism in agrarian structure and the notion of second serfdom lasting unchanged for 300 years can no longer be maintained as a general interpretation' (Cerman, 2012: 130).

In the majority of the regional and local landlord-peasant relations variations, peasants had the possibility, and enacted it, to produce agrarian surplus and industrial cultures, to market them, to engage in non-agrarian activities for the market, to inherit, buy, and sell holdings and plots of land and so on. In brief, the variegated agrarian regimes left enough room for peasant economic agency. 'Studies available for Brandenburg, Silesia, Poland, Hungary, Bohemia, Moravia and Russia show economic independence, successful market participation, taking advantage of market swings and price movements and a high degree of market involvement of tenant farmers and smallholders, some of whom grew wealthy in the process.' There is wide evidence that peasants in central-eastern and eastern Europe were 'far from market-averse'. There were numerous 'areas with proto-industrial production', and 'substantial proportions of the rural population were active outside arable agriculture'. In Cerman's own words, 'the most important conclusion to be drawn is that villagers engaged in markets regularly and were able to make independent decisions about production and economic strategies, even in areas of demesne lordship and a commercial demesne economy' (Cerman, 2012: 108-111).

Cerman's shareable criticism towards old dualistic views on rural societies, on a generalized backwardness and lack of freedom of enterprise in the east, and his convincing argumentation that economic agency was to be found to a large extent among the peasantry of central-eastern and eastern Europe as well, should not overshadow the indisputable fact that in the east as in other regions of the continent the scope of peasant agency was influenced by the regional and local institutional environment (agrarian structure, legal regime). 'Individual choices by peasants', as Ogilvie stressed, 'do not imply, either in theory or in practice, that manorial constraints on those choices were irrelevant'. In fact, landlords might intervene and impose regulations that limited the enacting of choices and 'most manorial systems [...] imposed some constraints'. Every specific situation was therefore the result of goals and actions by peasants and lords in a constant interaction of peasants' choices and landlords' constraints. (Ogilvie, 2014: 288-289). The best way to tackle similarities and differences in economic agency across Europe is the comparative approach, accompanied by 'more attention' to peasants' non-agrarian activities in east-central and eastern Europe (Cerman, 2011; Cerman, 2012: 129).

V. The Integrated Peasant Economy: a concept and a comparative approach

The traditional peasant economy is often still labelled as tendentially autarchic and with marginal connections to the market. Because of the prevailing interest in seemingly more important processes in rural Europe, such as the appearance of conditions for modern industrialization or the challenges brought on rural society by economic modernization, the peasant economy was mostly addressed instrumentally, incidentally, and partially.

For many economic historians, the peasants who lived autarkically are an annoying apparition. Those who lived on subsistence farming are discarded. Those who seasonally migrated are destitute. Those who worked on something besides agriculture are poor fellows in want. Whatever such a peasant might have done or how he strived, he had no chance to improve his living or social standards. 'Social promotion in this kind of rural society is a myth' (Thoen 2001, 145). Such a peasant is an obstacle on the path of modern development, the wrong child of European economic history.

The peasant is good and interesting only if and when he is functional to modern development or conducts specialized farming for the market. To be positively noticed and addressed, he should better contribute to capitalistic development. Such a view has two problems: on the one hand it is anachronistic, on the other it is teleological. What if we addressed the peasant economy for what and how it was, not from the perspective of its possible contribution to modern development?

V.1. The premises of the integrated peasant economy

In fact, some of the concepts and approaches examined so far also deal with peasant economy instrumentally, their main research interest being elsewhere, notably in development. In some cases, peasant economy is understood as something to be overcome. Yet many offer useful tools to disentangle the peasant economy from a view which is biased by the paradigms of misery, stillness, and passivity, by the consequent perception of peasant society as immobile and of peasants as passive actors who only respond to outside impulses.

A nearly uncountable mass of research on proto-industry, pluri-activity and other topics testifies to the fact that the engagement of peasants in non-agrarian sectors is one of the most prominent features in the history of the European countryside. Whichever our topic, as if by accident peasant income integration practices keep emerging on the surface of rural history. In spite of that, this evident common feature of rural Europe was rarely the object of specifically focused and comparative research for its own sake.

The aim here is to develop and test a conceptualization of peasant economy that would allow a step forward from terminology and models with a segmentary focus or selective applicability, and which would furthermore enable better comparability between regions and over time. The starting point was represented by the acknowledgement, well present in scholarship but more rarely brought to its interpretative consequences, that in several areas peasant populations did not live on subsistence agriculture but showed rather diversified income patterns. The proposed term to define this is 'integrated peasant economy', a concept which emerged from the conjunction between Slovenian and Italian historiographies. But the very beginning had indeed been in Slovenia, a mostly Alpine and hilly land in which smallholdings and cottages strongly prevailed, and where a tradition of studies regarding 'peasant trade', 'peasant transport' and 'additional activities' produced substantial evidence on the combination of different activities by the peasant population. Peasant activities in the secondary and tertiary sectors had macroeconomic dimensions and were largely export-oriented; thus, in pre-industrial Slovenia we might speak of an export-led peasant economy (Panjek 2017, 13-20).

What prompted peasants, in Slovenia and all over Europe, toward an apparently widespread orientation to combining market-oriented activities in different sectors? Their involvement in a mixture of agriculture, industry, trade, and transport was undoubtedly a necessity: for many peasants the acquisition of off-farm income represented a strategy whereby they could achieve both a level of subsistence and be able to pay their dues and taxes. But the fact that it was a necessity does not necessarily mean it was a passively accepted solution, nor that it simply represented a way out of need.

In many areas of Europe, a consistent part of the holdings was often too small to grant a living from their own agricultural produce. Throughout the early modern period, strata of rural population and forms of households with little land grew in numbers. We may observe an increase in the foundation of agriculturally self-insufficient households, both as cottagers with little land and through the progressive fragmentation of older and larger farm units. Is it reasonable to think that through several centuries peasants drove the system towards their own economic ruin without taking any measure, such as adjusting the marriage age and inheritance pattern? Or might we more reasonably suppose that, on the contrary, the multiplication of households beyond the level of subsistence provided by land alone indicates that the rural population counted on and exploited the possibility of access to alternative activities? This would mean that the economic rationality behind the fragmentation of farm units lay in the expectation and opportunities offered by income integration through market-oriented activities. Consequently, at a system level, non-agricultural and, in general, market-related income sources represented an element in a more complex and comprehensive economic strategy. Peasants counted on and systematically used the possibility of access to other activities. This possibility must have been one of the aspects taken into consideration in household planning: had it not been so, we would not encounter so many agriculturally self-insufficient units.

A variety of non-agricultural income sources allowed the rural society to structurally overcome environmental, technological, and other possible constraints – this supports the interpretation that non-agricultural and market-oriented activities were not necessarily subordinated to self-consumption agriculture. Is it then acceptable to think of such activities simply as a measure to overcome momentary or conjunctural insufficiencies of agricultural subsistence? The answer embedded in the concept of integrated peasant economy is negative. It is then reasonable to make a fundamental shift in perspective, from the interpretation that market oriented and non-agricultural activities were undertaken because holdings were too small and agricultural income consequently insufficient, to the acknowledgment that holdings were small because peasants had different income sources. Integrated peasant economy is the proposed definition of this reality. It is an economy in which peasant populations and households made their living by combining self-consumption agriculture with market-oriented activities; in fact, even agricultural activities may have been (at least partly) market oriented. Moreover, well-off peasants also engaged in off-farm income integration practices.

While thus far it was 'a concept in progress' (Panjek 2017), it is now possible for me to outline the theoretical premises of the integrated peasant economy, as follows:

1 The integrated peasant economy stems from a programmatic shift in perspective, that is, by adopting one in which the primary focus is on the peasant economy itself, not on its implications and effects on the wider economy or on economic development of sectors or regions.
2 The integrated peasant economy adopts an inclusive comprehension of the meaning of 'peasant', by including those who had virtually no land and those endowed with many hectares, as well as anyone in between, regardless of their belonging to different social and economic strata

and categories, and no matter how named in various European social and institutional environments and languages.

3 The integrated peasant economy regards the peasant society and economy not as closed and autarchic, but fundamentally open. Not even on the highest mountain was the village an isolated and self-sufficient economy and society. Individuals, families, and communities had social and economic relations with closer neighbours as well as with the wider world of villages, towns, cities, regions, and states, based on kinship, alliance, trade, and migration.

4 The integrated peasant economy stems from and adopts a holistic approach to peasant economy: its basic assumption is that different income sources were part of a comprehensive economic strategy, in which peasants counted on and exploited the opportunities of access to alternative activities. Consequently, the peasant economy based on income integration needs to be regarded in its entirety, as a system.

5 The integrated peasant economy encompasses and comprises all the activities and forms of labour from the primary, secondary, and tertiary sectors which are not directed to self-consumption and self-use, but are market oriented, and their income is the result of a marketed transaction of goods (from crops and raw materials to finished products), labour, or services. For the rest, it neither sets limits in terms of necessary combinations between sectors, nor excludes them. Also, the cultivation of a crop intended for selling represents a market-oriented activity, a form of specialization and an expression of the will and ability to exploit opportunities on the market.

6 The integrated peasant economy challenges the assumption that the peasant household economy aimed purely at subsistence and survival, as well as that the recourse to activities different from on-farm self-sufficiency agriculture was only or mainly out of need. In parallel, it questions the mirrored image that income integration was a practice relegated to the less affluent strata of the rural population. It states by contrast that peasants, both rich and poor, were able and willing to pursue improved living standards and social mobility, and that this motivation was at the origin of income integration practices, which may well lead to such improvements.

7 The integrated peasant economy renders agency to the peasants and recognizes them in a role of active actors in rural history, who do not only passively react to external impulses and influences. Peasants chose income integration practices, chose the activities in which they would get involved and chose to change and replace them when necessity or opportunity arose.

8 The integrated peasant economy recognizes that peasants implemented industriousness by optimizing the labour resources, skills, time and even geographical reach of all family members, considering age, gender,

and life-cycle variables, in order to make their living and possibly a better living, not disdaining motivations concerning consumption improvement.

9 The place where the integrated peasant economy manifests itself is the household, but it is not only the household's head who determines the presence of income integration, it is all the family members. Each of them may engage in activities other than on-farm cultivation and husbandry on a full-time, part-time, seasonal, or temporary basis. The integrated peasant economy is the result of combining all their labour activities, both according to age and gender or in situations where gender-specific tasks are blurred. Since the sources which allow an insight into the economy, labour division, and budget formation of single families are rare in earlier periods, the object or area of observation in which to detect the integrated peasant economy may also be the village or a region. Smaller areas, such as villages or groups of villages, are preferred in terms of accuracy of results, because larger ones may distort the estimations. On the other hand, wider regional surveys are useful to detect the presence and the general pattern (types and modes) of income integration.

10 The integrated peasant economy includes all the forms of labour and many findings of earlier concepts and approaches in economic-historical research, such as proto-industry, pluri-activity, the Alpine integrated economy, Chayanov's peasant family economy, migration studies, industriousness, and agency. On the other hand, it refuses their possible instrumental or incidental interest towards the peasant economy, chronological limits, as well as interpretations that assert exclusivity based on considerations of geographical, institutional, or cultural limitations. The integrated peasant economy upgrades them through its holistic approach and its focus on the peasant economy as such and for its own sake.

11 The integrated peasant economy is a long-term character of peasant economy in Europe, stretching (at latest) from the late Middle Ages through the twentieth century, which overcame periods of development, stagnation, and crisis, enabling peasants to take advantage of, or to overcome them, too.

12 The integrated peasant economy is geographically inclusive and has been demonstrated to be applicable throughout Europe, regardless of institutional and cultural variables. Existing literature on proto-industry, pluri-activity, economic agency, and industriousness allows extending it to the whole of western and central Europe. Its presence is confirmed by specific regional case studies on Slovenia, northern and central Italy, Sweden, and Scandinavia in general, and now also Poland, the Czech Republic, Serbia, Bosnia (with peculiarities) and the Russian Empire.

V.2. The features of the integrated peasant economy

The integrated peasant economy is not only a theoretical approach, but also the way the peasant economy functioned in practise. As such, it has some distinctive, defining features.

Peasants combined self-consumption agriculture and market-oriented activities to make their living, as with every human economic activity. Apart from this basic reality, to which peasants may not be simplistically bound and limited, they also adopted labour and income diversification strategies to improve their living standard. The existence of such improvements based on income integration practices is proved by empirical evidence, as are cases of upward social mobility both within the peasant social group and through its boundaries, passing to other social groups or statuses. This observation does not imply that resorting to income integration was never a solution to want and need, but that this was not its defining trait. Through the decades and centuries, economic conjunctures and the spectre of opportunities varied and changed, and what had earlier been a choice might have become a must. But to identify peasant income integration only with a must is simplistic and simply wrong.

Agriculture did not necessarily represent the basis of the peasant economy, nor were market-oriented activities simply supplementary. For this reason, market activities represented a basically equal income source to agricultural production aimed at self-consumption. The integrated peasant economy takes into consideration the three economic sectors (primary, secondary and tertiary), and regards them as, in principle, equal ingredients of a whole. The coexistence and combination of activities belonging to different sectors is inscribed in the very meaning and sense of the term 'integrated economy': what the integrated peasant economy integrates are activities and income sources from different economic sectors. This means we are not simply coping with peasants who consumed their own produce and additionally did some industry in winter months (although they fit in the concept, too), or engaged in some additional activity in bad harvest years, but with peasant households that systematically used the plough (or shovel), engaged in crafts and hit the roads, their income sources ranging from working as day labourers in agriculture to illegal trafficking, passing through industrial and transport activities. The integrated peasant economy system was flexible: single activities could be adopted, increased, decreased, or abandoned; their role in the peasant household's income structure could change over time and space. Although the forms in which it appears may consequently vary and change, income integration remains a basic feature of the peasant economy.

In the previous, already 'upgraded', list of the integrated peasant economy's features, the role of the commons was recognized as an important pool of resources available for income integration practices (Larsson,

2017; Mocarelli-Tedeschi, 2017). This trait may be confirmed by many examples. For this reason, it was included among the general features of the integrated peasant economy. Undoubtedly the commons, where they existed, played an important role in income integration in two ways: on the self-sufficiency side by integrating crops from cultivation with foodstuff from animal husbandry, by providing firewood and construction materials, and on the income integration side by offering the opportunity to market the goods produced on the commons (meat, cheese, wool, firewood, charcoal, lime, timber, etc.). For this reason, in many areas they played a central role, granting social and economic stability to the richer and even more so to the poorer, as is well known. Yet, the commons are not a necessary feature, since there are cases in which peasants perform income integration practices without counting on common assets. Moreover, at least part of the same resources (e.g. wood, timber, stone, grassland) may also have been accessed, through rights of use or illegally, outside common areas.

Considering the lessons of seasonal and temporary migration and of industriousness, we may make a further step in conceptual abstraction and conclude that commons, human resources, and mobility share a fundamental trait within the peasant economy: they all represent forms of activation of available assets and resources. We even found that peasants were able to create new assets, as in the case of migration. We may therefore conclude that a distinctive feature of the integrated peasant economy is that it activated a wide range of assets and consequently combined income from local resources and natural assets (including the commons) with earning opportunities in a wider space, as was the case of trade, transport, and various forms of migration. What is therefore distinctive of the integrated peasant economy is that it activates and even creates assets in order to widen the scope of income sources and increase earning possibilities.

As a result of the aforementioned features, the integrated peasant economy enabled rural societies to overcome natural and technical limits, and to significantly raise the carrying-capacity of their environment. Income integration allowed sustaining a peasant population well beyond the level that would have been possible based solely on agricultural land and the self-consumption of its produce.

In commenting on the integrated peasant economy, several scholars have explicitly or implicitly proposed that the influence of external markets and external demand has to be taken in due consideration. Besides this, other factors external to the local peasant economies must be considered, such as general economic and political changes and developments. These accelerated from the eighteenth and nineteenth centuries onward, but were not absent in earlier centuries. The influence of exogenous factors might have represented a link to positive opportunities in one period and later become 'a reason of weakness' (Mocarelli-Tedeschi, 2017, Bulgarelli, 2017; Larsson, 2017; Morell, 2017; Lazarević, 2017). This observation is correct and coherent with the theoretical premises of the integrated peasant economy, which is open to the outside world. An open peasant economy is surely influenced by external and exogenous factors, in the form of demand, opportunities, and challenges.

What has just been said may be summarized as follows:

Features of the integrated peasant economy

1 Peasants combine agriculture and market-oriented activities to make their living and/or raise their living standard.
2 Market-oriented activities represent an equal (may be minor or major) income source compared to subsistence agriculture.
3 The adopted activities and income sources belong to the three economic sectors (primary, secondary, and tertiary).
4 The system is dynamic and flexible, and adapts to changes in the availability of income sources and the market conditions, in the population and in family structure through time.
5 Peasants activate available natural assets, human resources, business and labour opportunities, and even create new assets, to broaden income sources.
6 The carrying-capacity of the environment is increased beyond the level of population possible based on agricultural land alone.
7 The integrated peasant economy is connected to external demand and to exogenous factors, a connection that may represent an opportunity or a challenge.

V.3. The comparative checklist of the integrated peasant economy

The integrated peasant economy was born equipped with a comparative tool, consisting in a scheme including the activities that brought a differentiation and increase in income, in relation to agricultural production for self-consumption. The initial list of activities was constructed by summing up those referred to by Coppola (1991) when discussing the 'integrated economy' in the Italian (southern) Alps, with those mentioned by de Vries in addressing rural 'industriousness' in western Europe (2008, 71-121, 169). The activities are grouped by economic sector (primary, secondary, and tertiary), in order to highlight the presence of work in different sectors. The result is a checklist that allows a graphic picture of the presence of income integration, as well as an easy comparison between different places and regions, or between different periods in the same area.

More recently, some areas of activity have been added to the checklist (works of trust, fishery, tourism, warfare, looting and banditry). The last addition to the list is credit, both for empirical and theoretic reasons. Credit was diffusely present in connection with income integration practices, since loans and leases often enabled peasants to engage in such activities (not only in mountaineers' peddling). At the same time, moneylending was per se a source of income for the better-off lenders in the form of interest. On a conceptual level, being involved in credit relations may be considered a sign of market-oriented behaviour and economic agency, as opposed to a supposed traditional peasant mentality which is expected to avoid debt and credit – and the integrated peasant economy is a display of economic agency.

The checklist and an example of its comparative use may be seen in the Introduction to this volume.

Funding

This paper was written within the project *Concepts of peasant economy: a theoretical and empirical comparative approach (15th-20th c.)*, financed by the Slovenian Research and Innovation Agency (ARIS).

Bibliography

Béaur G., (eds) 2013, *Property Rights, Land Markets and Economic Growth in the European Countryside (Thirteenth–Twentieth Centuries)*, Turnhout.

Béaur, G. (2017), 'Introduction: Was there really an "Industrious Revolution"?' Revue d'histoire moderne et contemporaine, 64, 4, pp. I-XVII.

Blanchard, I. (1997), 'Eighteenth-Century Russian Economic Growth: State Enterprise or Peasant Endeavour?' *Jahrbücher für Geschichte Osteuropas*, N. F., 45, 4, pp. 541-551.

Broad, J. and Schuurman, A. (eds) (2014), *Wealth and Poverty in European Rural Societies from the Sixteenth to the Nineteenth Century*, Turnhout.

Bulgarelli Lukacs, A. (2017), 'The Equilibrium of the Mountain Economy in the Apennines: The Regional Case of Abruzzo in the Kingdom of Naples (16th-19th Centuries)', Panjek, A., Larsson, J. and Mocarelli L. (eds), *Integrated Peasant Economy in a Comparative Perspective: Alps, Scandinavia and Beyond*, Koper, pp. 161-190.

Cafagna, L. (1989), 'L'occasione del filugello. Note sul settore serico nella prospettiva di una esplorazione delle pluriattività nella storia delle economie regionali italiane tra Sette e Ottocento', *La pluriattività negli spazi rurali: ricerche a confronto. Annali dell'Istituto Alcide Cervi*, 11, Roma-Bologna, pp. 79-86.

Cerman, M. (2011), 'Demesne lordship and rural society in early modern East Central and Eastern Europe: comparative perspectives', *The Agricultural History Review*, 59, 2, pp. 239-258.

——— (2012), *Villagers and Lords in Eastern Europe, 1300-1800*, New York.

Chayanov, A. V. (1986a), 'On the Theory of Non-Capitalist Economic Systems', Thorner, D., Herblay, B. and Smith, R. E. F. (eds), *A. V. Chayanov on the Theory of Peasant Economy*, Manchester, pp. 1-28.

——— (1986b), 'Peasant farm Organization', Thorner, D., Herblay, B. and Smith, R. E. F. (e.d.s.), *A. V. Chayanov on the Theory of Peasant Economy*, Manchester, pp. 29-269.

Coleman, D. C. (1983), 'Proto-Industrialization: A Concept Too Many', *The Economic History Review*, N. S., 36, 3, pp. 435-448.

Coppola, G. (1991), 'Equilibri economici e trasformazioni nell'area alpina in età moderna: scarsità di risorse ed economia integrata', Coppola, G. and Schiera, P. (eds), *Lo spazio alpino: area di civiltà, regione cerniera*, Napoli-Pisa, pp. 203-222.

Ebert, J. and Troßbach W. (eds) (2016), *Dörfliches Erwerbs- und Nutzungsorientierungen (Mitte 17. bis Anfang 19. Jahrhundert). Bausteine zu einem überregionalen Vergleich*, Kassel.

Federico, G. (1989) 'Pluriattività e offerta di forza-lavoro contadina: una analisi microeconomica', *La pluriattività negli spazi rurali: ricerche a confronto. Annali dell'Istituto Alcide Cervi*, 11, Roma-Bologna, pp. 87-100.

Fontaine, L. (1996), *History of Pedlars in Europe*. Cambridge.

——— (2005), 'Montagnes et migrations de travail. Un essai de comparaison globale (XVe-XXe siècles)', *Revue d'histoire moderne et contemporaine*, 52, 2, pp. 26-48.

Fornasin, A. (1998), *Ambulanti, artigiani e mercanti. L'emigrazione dalla Carnia in età moderna*, Verona.

Garrier, G., Goujon, P. and Rinaudo, Y. (1988), 'Annexe: notes d'orientation de la recherché', Garrier, G. and Hubscher, R. (eds), *Entre faucilles et marteaux. Pluriactivités et stratégies paysannes*, Lyon-Paris, pp. 233-237.

Ginzburg, C. (1980), *The Cheese and the Worms. The Cosmos of a Sixteenth-Century Miller*, Baltimore.

Hubscher, R. (1988), 'Presentation', Garrier, G. and Hubscher, R. (eds), *Entre faucilles et marteaux. Pluriactivités et stratégies paysannes*, Lyon-Paris, pp. 7-17.

Isaacson, M. and Magnusson, L. (1987), *Proto-Industrialisation in Scandinavia. Craft Skills in the Industrial Revolution*, Leamington Spa.

Kalc, A. (2024), 'Historical, Social, Economic, and Political Aspects of Migrations', Kalc, A., Milharčič Hladnik, M. and Žitnik Serafin, J. (eds.), *Daring Dreams of the Future. Slovenian Mass Migration 1870–1945*, Lausanne-Berlin.

Kriedte, P. (1981), 'The origins, the agrarian context, and the conditions in the world market', Kriedte, P., Medick, H. and Schlumbohm, J., *Industrialization before Industrialization. Rural Industry in the Genesis of Capitalism*, New York.

———, Medick H. and Schlumbohm J. (1981), *Industrialization before Industrialization. Rural Industry in the Genesis of Capitalism*, New York.

Larsson, J. (2017), 'The Importance of Commons in an Integrated Peasant Economy in Early Modern Northern Scandinavia', Panjek, A., Larsson, J. and Mocarelli L. (eds), *Integrated Peasant Economy in a Comparative Perspective: Alps, Scandinavia and Beyond*, Koper, pp. 117-136.

Lazarević, Ž. (2017), 'Peasant Economy in Interwar Slovenia – Policies of Income Diversification', Panjek, A., Larsson, J. and Mocarelli L. (eds), *Integrated Peasant Economy in a Comparative Perspective: Alps, Scandinavia and Beyond*, Koper, pp. 351-373.

Levi, G. (1971), 'Mobilità della popolazione e immigrazione a Torino nella prima metà del Settecento', *Quaderni storici*, 6, 17, 2, pp. 510-554.

——— (1988), *Inheriting Power. The Story of an Exorcist*, Chicago.

Lucassen, J. (1987), *Migrant Labour in Europe, 1600-1900: The Drift to the North Sea*, London.

Mayaud, J.-L. (1999), 'De la pluri-activité paysanne à une re-définition de la petite exploitation rurale', *Annales de Bretagne et des pays de l'Ouest*, 106, 1, pp. 231-248.

Mendels, F. (1972), 'Proto-Industrialization: The First Phase of the Industrialization Process', *The Journal of Economic History*, 32, 1, pp. 241-261

——— (1975), 'Agriculture and Peasant Industry in Eighteenth-Century Flanders', Parker, W. N. and Jones, E. L. (eds), *European Peasants and Their Markets. Essays in Agrarian Economic History*. Princeton.

Mocarelli, L. and Ongaro, G. (eds) (2020), *Pluriactivité – Pluriattività – Pluriaktivität. Histoire des Alpes*, 25, pp. 17-115.

——— and Tedeschi, P. (2017), 'Household Income Strategies in the Lombard Valleys: Persistence and Loss of a Traditional Economic Equilibrium in an Alpine Area (end of 18th–early 20th Centuries)', Panjek, A., Larsson, J. and Mocarelli L. (eds), *Integrated Peasant Economy in a Comparative Perspective: Alps, Scandinavia and Beyond*, Koper, pp. 375-394.

Moch, L. P. (1992), *Moving Europeans: Migration in Western Europe Since 1650*, Bloomington-Indianapolis.

Morell, M. (2017), 'Pluriactivity, Proto-industrialisation or Integrated Peasant Economy? Scandinavia in the 18th-20th Centuries', Panjek, A., Larsson, J. and Mocarelli L. (eds), *Integrated Peasant Economy in a Comparative Perspective: Alps, Scandinavia and Beyond*, Koper, pp. 395-414.

Ogilvie, S. 2014. 'Choices and Constraints in the Pre-Industrial Countryside', Briggs, C., Kitson, P. M., and Thompson, S. J. (eds), *Population, Welfare and Economic Change in Britain, 1290-1834*, pp. 269-305, Cambridge.

——— and Cerman, M. (1996), 'The theories of proto-industrialization', Ogilvie, S. and Cerman, M. (eds), *European proto-industrialization*, New York, pp. 1-11.

Panjek, A. (2017), 'The Integrated Peasant Economy as a Concept in Progress', Panjek, A., Larsson, J. and Mocarelli L. (eds), *Integrated Peasant Economy in a Comparative Perspective: Alps, Scandinavia and Beyond*, Koper, pp. 11-49.

———, Larsson J. and Mocarelli L. eds (2017), *Integrated Peasant Economy in a Comparative Perspective: Alps, Scandinavia and Beyond*, Koper.

———, and Lazarević, Ž. eds (2018), *Preživetje in podjetnost. Integrirana kmečka ekonomija na Slovenskem od srednjega veka do danes*, Koper.

Pingaud, M.-C. (1981), 'La pluriactivité des familles agricoles est-elle une condition de survie pour le monde rural?', *Études rurales*, 84, pp. 113-120.

Ploeg van der, J. D. (2013), *Peasants and the art of farming: a Chayanovian manifesto*, Winnipeg.

Poitrineau, A. (1962), 'Aspects de l'émigration temporaire et saisonnière en Auvergne à la fin du XVIIIe et au début du XIXe siècle', *Revue d'histoire moderne et contemporaine*, 9, 1, pp. 5-50.

Pollard, S. (1981), *Peaceful Conquest: The Industrialization of Europe, 1760-1970*, Oxford.

Poni, C. (1983), 'Premessa', *Quaderni storici*, 18, 52, 1, pp. 5-10.

——— (1985), 'Proto-Industrialization, Rural and Urban', *Review Fernand Braudel Center*, 9, 2, pp. 305-314.

Rinaudo, Y. (1987), 'Un travail en plus: les paysans d'un métier à l'autre (vers 1830 – vers 1950)' *Annales. Économies, Sociétés, Civilisations*, 42, 2, pp. 283-302.

Sahlins, M. (1972), *Stone Age Economics*, New York.

Schlumbohm, J. (1996), 'Proto-industrialization as a research strategy and a historical period – a balance sheet', Ogilvie, S. and Cerman, M. (eds), *European proto-industrialization*, New York, pp. 12-22.

Shanin, T. (1986), 'Chayanov's message: Illuminations, Miscomprehensions, and the Contemporary "Development Theory"', Thorner, D., Herblay, B. and Smith, R. E. F. (eds), *A. V. Chayanov on the Theory of Peasant Economy*, Manchester, pp. 1-24.

Sreenivasan, G. P. (2004), *The Peasants of Ottobeuren, 1487-1726. A Rural Society in Early Modern Europe*, Cambridge.

Tannenbaum, N. (1984), 'The Misuse of Chayanov: "Chayanov's Rule" and Empiricist Bias in Anthropology', *American Anthropologist*, N. S., 86, 4, pp. 927-942.

Thoen E. (2001), 'A "commercial survival economy" in evolution. The Flemish countryside and the transition to capitalism (Middle Ages – 19th century)', Hoppenbrouwers, P. and Luiten van Zanden, J. (eds), *Peasants into farmers? The transformation of rural economy and society in the Low Countries (Middle Ages – 19th century) in light of the Brenner debate*, Turnhout, pp. 102-157.

Vries, J. De (1974), *The Dutch Rural Economy in the Golden Age, 1500-1700*, Yale.

Vries, J. De (1975), 'Peasant Demand Patterns and Economic Development: Friesland, 1550-1750', Parker, W. N. and Jones, E. L. (eds), *European Peasants and Their Markets. Essays in Agrarian Economic History*. Princeton, pp. 205-266.

——— (1994), 'The Industrial Revolution and the Industrious Revolution', *The Journal of Economic History*, 54, 2, pp. 249-270.

——— (1999), 'Great Expectations: Early Modern History and the Social Sciences', *Review Fernand Braudel Center*, 22, 2, pp. 121-149.

——— (2008), *The industrious revolution: consumer behavior and the household economy, 1650 to the present*, New York.

PIOTR GUZOWSKI AND
RADOSŁAW PONIAT

3. Non-agricultural Sources of Polish Peasants' Income

I. Introduction

The development of the Polish economy in the Golden Age of the sixteenth century was not only connected with enrichment of the nobility and great landowners (magnates), but also widened opportunities for the economic advancement of the peasant population. The dynamic growth in the export of Polish grain and cattle, integration with European markets, and the development of the internal market contributed to the increase in commercialisation of peasant farms (Topolski, 2000:18). So far, the attention of historiography has been primarily directed towards peasants' agricultural activity, which was impeded by nascent elements of the serfdom system, such as the restriction of mobility and the development of serfdom. Attempts at constructing models of peasant budgets covered a relatively versatile resource of peasants' burdens/expenses, but due to source limitations regarding incomes, they were primarily based on calculations of incomes from farming, mainly grain cultivation (Wawrzyńczyk, 1962; Wyczański, 1966; Żytkowicz, 1969; Guzowski, 2005; 2008). To a lesser degree incomes from breeding were taken into account, which resulted from a conviction that the lack of historical materials does not even allow estimation of the scale of potential incomes from other sources.

The concept of the Integrated Peasant Economy (IPE), underscoring that peasants used the resources gained in different activity sectors: agriculture, manufacturing, and service (Panjek, Larsson, Mocarelli, 2017), forces us to revise the business activity of Polish peasants and search for new incomes, exceeding the traditional accountancy material, inventories of goods or court books. The objective of this chapter is to examine how the extra-agricultural business activity of peasants was perceived by the noble elite, i.e. the most important social group in the society of that period, with a decisive influence on the economic life and politics of the country. Their role was so considerable that sometimes the early modern

Integrated Peasant Economy in Central and Eastern Europe, ed. by Aleksander Panjek, Rural History in Europe, 18 (Turnhout: Brepols, 2024), pp. 67–80
BREPOLS PUBLISHERS 10.1484/M.RURHE-EB.5.142464

Polish-Lithuanian Commonwealth is called the Republic of Nobles. The basis of the analysis comprises two types of sources: one is the most popular husbandry manual (*Gospodarstwo/Farm*) written by Anzelm Gostomski, a rich nobleman, royal official and owner of vast land estates, the other being tax rules referring to villagers, prepared and passed in the parliament by representatives of the nobility in consultation with the king, as well as tax registers.

II. Agricultural handbook

Anzelm Gostomski lived in the period 1508-1588, and was the author of the first agricultural book written in Polish, titled *Gospodarstwo* (*Management/Farm*) (Gostomski, 1951). We do not know anything certain about his education. In his youth and adulthood he was associated with the royal court of Sigismund II Augustus and consequently held several increasingly higher offices in Mazovia. In 1562, he was Wyszogród castellan, in 1564 Płock castellan, in the years 1565-1572 he was Rawa starost, and from 1572 on he held the function of Rawa voivod. The offices secured him a place in the Senate. He participated in the war with Moscow in 1564, leading a unit funded by himself, and in the Polish-Russian negotiations concluding the Polish-Russian conflict in the 1580s. Anzelm Gostomski was Reformed Evangelical and showed himself to be a defender of religious tolerance in the Commonwealth. He was considered a perfect estate manager. He inherited 29 villages, and leased a further 36 villages with 2 towns (Podraza, 1959-1960:362-364). He started writing his work towards the end of his life. It was first published posthumously; in the subsequent century it was republished twice, and in the nineteenth century three times (Inglot, 1951: XXXVII).

Gospodarstwo, also published under the title *Ekonomia albo gospodarstwo ziemiańskie* (*Economy or land farm*), is a very original agronomic work, whose author did not focus on the issues of farming technologies, but on questions connected with the organisation and management of land estate, as well as relations between the noble owner and his peasant subjects (Topolski, 1952:46-47). Gostomski included therein several tips resulting directly from his experience, representing the point of view of the successful economic elite, which on the one hand used a good economic situation and foreign demand for Polish grain, and on the other hand the political and social advantage of the nobility in introducing elements of the serfdom system: mobility restriction and serfdom. For this reason he was presented in Marxist literature as a brutal feudal, firmly executing peasant duties of serfdom work and tributes, but at the same time a pro-capitalist, obsessed with profit, an entrepreneur promoting commercialisation (Lipiński, 1956). Simultaneously, the author of this agricultural manual was an attentive observer of economic life and drew rational conclusions. In the context of the peasant population, he wrote: 'Peasant labour is the greatest income in Poland everywhere, and the nobleman should manage it in such a way that it does not impoverish the peasants but leads to greater benefits every year' (Gostomski, 1951: 19-20). The main attention of Gostomski was focused on the farming economy and peasant labour division between the landowner's manor farm and the peasants' own farms. Thus, he advised: 'The peasants, whom the nobleman does not want to drive into poverty, must have so much land that even after deducting tithes, they have a harvest greater than the nobleman on the manor' (Gostomski, 1951: 106). Moreover, the book contains tips referring to the comprehensive development of the complex of property, not only villages but also towns, underscoring potential opportunities for increasing incomes of the nobles. Gostomski also mentioned the economic activity of peasants, primarily in farming. On the margin of his considerations, however, he noted other sources of peasant incomes, which complemented incomes from agriculture, and in a way distracted peasants from work on the farm.

In the chapter devoted to relations of manor officials with the subjects, he described peasants active in crafts, among which blacksmithing, cooperage, and innkeeping were considered the most important. In this case Gostomski expressed concern about the provision of appropriate materials, including particularly wood, the appropriate quality of which should be available in the master's forests (Gostomski, 1951:35). In many places in the work linen makers, tanners, furriers, and potters also appear, as an important element of market relations. Gostomski even wrote that it is important to increase the number of craftsmen, but underscored that they should be gathered in small towns, because 'they create the market' (Gostomski, 1951:101).

However, peasants' activities in the field of transportation services and hiring themselves out as a workforce did not raise the author's enthusiasm. The master's official should make sure that such a side activity did not take place at the cost of work for the master. Occupied with services for other employers, the peasant 'will soon neglect the work he is due to do' (Gostomski, 1951:37). Among the transportation services provided by peasants was also river rafting. Gostomski, realising that, particularly near the Vistula and its largest tributaries, the demand for river transport of forest goods and grain dispatched to bigger cities, including Gdańsk, was high, warned that peasants' multi-day rafting services carried out at the cost of work on the masters' farm should be compensated by the peasants with cash (Gostomski, 1951:42).

Focusing on agriculture and breeding on his farms, Gostomski did not ignore forest economy. He believed that '[h]e who has the woods, and does not want to or cannot found villages there, and is not indebted, will leave to his offspring a treasure more certain than money in the chest: if he does not loot it' (Gostomski, 1951:109). In this context he wrote about peasants who use the forest as the source of fuel and timber. Therefore, he instructed officials that peasants should use brushwood and fallen trees, and for construction the ones marked by competent officials. Nevertheless, he also wrote: 'At the woods everyone gathers craftsmen working in wood' (Gostomski, 1951:100). The peasants should also be well equipped with the tools used in the forest: 'For cutting trees: axes, a drill, and other stuff' (Gostomski, 1951:35).

Gostomski also mentions peasants' commercial activity. He does it through describing the ways of enhancing the organisation of land estates and increasing their profitability. Several times he points out the economic significance of urban centres as a destination of peasants who go there to markets, fairs, or even travel to Torun (i.e. a very large city) (Gostomski, 1951:129). Approving peasants' participation in trade, he instructed officials to make sure that 'the peasant farmers did not rapidly sell draft animals, cattle, [or] herds, because a wealthy one will soon be poor' (Gostomski, 1951:43). Gostomski also notes in the text that in his time not only towns played the role of a local market but primarily there had emerged a great number of market villages, where commerce flourished (Gostomski, 1951:101).

Gostomski's landed estates were located in Mazovia. There he managed also the complexes of royal estates. Among them was the Rawa starosty, which included, in addition to the town of Rawa, nine surrounding villages. With four manors, the estate was oriented towards agricultural production. A description of this estate from 1564 provides data on 328 peasant farmers (Kędzierska, 1959:9-25). Peasants with hereditary holdings dominated among them (226), accounting for 69% of all heads of households. The text also mentions 58 peasant-gardeners (17.7%), whose main occupation was hired labor. They lived in 8 of the 9 villages of the starosty. As many as 36 innkeepers (11%) and 3 millers (1%) also lived in the villages described. The source also mentions 23 permanent wage earners in the manors, and provides information indicating an extensive usage of fishponds and forests, which means that local residents must have used these resources as additional sources of income.

The social structure of the villages of the starosty of Rawa was characterized by features common to all of Mazovia, a district whose economy was geared toward floating grain down the Vistula to Gdansk.

The average acreage of land in the hands of peasants was 0.6 mansus (*lan*) per farm (Wawrzyńczyk, 1962: 41), while the level ensuring self-sufficiency for a peasant family is defined as 0.25 mansus (Guzowski, 2012). Data from Mazovian tax registers indicate that, on average, there was 1 rural artisan per 8-9 mansi of land in peasant hands, and this did not differ from nationwide standards (Boroda, 2016: 703). However, some regions of Mazovia were characterized by an above-average number of gardeners living in villages (Boroda, 2016:299). In the Rawa area, gardeners, typically working as manor labourers, resided in as many as 85% of villages (Wawrzyńczyk, 1962: 41). We can infer the non-agricultural sources of peasant income from information about charges to village owners that were not related to serfdom or rent in money. Prominent among them are the fees paid by peasants for using forest areas (not only for their own consumption), brewing and selling beer and grain milling (Wawrzyńczyk, 1962:108-113).

More detailed studies of peasants' economic activity were conducted for other districts of the country than the Mazovian region described by Gostomski. Andrzej Wyczański found a confirmation of Gostomski's observations in accounts and inventories of the Korczyn county. In his two books, studying the organisation and profitability of the complex of royal land estates, the author also dealt with changes in the social structure of its inhabitants, providing data referring to their incomes from beyond their own farm businesses (Wyczański, 1964; 1977). In the light of the data of 1556, 40 royal villages were inhabited by 476 farm owners, of whom 391 (82.1%) were recorded in sources as peasants possessing hereditary farm plots of middle and large size, 47 peasants (9.9%) had only farms and small nearby plots, 2 of them were just house owners, i.e. they had only houses without fields, and three were village heads (*sołtys*), that is, well equipped peasants with their own manor farms. The group of 443 big, middle, and small farmers (93.1%) were complemented by 5 millers, 25 innkeepers, 2 fishermen, and a guardian of manor ponds (Wyczański, 1977:88-89). The authorities of the county made an income not only from rents resulting from peasants' use of hereditary farms, but also from leasing various objects to peasants. No wonder that peasants were most eager to enlarge their plots through leasing additional fields, meadows, and farms; plebeian inhabitants of the Korczyn country also leased lakes, woods, rivers (banks), a ferry, wild beehives, and a toll (Wyczański, 1977: 99). Within the structure of additional resources acquired by the county authorities thanks to leasing various objects to peasants, 57.6% came from fees for fields, 14.8% for meadows, and 0.9% for farms, i.e. 73.3% of all additional revenues came from typical farming and breeding activities. Another important grouping of interest to peasants was lakes and rivers, which partly resulted from local geographic conditions (the confluence of two rivers: the Vistula and the Nida, as well as floodplain lakes), but also from developed fishery, which brought the starosts 20.1% of additional income. The ferry on the Vistula in peasant use generated 4.3% of revenues from leases, the bridge toll 1.2%. The royal officials gained considerably less, just symbolic sums, thanks to the peasants' use of wild beehives and the woods (Wyczański, 1977:101).

III. Mansus tax

From the perspective of the landowner, agriculture and breeding remained the peasants' basic occupations, but it was commonly noticed that the economic development in the sixteenth century led to an increase in peasants' commercial activity in different sectors of the economy. Both the king and noble elites in the parliament, modernising the state under the influence of the military revolution, saw the chance of increasing revenues of the public treasury in the taxation of ever new social groups inhabiting the countryside, as well as in taxing business activities of the rural population. The fundamental tax paid annually by the rural population, the plough tax (Polish: *poradlne*; Latin: *exactio regalis*), having constantly been in force since 1374, was collected from the peasants, and the base of its amount was the size of the hereditary arable area. Over the fifteenth century, extraordinary taxes were imposed upon the rural population, usually at crisis moments, e.g. military conflicts. The basic one was the mansus tax (Polish: *łanowy*; Latin: *exactio*), which theoretically was also to be paid from the arable area (Guzowski, Sowina, 2022: 359-361). However, as early as 1440, besides peasants, village heads and noblemen who worked on their farms themselves, i.e. people making a living from agriculture, inns and mills were taxed. In 1468 the list of mansus tax payers was extended to gardeners or people having gardens and living from hired work, Vlachs, i.e. the cattle-breeding population in Podkarpacie. Moreover, windmills, fuller's workshops, and sawmills were taxed. With time, they added to the taxation categories day workers (1526), and in 1563 also craftsmen and vendors. Subsequent fiscal reforms imposed tributes for the state on villagers who did not have their houses, who lived in a 'chamber' with peasant householders and made a reservoir of hired workforce. A tax was also imposed on rural distilleries, ironworks, paper mills, and tar furnaces (Boroda, 2007:168-170). Tax amendments introduced in 1578 concluded the process of covering with an extraordinary tax all social groups living in the countryside (Grodziski, Dwornicka, Uruszczak, 2005; 420-430). In the case of many inhabitants of villages, various economic activities were combined, but at the moment of tax payment and register entry, they selected one trade, not always the one dominating or bringing the most profits, but often that guaranteeing a lower tax. In their subsequent statements the taxpayers could change their declarations; hence historians often observe considerable differences in the declared socio-economic structure of particular places. Thus, despite certain imperfections of the preserved tax registers of the sixteenth century, they allow us to scrutinize the structure of fiscal revenues in terms of the importance of agricultural and extra-agricultural incomes of the peasant population. Registers from Greater Poland (Polish: *Wielkopolska*) from the period of 1578-1583 will serve as a case study. Thus, we will look at a relatively well-developed region of the country at an important time of introducing fiscal reforms, which was characterised by the preparation of exceptionally reliable tax registers.

In terms of territorial division, Greater Poland consisted of two provinces (voivodeships, Polish: *województwa*): the Kalisz Province and the Poznan Province. There were 6 districts (Polish: *powiaty*) in the Kalisz Province: Gniezno, Kalisz, Kcynia, Konin, Nakło, and Pyzdry, while the Poznań Province comprised 4 districts: Poznań, Kościan, Wałcz, and Wschowa. The districts differed from one another in the level of settlement, economic development, social structure, and the size of public treasury revenues (Table 1). The highest amount was paid into the state treasury in the Poznań district (5711 florins), which also had the most taxed arable land (3773 mansi; 1 mansus = 16.8 ha). The smallest amount was paid in the Wałcz district, where only 647 florins of tax was collected and 372 mansi were taxed, i.e. ten times less land was entered in the tax registers than in the Poznań district. The land registered in the sources was used by peasants, village heads and, very rarely, by the nobility who farmed the land on their own. The registers do not provide information about the land in the manor farms, as it was not taxed.

In spite of the fact that the analysed registers concern the tax originating from the mansus tax, i.e. that primarily taxing the land used by peasants, towards the end of the sixteenth century, fiscal revenues resulting directly from farming were not the majority of income everywhere. Depending on the county, in Wielkopolska the łan taxation was related to 30.6%-85.6% of fiscal revenue, on average 59% (Graph 1). It is worth underscoring that the low percentage share of land taxes was not correlated with the size of the arable area in a particular county. The remaining resources were paid from proto-industrial facilities, such as mills and fuller's workshops, from inns, through craftsmen, fishermen, pedlars and landless peasants, constituting a reservoir of workforce, and from sheep breeding. Their importance grew over the sixteenth century. They were noticed by the nobility debating in the parliament and defined as a serious reinforcement of the state's financial potential in tax regulations and fiscal practice.

IV. Poll tax

The diversification of income sources of the rural population was also noted in acts of law introducing another extraordinary tax, the poll tax. It was applied merely twice in the sixteenth century, in the years 1520 and 1590 (once in the previous century) (Weyman, 1956). In the context of these reflections, the fact that the rates of the tax diversified according to the socio-professional group of a particular taxpayer

Table 3.1. Tax and taxed land in Greater Poland in the years 1578-1583

District	Province	Year	Tax (in Polish florins)	Taxed land (in mansi)
Gniezno	Kalisz	1579	2576.4	2427.7
Kalisz	Kalisz	1579	3808.1	2121
Kcynia	Kalisz	1579	2801.7	2120.8
Konin	Kalisz	1578	2162.2	1283.4
Nakło	Kalisz	1579	3052.9	2263.85
Pyzdry	Kalisz	1578	4084.4	2333.14
Kościan	Poznań	1580	4380.3	2752.82
Poznań	Poznań	1583	5711.8	3773
Wałcz	Poznań	1579	647.6	372
Wschowa	Poznań	1579	1651.9	560.35

Sources: *Rejestry poborowe województwa kaliskiego w XVI w. Atlas Źródeł i Materiałów do Dziejów Dawnej Polski*, nr 2 ed. M. Słoń, Instytut Historii PAN im. Tadeusza Manteuffla 2015 available at: https://atlasfontium.pl/rejestry-poborowe-kaliskie/; *Rejestry poborowe województwa poznańskiego w XVI w. Atlas Źródeł i Materiałów do Dziejów Dawnej Polski*, nr 3 ed. M. Słoń, Instytut Historii PAN im. Tadeusza Manteuffla 2015 – available at: https://atlasfontium.pl/rejestry-poborowe-poznanskie/

is of special significance. In practice, every time the tax was imposed, the parliament which introduced it had to divide the population of the country into income categories, from which very different amounts were to be collected. Thus, in 1590, the highest tax of 600 florins (1 Polish florin =30 groshes) was to be paid by the Gniezno archbishop (it is important to note that a special, individual tax category was created for him). Rich merchants were to pay 15 florins each, and, for example, musicians 6 groshes per person (Senkowski, 1970). The examples cited here, which are supposed to demonstrate a considerable range of required tax amounts, also nicely show the precision of divisions into socio-professional groups applied therein. Every time the poll tax was imposed, such groups were defined in a slightly different way, but this always meant hundreds of categories of taxpayers. For instance, in the 1520 poll tax, 189 main socio-professional groups were distinguished (Grodziski, Dwornicka, Uruszczak, 1996:356-366). Thus, the peasant population was subject to the division into subgroups. Even though in comparison with, for example, the clergy, in its case clearly fewer socio-professional groups were distinguished, it still meant differentiating several categories among the peasants. Some of

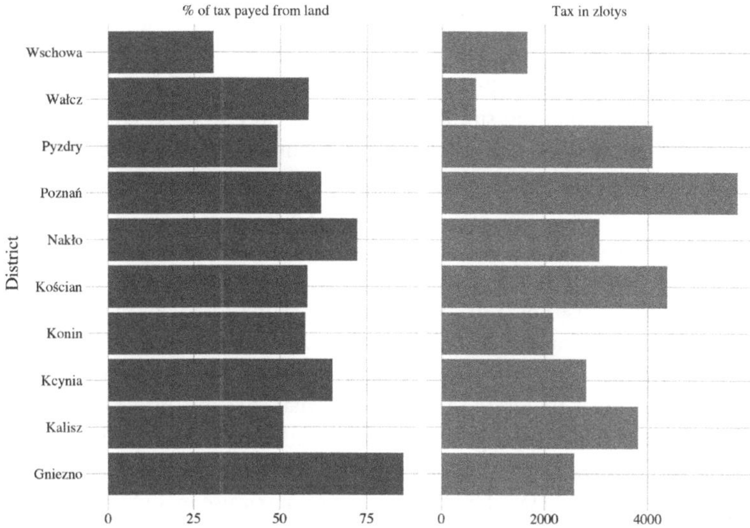

Graph 3.1. Share of tax from land in total tax paid by the rural population in Greater Poland in the years 1578-1583
Sources: as in Table 1.

them were determined by land possession, some of them were of more local character connected, for example, with living in places which were recently destroyed by warfare or fires, but it is also possible to indicate categories of the rural population defined on the basis of their performance of works not directly connected with grain production, for example, people dealing with shepherding, fishing or commerce. Particularly, millers stood out (by the way, in 1590 divided into 3 subcategories related to the size of the mill they possessed), but perhaps still more interesting a category is the rafters or people involved in water transport, distinguished in the 1520 tax. In addition, in each of the discussed taxes servants appear (male and female), sometimes described as a separate group of taxpayers, and sometimes treated as members of their employers' households. In the latter system, the fee from a servant began to vary depending on whether he worked for, for example, a village head or a farmer.

Although the sources preserved till our times do not allow us to determine how numerous on the scale of the country particular categories of peasant taxpayers were, the very fact of their distinguishing clearly shows the internal differentiation of the peasant estate. The terminology applied by the authors of tax proclamations also clearly indicates that in certain cases particular groups of the rural population were distinguished by their source of income, which did not always have to come from grain cultivation. Rural commerce, breeding, crafts, or transport must have been occupations so popular and perceptible by parliamentarians of noble origins, that they were worth distinguishing in acts of law and covering with other financial obligations. Also, frequent mention of peasant servants in the sources should be similarly perceived: they were so common and numerous that special attention had to be devoted to their taxation.

V. Conclusions

Both Anzelm Gostomski as well as other representatives of the noble elite sitting in parliament and making the tax system noticed the complex socio-economic structure of the peasant community in sixteenth-century Poland. They also understood that the formal division into professional categories distinguished legally were followed by different sources of income, and in everyday practice a norm was combining many activities. Their actions were dictated by the striving to maximise incomes from their own land estates through the use of their legal and economic advantage over the plebeian population, simultaneously restricting the level of peasants' tax extraction. The representatives of the noble elite did not know the theory of the Integrated Peasant Economy, but looked at peasant activity as if they co-created this theory. In his manual, Gostomski expressed observations on different sources of peasant incomes on the margin, and the tax laws used a simple and clear language, which did not allow for nuancing the reality, but both types of sources allow for tentative assessment of the nobility's perspective. Certainly, the nobility realised that the basis of peasant economy was farming, and Gostomski assessed it as more effective than manor farming and strived for supporting his subjects rather than their soulless exploitation. Both Gostomski and the tax legislators also saw the potential of other peasant activities in the primary sector: sheep and cattle breeding, exploitation of forests, fishing, wage day-labour in agriculture, and long-term farmhands at larger farms. Among the peasant activities in second and third sector, the nobles' attention was attracted by activities connected with crafts, transport, and commerce.

The tendency noted by historians for the share of smallholders and landless peasants to increase in the population structure in subsequent centuries (especially in the 18th century) must have been related to the growing importance of non-agricultural sources of peasants' income (Klein, Ogilvie, 2016). This situation was not typical only for Polish lands; the share of part-time farmers in rural communities was greater than in Poland in Silesia, Brandenburg or Mecklenburg (Cerman, 2012: 127), where the serfdom system also developed. Unfortunately, no studies are yet available that explain the long-term increase in the level of inequality among peasants and their non-agricultural activity as well. It can be assumed that such factors as the size of the village, access to land, the number of smallholders and cottagers, the presence of external entrepreneurs such as Jews, and the farming model preferred by the landowner must have influenced the economic activity of the peasants and their search for non-agricultural sources of income, but the situation of the rural population should be considered not as stable, but as changing over time. It is worth noting that the Polish peasants functioned under different conditions in the 16th century, which was the period of economic boom and peace, whereas their situation changed dramatically during the wars of the 17th and early 18th centuries.

Funding

This paper was written as part of the project 'Wealth inequalities in the Polish-Lithuanian Commonwealth and their socio-political consequences', financed by the National Science Centre (2018/31/D/HS3/00904).

Table 3.2. Integrated peasant economy activities checklist: sixteenth century Poland

Activity	Check
Primary sector	
Agricultural specialisation	x
Intensification of cultivation (no fallow, mixed-cropping, …)	
Wage day-labour in agriculture and longer-term farmhands on larger farms	x
Extension/intensification of animal husbandry	x
Intensification of forest exploitation (in primary sector, but also secondary and tertiary)	x
Extension of cultivated land (reclamation of commons and woods)	
Quarries	x
Fishing	x
Secondary sector	
Transformation of primary resources/products (e.g. wine, cheese, meat products; charcoal, lime)	x
Rural crafts	x
Domestic, putting-out system (proto-industry)	x
Work in 'centralized' industries and plants (manufactures, mining, etc.)	
Migrant/mobile craftsmen (e.g. bricklayers)	x
Wage labour in the industrial sector	
Tertiary sector	
Services in the field of long and medium distance trade (draft animal lease, fodder, lodging, inns)	x
Transport of other people's products and goods over short to medium distances	x
Trade with own products and goods over short to medium distances	x
Peddling	
Smuggling	x
Migrant/mobile workers (dock-workers, etc.)	x
Works of trust (estimation of land value, testimonies, etc.)	
Tourism	

Bibliography

Boroda, K. (2007), 'Kmieć, łan czy profit? Co było podstawą poboru łanowego w XV i XVI wieku', Guzowski., P., Liedke, M. (eds) *Człowiek wobec miar i czasu w przeszłości*, Kraków 2007, pp. 152-170.

Gostomski, A. (1951), *Gospodarstwo*, ed. S. Inglot, Wrocław 1951. Grodziski, S., Dwornicka, I., Uruszczak, W.(eds) (1996), *Volumina Constitutionum*, part I, vol. 1 (1493-1526), Warszawa.

Grodziski, S., Dwornicka, I., Uruszczak, W. (eds) (2005), *Volumina Constitutionum*, part II, vol. 1 (1550-1585), Warszawa.

Guzowski, P., (2005) *Changing Economy – Models of Peasant Budgets in 15th and 16th century Poland*, 'Continuity and Change' 20, 1, pp. 9-25.

——— (2008),*Chłopi i pieniądze na przełomie średniowiecza i czasów nowożytnych*, Kraków.

———; Sowina, U. (2022), 'Kingdom of Poland and the Grand Duchy of Lithuania', Menjot D., Caesar, M., Pijuan, P.V. (eds), *The Routledge Handbook of Public Taxation in Medieval Europe*, Abington, pp. 356-371.

Inglot, S. (1951), 'Wstęp', Gostomski A., *Gospodarstwo*, Wrocław, pp. I-XXXIX.

Lipiński, E. (1956), 'Anzelm Gostomski – ideolog wilczego głodu produktu dodatkowego', Lipiński, E., *Studia nad historią polskiej myśli ekonomicznej*, Warszawa, pp. 142-148.

Panjek, A., Larsson J., Mocarelli, L. (eds) (2017), *Integrated Peasant Economy in a Comparative perspective. Alps, Scandinavia and Beyond*, Koper.

Podraza, A. (1959/60), '*Gostomski Anzelm*', *Polski Słownik Biograficzny*, vol. 8, Wrocław-Kraków-Warszawa, pp. 362-364.

Rejestry poborowe województwa kaliskiego w XVI w. Atlas Źródeł i Materiałów do Dziejów Dawnej Polski, nr 2 ed. M. Słoń, Instytut Historii PAN im. Tadeusza Manteuffla 2015 available at: https://atlasfontium.pl/rejestry-poborowe-kaliskie/.

Rejestry poborowe województwa poznańskiego w XVI w. Atlas Źródeł i Materiałów do Dziejów Dawnej Polski, nr 3 ed. M. Słoń, Instytut Historii PAN im. Tadeusza Manteuffla 2015 – available at: https://atlasfontium.pl/rejestry-poborowe-poznanskie/.

Senkowski, J. (1970), 'Uniwersał poboru pogłównego z 1590 r.', *Kwartalnik Historii Kultury Materialnej* 18, 3, pp. 61-84.

Topolski, J. (1952), 'O literaturze i praktyce rolniczej w Polsce na przełomie XV i XVII wieku', Roczniki Dziejów Społecznych i Gospodarczych, p. 43-106.

——— (2000), *Przełom gospodarczy w Polsce XVI wieku i jego następstwa*, Poznań.

Wawrzyńczyk, A. (1962), *Gospodarstwo chłopskie na Mazowszu w XVI i na początku XVII wieku*, Warszawa.

Weyman, S. (1956), 'Pierwsze ustawy pogłównego generalnego (rok 1498, 1520) na tle ówczesnego systemu podatkowego', *Roczniki Dziejów Społecznych i Gospodarczych* 18, pp. 11-68.

Wyczański, A. (1964), *Studia nad gospodarką starostwa korczyńskiego w latach 1500-1660*, Warszawa.

——— (1966), 'Próba analizy matematycznej ekonomii gospodarstwa chłopskiego w Polsce XVI-XVIII w.', *Studia z Dziejów Gospodarstwa Wiejskiego*, vol. VIII, Warszawa, pp. 341-344.

——— (1977), *Uwarstwienie społeczne w Polsce XVI wieku*, Wrocław.

Żytkowicz, L. (1969), *Studia nad wydajnością gospodarstwa wiejskiego na Mazowszu w XVII wieku*, Warszawa.

JOSEF GRULICH

4. Rural Non-Agricultural Activities in South Bohemia During the Second Half of the Seventeenth and in the Eighteenth Century

I. Introduction

South Bohemia is a region with not very fertile land. Consequently, non-agricultural activities have always represented an important source of livelihoods for its rural inhabitants. This study[1] investigates non-agricultural rural activities in Southern Bohemia through a detailed quantitative analysis of land registers which recorded the main livelihoods of the inhabitants. It demonstrates the existence of a wide range of important non-agricultural activities in this region in the seventeenth and eighteenth centuries. The study focuses on three historic regions of Southern Bohemia and finds that non-agricultural activities arose in response to specific local conditions, particularly landscape, microclimate, road and water networks, the presence of forests, and availability of raw materials. The study demonstrates that rural non-agricultural activities were very important in South Bohemia, even though this was a region that was never one of the important proto-industrial areas of the Czech lands.

1 The research for this article was supported by the Czech Science Foundation/Grantová agentura České republiky (project No 21-16050S, 'Recruits, deserters, invalids and veterans. Military service and its influence on the structure of rural family in South Bohemia, 1780-1830'). I would like to express my thanks to Professor Sheilagh Ogilvie, FBA, Chichele Professor of Economic History, All Souls College, University of Oxford, for her very important comments on the text as well as her proof-reading of the content and English language. My thanks also go to Mgr. Václav Černý, Ph.D. for discussions of the topic of 'Soldiers – "away from the village"', as well as the creation of the map in the appendix.

Integrated Peasant Economy in Central and Eastern Europe, ed. by Aleksander Panjek, Rural History in Europe, 18 (Turnhout: Brepols, 2024), pp. 81–114
BREPOLS PUBLISHERS 10.1484/M.RURHE-EB.5.142465

II. Czech and European historiography on rural non-agricultural activities

Rural non-agricultural activities were discussed by Czech Marxist historians as early as the 1950s and 1960s. They were mostly considered in connection with the expansion of the putting-out-system and dispersed manufacturing. These were regarded as components of the first stage of industrialization, so the cottage-industrial producers of the eighteenth and nineteenth centuries were seen as 'a manufacturing working class' that became a predecessor of the modern proletariat (Klíma, 1955; Purš, 1965). The trouble was, however, that the statistics of that period, which were used by historians, reported the numbers of individuals making a living by industrial work only very partially. When people did industrial work only seasonally or occasionally, they did not constitute a working class in the modern sense but rather mainly comprised poorer groups within the rural population in a period in which agriculture was still the dominant rural activity (Machačová-Matějček, 2010: 79-82).

The phenomenon of 'proto-industrialization' was brought to the attention of Czech historians by Milan Myška (Myška, 1994a; 1994b). This theoretical concept had been invented by the Belgian-American researcher Franklin F. Mendels in the late 1960s, based on his research into demographic behaviour in a region of Flanders in the seventeenth and eighteenth centuries. Mendels pointed out that rural workers in this region were involved in cottage manufacturing, were not limited by guild regulations, and addressed demand on international markets. This is supposed to have given rise to a process of regional specialization, whereby some areas specialized in rural crafts and others in agriculture (Mendels, 1972; 1981). According to Mendels, regions that developed such cottage-industrial production later became centres of factory industry. The similarity of proto-industrial regions to regions of later factory-industrial production was visible in their demographic behaviour, he argued, as well as in the character of their population growth. Rapid population growth was connected to better material living standards. This made it possible for people to marry earlier, thereby lengthening the woman's fertile lifespan: in general, fertility rose, while mortality remained the same as in agricultural areas.

This concept was questioned by the American historians Charles and Richard Tilly, who, unlike Mendels, referred to 'industrialization before the factory system' (Tilly-Tilly, 1971). Another impulse for the debate about proto-industrialization was a book by three Göttingen historians, *Industrialization before Industrialization* (Kriedte, Medick and Schlumbohm, German original 1977; English translation 1981). For these authors, rapid population growth was the basis and driving force of the process of proto-industrialization. Hans Medick argued that proto-industry meant that security of livelihood was no longer dependent on an inherited landholding, i.e. on crop cultivation and cattle raising. Rural non-agricultural activity led to much earlier independence of villagers than was usual with an agricultural population. A couple did not have to wait to obtain the family landholding before marrying, so they married on average at a much lower age. Therefore, they were able to start a family earlier, and their children were a welcome addition to the familial labour force (Medick, 1976). This argument was also put forward for England by David Levine (1984).

During the 1980s, a number of historians argued against the idea that proto-industrialization was a driving force for population growth (Wrigley and Schofield, 1989). During the 1990s, both Mendels' concept and the Göttingen model of proto-industrialization received so much criticism that it was necessary to revise the most controversial topics, e.g. the matter of changes in population behaviour or transformations of social structure, which might have been both prerequisites and outcomes of proto-industrialization (Ogilvie, 1993; Cerman and Ogilvie, 1994; Kriedte, Medick and Schlumbohm, 1998). At the end of the twentieth century and at the beginning of the twenty-first century, researchers applied the existing proto-industrialization theories to different European regions, thereby initiating a new debate about proto-industrialization (Schlumbohm, 1994; Medick, 1996; Ogilvie, 1997; Marfany, 2012).

Czech proto-industrial regions were primarily studied by Arnošt Klíma (Klíma, 1955; 1957; 1963; 1979; 1991). Further research on these questions was carried out by Purš in connection with the Czech Industrial Revolution (Purš, 1965). The influence of rural cottage industries on the economic and demographic transformation of Bohemian regions was analysed by Ludmila Kárníková (Kárníková, 1965). However, none of these historians worked with the concept of proto-industrialization. Textile production (especially linen manufacturing), which in the eighteenth and in the first half of the nineteenth century was concentrated in the north-east of Bohemia and in the northern parts of Moravia and Silesia, managed to form early connections with the European market. These local cottage industries needed a huge labour force that was provided by serf families. Whereas the 'Göttingen model' argued that proto-industry caused the decline of the feudal system or even its destruction, in the Czech lands most of the noble overlords engaged in this business within their demesne economy. In some Bohemian regions, textile production was a supplementary activity to the dominant agricultural system; in other locations it turned into the main or sole source of livelihood for rural people. At the same time, the national Bohemian pattern should not be ignored: the Czech-speaking population prevailed in the agricultural regions, whereas the German-speaking population was dominant in the proto-industrial (mountain and submontane) areas.

Kriedte, Medick, and Schlumbohm argued that feudal lords who had withdrawn from involvement in business enabled capitalist factors and manufacturers to carry on proto-industrial activities in their dominions. These feudal lords were later rewarded by financial payments that they collected both from the capitalist factors and from the serfs. For the Czech lands, the 'Göttingen model' was criticized on the basis of evidence from rural regions of Bohemia where the economic activities of the noble overlords were combined with the 'second serfdom'. Specific research studies conducted for Bohemia, Moravia, and Silesia demonstrated that local noble overlords became actively involved in proto-industrial activities by financing and organizing them in their dominions. This business brought the noble landlords similar profits to those that were generated in the lands of typical proto-industrialization in which merchant capital predominated. Milan Myška illustrated this based on the examples of textile production (Myška, 1984) and iron and steel manufacturing (Myška, 1979).

During the 1990s, proto-industrialization was also studied within the international research project 'Social Structures in Early Modern Bohemia' (Cerman, 1999). Its results demonstrated not only the existence of regional differentiation but also the need to go beyond the assumption that there was a strict dichotomy between proto-industrial and agricultural areas. At the same time, this project also demonstrated the significance of social strata (e.g. smallholders) that managed to stimulate structural changes even within feudal estates (Cerman and Zeitlhofer, 2002; Cerman and Luft, 2005). The questions of non-agricultural and trade activities by serfs was researched, e.g. for the north-Bohemian estate of Frýdlant (Cerman, 1997; 2002; Ogilvie, 2002). For the region of the borderland between Bohemia and Upper Austria (the village of Kapličky) it was successfully demonstrated there had been mixed serf activities, i.e. agriculture alongside the timber trade, and the growing and subsequent processing of flax (Zeitlhofer, 2014: 86-115).

On the basis of quantitative analysis of the first Czech tax cadaster – the 1654 'Berní rula' – it was successfully demonstrated for the whole area of the Czech lands that non-agricultural activities observed in seventeenth-century Bohemia arose overwhelmingly from the initiative of villagers themselves. Noble overlords permitted those non-agricultural activities by serfs from which they themselves could extract rents (Klein and Ogilvie, 2016: 517-518). A similar situation can also be demonstrated for other European regions, e.g. in Slovenia where this process began earlier – in the sixteenth century – but then went into crisis in the seventeenth century (Panjek, 2011). In the area of north-east Bohemia, microhistorical research documented a two-way link between changes in social structure and increases in the non-agricultural activities of the village population. At the beginning of the eighteenth century, peasants (i.e. those holding enough arable land to support the entire household) and smallholders (those holding at least some arable land) prevailed among the inhabitants of the village of Stružinec. As a result of population growth, there was an increase in the number of cottagers during the eighteenth century. These belonged to the lower stratum of the village population which only owned a small house, sometimes a small piece of land, a so-called 'garden'. As early as the first half of the nineteenth century, members of this social stratum owned half of all landholdings in this locality. Most of them did not own any arable fields so they made their living by weaving, a craft that was supported by the local noble overlord as early as the first half of the eighteenth century (Nekvapil Jirásková, 2015; 2019: 280).

III. Sources

III.1. The 1654 'Berní rula' tax cadaster and social stratification in Bohemia

The great tax cadaster of 1654, which was called the 'Berní rula', was the outcome of a long series of negotiations between the sovereign and the Bohemian 'Estates' (i.e. parliament). The idea was that this systematic description of the country would be used as a basis for quantifying the number of taxpayers in the country. The 1654 tax cadaster recorded an enormous amount of information about each taxpayer, including his or her name (each farmer in a village, each burgher or craftsman in a town); how much arable land he or she owned (measured in 'strich', equal to about 0.285 hectares); how much land the farmer sowed in the autumn and in spring; how many deserted fields and houses there were in each village and town; the number of burned-down villages and 'burnt-out' farmers, because they were tax-exempt for two or three years; and the occupations of the taxpayers. A Bohemian subject paid taxes on almost everything he or she owned. For this reason, the tax cadaster also listed each taxpayer's livestock – teams of horses or oxen, cows, heifers, sheep, pigs, and sometimes also goats. Ownership of draft teams of horses or oxen was an important characteristic by which the tax-commissioners assigned farmers to different social strata (Matušíková and Ogilvie, 2006: 3-4).

In Bohemia, as in many other parts of central and eastern Europe, social stratum was not defined economically (in terms of occupation or wealth) or socio-culturally (in terms of education, speech, or consumption habits), but institutionally and legally. At the top of the village hierarchy were the 'peasants' (Czech *sedlák* or *rolník*, German *Bauer*), who owned enough arable land for the family to subsist entirely from agriculture, paid the highest manorial dues and state taxes, and owed the most forced labour to the overlord, often with draft animals as well as human workers. Then came the smallholders (Czech *zahradník*, German *Gärtner*), who had some arable land but not enough to subsist from, paid lower dues and taxes, and owed services to the landlords with human labour only. Finally, the cottagers (Czech *chalupník*, German *Häusler*) held only their own cottages and gardens, paid minor dues and taxes, and owed lighter (though increasing) labour services. All other Bohemian serfs lived in households headed by members of these three official strata, as family members, servants, or inmate-lodgers (Czech *podruh*, German *Freibauer*). Jews (Czech *žid*, German *Jude*), also dwelt in Bohemian villages under manorial 'privileges' (Klein and Ogilvie, 2016: 505; Matušíková and Ogilvie, 2006: 4).

The commissioners also recorded the quality of the land in each village in three categories: rich, medium and poor. This proved very useful when taxes were collected, since the quality of the land affected the productivity of the farm and the farmer's ability to pay taxes. The historical background to the creation of this great tax cadaster of 1654 was the loss of population in Bohemia during the Thirty Years' War between 1618 and 1648 (Fialová et al., 1996: 100-105). This led to a huge increase in the number of deserted houses and farms in every village and town in the country. In turn, this generated strong pressure for the overlords to compel their serfs to stay on the estate, in order to fill up and cultivate the deserted landholdings. The overlords were supported in this by the sovereign, who wanted to keep his subjects settled and paying taxes (Matušíková and Ogilvie, 2006: 4).

The 1654 tax cadaster was drawn up for the entirety of Bohemia, and provides valuable information on the structure of the local economy. The historiography contains occasional speculations that the numbers of rural people engaged in non-agricultural work may be a slight under-estimate because taxation was based mainly on landholding, which was the primary focus of these land registers. Nonetheless, both the Czech and the international historiography have concluded that these documentary records are trustworthy sources on the economic and social realities of Bohemian society in the seventeenth and eighteenth centuries.

III.2. The 1710-1713 'Theresianum' tax cadaster

At the beginning of the eighteenth century, economic development and changes in social conditions in Bohemia called forth a fiscal reform. This was the origin of the second great Bohemian tax cadaster of 1710-1713, which we call Theresianum (after Empress Maria Theresa who ordered it to be drawn up). The first phase of this great early-eighteenth-century tax reform gave rise to a document called the 'Fasse'. This was the income return, prepared by the overlord's main office on each feudal estate. This document included the names of the landowners; the number of their arable fields with information about the quality of land; the quantity of pasture on the estate (measured in terms of the numbers of cartloads of hay they produced); the number of livestock (teams of horses and oxen, cows, heifers, sheep, and pigs); and other sources of income of the inhabitants, for instance from crafts, small plots of forest, fishponds, and small businesses such as those of teamster or carter. The information provided in the 'Fasse', or income return, was later checked by special commissioners, and the annual tax levy was based on their results. However, the preparation of the great new Theresianum tax cadaster was a very long process because there were numerous complaints against the registration, which were repeatedly referred back to the commissions. So the final version – the so-called 'Elaborate' – was only finished in 1748 and only published in 1757 (Matušíková and Ogilvie, 2006: 5).

IV. The 'second serfdom', craft production, inheritance practices, and population growth

During the Thirty Years' War (1618-1648), most rural areas of Bohemia were devastated. It is estimated that the population fell by one quarter to one third; many rural holdings remained vacant. This demographic crisis contributed to intensifying the so-called 'second serfdom', during which the power of the landlords over the serfs was reinforced (Maur, 1985: 241-247; Ogilvie, 2005: 80-91). The landlords compensated for the loss of labour by increasing their extraction of forced serf labour and by limiting the personal freedom of their serfs. Besides working in the fields, peasants were required to transport their overlord's goods to markets even beyond the borders of the estate. The lord's officers monitored the serfs to see if they were farming their holdings well and were not neglecting their fields, because the lord's administrators often bought the serfs' surplus, which they sold at a profit. The lord also wanted serf holdings to be in a good economic condition so that serfs would be able to buy goods from the lord's demesne production (e.g. beer from the manorial brewery, fish from the manorial fishponds) and to pay for manorial services (e.g. for grain milling). The serfs had to be able to make money in order to pay money rents to the landlord, the church, and the state (Mikulec, 1993: 9-54).

The eighteenth century saw an increase in the importance of craft production in Bohemia. Most full-size towns and small market-towns continued to be the local centres of crafts and trades. The most important source of income for local inhabitants was still farming. Only towns which specialized in textile production for distant markets or in exporting abroad grew at a faster pace (Jindra and Jakubec, 2015: 254). In the area of the Bohemian-Moravian Highlands this trend can be illustrated by the example of some full-size towns (such as Jindřichův Hradec and Počátky) and a few smaller towns (such as Nová Bystřice) which built their prosperity on woollen-weaving (Martínek, 2000: 157). The production of woven fabrics of flax (linen) was concentrated in smaller but fast-growing towns (Kunžak, Strmilov) from which it spread into neighbouring villages. There arose a symbiosis between manufactory systems and guild production which also involved rural weavers. The production of woollen and linen yarn was a source of livelihood mainly for cottage weavers in overpopulated and not very fertile mountain and submontane areas with large numbers of landless persons. The higher population density that prevailed in these regions directly reflected the existence of work opportunities, specifically the possibility of linen processing and weaving. In places where the fields were so infertile that they did not provide sufficient livelihoods, rural people did not behave passively, but instead actively sought out opportunities in proto-industrial production. Local inhabitants engaged in weaving both full-time and as a by-employment (Jindra and Jakubec, 2015: 254).

The government tried to support the growth of export crafts by dismantling old-fashioned forms of production. During the reign of Empress Maria Theresa (1740-1780), the Bohemian state gradually changed the privileges of the guilds. Restrictions on the number of workshops, masters, journeymen and apprentices, or on total output, were gradually dismantled, and new production processes began to be permitted. In contrast to the so-called 'regulated' (*Polizei*) crafts supplying the local market (e.g. the food and clothing crafts), the state defined a set of so-called 'commercial' crafts, producing goods for wider markets within the entire province or beyond the borders of the Habsburg Monarchy, controlled by the provincial authorities. Between the 1750s and the 1770s, textile production was placed among the so-called 'free' crafts. However, the guild organization was not abolished until 1859 because the state saw it as a means for maintaining public order (Jindra and Jakubec, 2015: 255).

During the reign of Maria Theresa (1740-1780) and her son Joseph (1780-1790), a long-term growth in population took place. For example, the South Bohemian town of Jindřichův Hradec grew to become one of the four largest rural towns in the Czech lands in the first half of the eighteenth century (Fialová et al., 1996: 130). The growth in population increased the supply of labour and at the same time contributed to a greater demand for food and industrial goods. As a result of using traditional methods of cultivating the fields and raising animals, agricultural production slowly reached its limits, leading to a great famine in 1771-1772 (Grulich, 2008: 140-145). Also, some owners of noble estates became aware of this unsustainability in the agricultural situation. A solution might have been to cultivate new crops, end crop monocultures, and move away from the traditional three-field crop-rotation system and the associated animal-raising practices, but this seldom happened. In rural areas, population growth resulted in a growing number of poor cottagers and also inmate-lodgers with very little or no land (Černý, 2021: 25).

These people made their livings by engaging in cottage production, not only in textile manufacturing but also in other types of production, such as glass carving and glass painting in the Šumava mountain range (also called the Bohemian Forest).

The inheritance law was another reason for the increase in the size of poorer groups among the rural inhabitants. In the interest of maintaining the productivity of the serf economy, the family holding was legally impartible. There was only one, usually male, successor who was allowed to take over the whole holding; all other heirs were supposed to be gradually paid off by means of inheritance shares (Procházka, 1963: 453-510; Velková, 2009: 150-174). The new holder was burdened heavily by the obligation to pay off inheritance shares to his non-inheriting siblings or by debts that had been incurred by the previous owner and were still attached to the holding. Neither the brothers nor the sisters of the person who inherited the holding had any guarantee of the date at which their financial claims would be paid off, and whether they would receive full or only part payment. The holder's ability to pay off his non-inheriting siblings depended on many factors, including the condition of the farm, fluctuations in the weather, and the uncertain perspective of the crops.

Although we observe an increase in the population of rural areas of Bohemia during the eighteenth century, the number of full peasant holdings did not change because of the limited extent of the land and the legal impartibility of farms. There arose only cottager holdings whose owners did not own any land and worked as inmate-lodgers and day-labourers. On the one hand, the abolition of serfdom (1781) helped to solve rural over-population and the impossibility of making a living in agriculture; on the other, it also solved the scarcity of labour in industrial production. By liberating the peasants and improving villagers' rights over their holdings, the state sought to achieve higher agriculture output and thereby increase revenues for the state treasury. The rise in rural consumer capacity was also supposed to support proto-industrial businesses.

V. The region under analysis: South Bohemia

Compared to its surroundings, South Bohemia has always seemed to be a little closed. The character of the landscape is mostly hilly; the local soil is mediocre or poor in quality; a colder climate prevails. Although most of the area of South Bohemia does not have suitable natural conditions for growing crops or raising animals, in the early modern period agriculture provided a livelihood for the majority of inhabitants. Trade in agricultural products was carried out not only within local markets, i.e. around the full-size towns and small market towns of the region. Land routes and also the rivers (especially the Vltava) made trade possible even over longer distances. South Bohemia, which consists of the regions of Budějovice, Tábor, and Prácheň, can be divided into four geographical areas: 1. the montane and submontane region of Šumava in the south-west; 2. the hilly landscape of the Bohemian-Moravian Highlands in the south-east and north-east; 3. the central flat fishpond area in the basin of Budějovice and Třeboň and the surroundings of the Vltava river; and 4. the rolling landscape of the Středočeská pahorkatina in the north-west.

The basis of agricultural production in South Bohemia consisted mainly in cultivating plants, even in hilly landscapes which also had cattle raising. Cereals, root crops, legumes, vegetables and fruit, along with flax and hemp, were used in four different ways. First, they were the basis of the diet of the householder and his family. Second, they provided fodder (oats) without which cattle would not survive winter. Third, they were sold on the market, since every householder had to sell at least a small share of his or her grain or other crops to be able to pay taxes to the state, the landlord, and the church, as well as to buy things necessary for the functioning of the household; rent in kind was rendered to the landlord mainly in the form of grain. Fourth, plant production was also useful for manufacturing. On every holding, family members spun yarn from flax for rough linen cloth. From flax seeds, rural people obtained oil for lighting and wheel greasing. Straw was used for making thatch or weaving baskets. In the seventeenth and eighteenth centuries, wheat comprised the main rural crop (for white flour sold to the towns); barley was produced for brewers' malt; rye and oats were sold less widely.

Cottage manufacturing in South Bohemia was not as extensive and important as in North-East Bohemia. Due to lower population density, it was observable here to a much lower extent. Most of the rural inhabitants were employed by the textile proto-industry, especially in the growing, processing, and (especially) spinning of flax, as discussed in detail above. South Bohemian spinners were concentrated in villages, especially around the full-size towns and small market towns which were the traditional centres of textile production, such as Jindřichův Hradec and Nová Bystřice. In this way, rural inhabitants had the opportunity to engage in seasonal work and earn welcome 'extra money' during the winter. Although South Bohemia was an important glassmaking region which also produced for export, the only cottage occupation related to this industry was the painting and cutting of glass in the Šumava mountain range and in Novohradské hory.

The richness of the forests in South Bohemia stimulated cottage manufacturing in the processing of wood as well. Its basis lay in the primitive division of labour of medieval small-scale production when people made simple tools and furniture for themselves. In the areas that were rich in forests, villagers cut down trees and made timber, craft wood, and fuel wood for transport to towns and forestless areas. In these cases, there was a mutual interrelationship among production for personal domestic consumption, wage-work, and craft businesses. These forms of production were described in the 1654 'Berní rula' tax cadaster when assessing the gainful opportunities of the population. The great Theresianum tax cadaster of 1710-1748 mentioned wood processing as an option for making money, not across the whole regional but just in some villages.

In rural areas, cottage manufacturing and crafts were practised by landless day-labourers and inmate-lodgers as well as by members of the poorer strata of the rural population (cottagers). A typical rural non-agricultural activity in South Bohemia was working as a carter. Draft animals such as oxen and horses were owned mainly by better-off peasants and to a lesser extent also by smallholders. Another profitable activity was salt importing from Upper Austria and Bavaria. As a result of the imposition of tolls and custom duties, the profitability of salt importing decreased so that during the eighteenth century carters lost interest in this activity. Exports from Bohemia included cereal, textile, and glass products and fish from the South Bohemian fishpond areas. The transporting of wood retained its long-term importance in South Bohemia. The wood was transported from forest districts to the locations in which it was consumed, mainly the urban centres of the feudal estates. If the wood was destined for a more distant market, it was carried on carts to the river and then floated downstream on rafts to Prague. These opportunities relied on the advantageous location of South Bohemia on the so-called Salt Road and also alongside an important water highway – the Vltava river.

In the second half of the seventeenth century and during the eighteenth century, rural non-agricultural activities in Bohemia were oriented around the interests and needs of the noble estates. Some activities were part of the coerced labour owed by serfs to their lords; these included bobbin lacemaking, mining, wood-transporting, transporting raw materials to ironworks, long-distance carting, and transporting the output of the landlord's demesne operations to the market. The Czech noble landlords permitted those non-agricultural activities by serfs from which they themselves could extort rents (Klein and Ogilvie, 2016: 518). On this basis, serfs could be used within the putting-out system. Villagers whose agricultural activities were not very profitable because of infertile soil or a colder climate finally started to bring money to the estate owner. A manufactory, via its factor, provided the noble landlord with a share of the profits. From rural non-agricultural activities, serfs obtained money for satisfying their own needs and also the financial demands of the state, the landlord, and the Catholic church. This study shows that rural non-agricultural activities had a great importance in South Bohemia, even though it was never one of the important proto-industrial regions of the Czech lands.

VI. The estate of Nová Bystřice (Neu Bistritz in German) – an example of relationships among landlords, factors, and spinners

Most Czech proto-industrial regions emerged due to a local source of raw materials – in the case of textile production, flax or wool. In the Czech lands it is possible to document the rise of proto-industries in submontane and mountain areas where the soil or weather conditions were less suitable for agriculture. In this case, the term 'proto-industry' is used not to refer to cottage manufacturing as a preparatory phase for later factory industrialisation, but rather to the putting-out-system which started to be practised in the Czech lands from the end of the Thirty Years' War onwards. Dispersed cottage manufacturing reached its peak in the Czech lands in the eighteenth century. In some Bohemian regions, part of the population made its living outside agriculture from as early as the seventeenth century. This situation is reflected in the 1654 Berní rula tax cadaster and the great Theresian tax cadaster of 1710-1748 for the South Bohemian estate of Nová Bystřice (BR 4, pp. 6-18, 24-27; TK 2, 354-355). Further information comes from the files of the Manufactory Collegium (hereafter ČG.com) in the records of the Czech Gubernium held in the National Archives in Prague. Reports from the regional commercial commissioner make it possible to explore the relationships among the landlords, the factors, and the spinners on this estate, as well as the connections between the textile proto-industry in South Bohemia and manufactories in Linz (Upper Austria), Schwechat (Lower Austria), and Šaštín (Slovakia), demonstrating the South Bohemian textile proto-industry's links with foreign markets.

Francis Stephen of Lorraine, the husband of Empress Maria Theresa, sought to support the development of textile production in Bohemia as in other parts of the Habsburg lands. On his Slovak estate of Šaštín, for instance, he established a manufactory for cotton fabrics in 1736, which obtained the same privileges as the manufactory in Schwechat in Lower Austria had secured ten years earlier, in 1726. Its factor, F. A. Dedlmayer from Dodersberg, entered into a contract with the owner of the estate of Nová Bystřice on 8 December 1762. Count Karl Ignatz Clary-Aldringen promised that during the period that his serfs worked as cotton spinners, he would protect the interests of the manufactory, or more precisely, he would arrange for a sufficient labour supply and ensure the quality of products. A similar contract with F. A. Dedlmayer, the factor of the manufactory in Šaštín, was also entered into by the owner of the neighbouring estate of Landštejn. Count Josef Jan Herberstein was the overlord of both the Bohemian estate of Landštejn and the Lower Austrian estate of Dodersberg. At the same time, Dedlmayer was a factor of the manufactory in Šaštín and a manorial administrator of the estate of Dobersberg which bordered on the estate of Landštejn. Via his person, the interests of the manufactory and the estate were closely knit together. The owner of the estate of Landštejn, Count Herberstein, also pledged to protect the interests of the manufactory in case anyone offered the spinners higher pay (Klíma, 1955: 375).

The end of the privileges for the manufactories in Schwechat and Šaštín in 1762 was an important milestone. In 1763, a principle of free enterprise came into operation, leading to the foundation of new manufactories, which often competed with each other. In the second half of the eighteenth century, a big problem for woollen and cotton manufactories in Bohemia was a scarcity of spinners. The government wanted to solve this situation by allocating all the village spinners, who worked from home, to the districts of particular manufactories. Within the economic policy pursued by the Habsburg monarchy, from the second half of the eighteenth century onwards, we observe a centralized manufactory system of this sort increasingly implemented side-by-side with the putting-out system. This was supposed to prevent competition among manufactories for workers. This intention failed to be implemented and from 1763 onwards there was competition not only in the localities where the finished products were sold, but also in those where the work was done, in a struggle to obtain new workers. There were plenty of new manufactories, all of which needed spinners.

The demand by consumers for cheap cotton cloth contributed to the development of new manufactories in the Czech lands. The cotton boom was supported by opportunities for a quick turnover of investments and high profits. Josef Bolza (who came from Milan), Francis Stephen of Lorraine's man of finance, who was awarded the title of count for his services in 1761, was fully aware of this. Due to his marriage, he came to central Bohemia where he started the production of cotton cloth in his manufactory in Kosmonosy in the spring of 1763 (Klíma, 1955: 390-391). The then owner of the estate of Nová Bystřice, Karel Ignác Count Clary-Aldringen, was tempted by a vision of a quick profit. Along with Count Bolza he established a spinning mill in Nová Bystřice that was supposed to work for the manufactory in Kosmonosy. However, immediately after its foundation the mill started to entice spinners away from other localities. The promise of higher pay made serfs from the neighbouring estate of Landštejn lodge a complaint against their overlord with the regional authorities (on 7 February 1764). The overlord was making them spin for factor Dedlmayer to supply the Šaštín manufactory, although they could have got higher pay by working for the spinning mill and the weaving mill in Nová Bystřice which supplied the Kosmonosy manufactory.

When the manufactory in Kosmonosy stopped operating in 1768, Count Karl Ignatz Clary-Aldringen entered into a new contract with a manufactory in Fridau in Lower Austria. He granted permission for the

Fridau manufactory to employ his serfs as spinners and weavers for six years. The manufactory made a commitment to supply Bohemia with cotton for weaving and spinning. To its employees it guaranteed stable jobs and fixed pay. Later, when the overlord got the opportunity to enter into a more profitable contract with the Schwechat manufactory in 1780, the old contract was not renewed. The factor of the Fridau manufactory was even forbidden to do business on the estate of Nová Bystřice, and was arrested and thrown in prison.

The noble overlords entered into contracts with manufactories because in agriculturally infertile areas there were few employment opportunities for their serfs. If serfs wove and spun, the overlord was entitled to receive payments from the manufactory, i.e. a percentage of the value of the output. Furthermore, the overlord had the certainty that he would also be able to collect dues on these activities from the serfs (Klíma, 1955: 377). A spinner or weaver did not work because the overlord compelled him or her to do so, but rather because it gave them the opportunity to make extra money in the quiet season of the year.

A special position within textile manufacturing was occupied by a wool manufactory established in 1672 in Linz in Upper Austria. This manufactory became the property in 1754 of a Vienna bank which was a financial enterprise of Maria Theresa's husband, Francis Stephen of Lorraine. According to an administrative report issued in 1773, the manufactory employed 11,783 people in the Czech lands, who were paid a total of 14,145 *Gulden*. The Linz manufactory had many factors in the region, some of whom came from the ranks of rich serfs. These factors distributed the raw material to cottage spinners, collected the yarn from them, and paid them. In 1776, there was a dispute in South Bohemia because one of the factors of the Nová Bystřice manufactory, the innkeeper Kašpar Dewert, had, in 1756, set up a cotton mill in Jindřichův Hradec. Then he began to persuade the spinners who worked for the Linz manufactory to start spinning cotton for a rival company in Nová Bystřice. The Linz manufactory lodged a complaint and the disputed issue was investigated by a regional commercial commissioner. It turned out that the factors from the Linz manufactory who complained against Dewert had stolen from the spinners and had not given them all the money paid by the Linz manufactory. As a result, a part of the spinners' salary had ended up in the Linz factors' pockets.

Dewert, as a factor of the Nová Bystřice manufactory, offered the spinners higher pay than they received from the factors of the Linz manufactory, so they preferred to work for him. Dewert expanded his mill by recruiting additional workers. According to a 1775 report by the commercial commissioner Svoboda from Tábor, Kašpar employed 500 wool spinners and 250 cotton spinners. He supplied woollen yarn to the Poneggen stocking-making manufactory in Lower Austria and cotton yarn to a restored manufactory in Kosmonosy. When it turned out that cotton spinning was more profitable, he ceased wool spinning and his employees only spun cotton. Dewert was very flexible in his business dealings, and later also cooperated with a manufactory in Šaštín in Slovakia (Klíma, 1955: 377-378).

VII. South Bohemian rural non-agricultural activity in the light of the land cadasters

Research conducted on the basis of the land cadasters for South Bohemia, specifically for the regions of Prácheň and Bechyně, casts light on rural non-agricultural activities. Maria Theresa's statute of 23 January 1751 divided the Bechyně region into two territories: Budějovice and Tábor. The published editions of the 1654 'Berní rula' tax cadaster (hereinafter BR) and the Theresian tax cadaster of 1710-1748 (hereinafter TK) were analysed with special attention to information about rural non-agricultural activities – not only cottage industry but all production activities of villagers outside agriculture.

VII.1. Work as a day-labourer

The most common job for the poorest strata of the rural population in all parts of South Bohemia was casual labour. Notes such as 'he works as a day-labourer – they earn their bread by everyday work – they made a hard living by manual work' – were common for persons recorded as inmate-lodgers or day-labourers. For instance, on the estate of Český Krumlov, the village of Skubice was recorded as having 'one day-labourer and four inmate-lodgers' (TK 1, p. 119). These belonged to the poorer strata of the rural population who found employment in the place of their residence or nearby, as in the village of Žďár on the estate of Protivín, where there were 'three inmate-lodgers for day-labour at the neighbour's, another three in cottages owned by the village community, one in his own cottage' (TK 2, p. 257). There were numerous day-labourers on Czech noble estates. On the small gentry estate of Chlum u Třeboně, they comprised one-third of all recorded persons (TK 1, p. 135), whereas on the estate of Jindřichův Hradec, they made up one-quarter of the total (TK 2, p. 337, 339, 341).
However, the particular type of work that day-labourers carried out was mostly not recorded in the cadasters. It was only mentioned sporadically, as in the village of Lodhéřov on the estate of Jindřichův Hradec, where there were '22 day-labourers making their living by flax-spinning' (TK 2, p. 337). In some cases, the specific type of work was recorded only for some individuals, as in the village of Strmilov on the estate of Kunžak, which recorded '6 day-labourers, 2 of them work as spinners' (TK 2,

p. 345). A day-labourer, as a casual worker, carried out various jobs according to necessity and opportunity. Non-agricultural work might be replaced, depending on local conditions, by seasonal agriculture jobs such as threshing.

VII.2. Domestic flax-spinning

A very common type of work for the poorer strata of the rural population, such as cottagers and inmate-lodgers, was cottage textile production, especially flax-spinning. It is possible to observe this activity in varying intensity across most of the South Bohemian area. In places where the raw materials were not sufficiently plentiful, it only served to satisfy local demand, as on the estate of Nové Hrady (Chalupa, 1969: 295). Growing and processing flax had economic significance for the estates of Český Krumlov (BR 5, p. 385) and Vyšší Brod (BR 5, p. 385), where it was often recorded that 'the serfs make a huge profit from linen and spinning'. Part of the south Bohemian textile output went to markets in Upper Austria (Linz) and Bavaria (Passau): 'Full peasant farmers also sow flax that they later sell either untreated or in the form of yarn or linen to the areas of Upper Austria and Passau' (TK 1, p. 117). Whereas on the estates of Český Krumlov and Vyšší Brod people had, apart from their relatively infertile fields, various other sources of livelihood (such as cattle raising, wood transporting, and salt transporting), the situation was different on the estate of Rožmberk, where, 'Earnings are low, [and] people usually make some extra money by spinning' (TK 1, p. 145). Where there was poor soil combined with a colder climate, flax-spinning was a welcome source of livelihood.

To varying degrees, members of all rural social strata profited from growing flax. Whereas peasants and smallholders sowed flax regularly, cottagers had to buy it from them to make their livings by spinning. Cottagers or inmate-lodgers, with very few exceptions, did not own any arable fields so they had no place to sow flax. On the estate of Kunžak, flax-spinning was mentioned as the main source of livelihood for the poor (Chalupa, 1969: 292). The preparation of fine yarn was connected to flax-drying in village hemp-kilns whose number was stated in the cadasters, e.g. in the village of Malíkov nad Nežárkou on the estate of Jindřichův Hradec, there was 'a communal hemp-kiln in the village; the householders grow flax' (TK 2, p. 339). Domestic textile production was a source of prosperity for some South Bohemian towns, e.g. in the town of Cetviny on the estate of Rožmberk, 'the serfs make extra money by linen bleaching and spinning' (TK 1, p. 145). The great importance of linen production emerges from documents for the area of the Bohemian-Moravian Highlands (Martínek, 2000: 142). The small towns in this area reported large numbers of linen-weavers: on the estate of Kunžak, there were 45 in the town of Kunžak and 51 in the town of Strmilov (TK 2, 345). On the estate of Jindřichův Hradec, linen production was more extensive in the villages than in the town of Jindřichův Hradec itself (which had only 39 linen-weavers) or in the town of Číměř (which had just 20 linen-weavers). There were 56 villages on the estate, with 134 linen-weavers, meaning that two-thirds of all linen-weavers on this estate were based in the villages (TK 2, p. 336-341).

VII.3. Lacemaking

Bobbin lace started to be made in the second half of the sixteenth century in the Ore Mountains (Krušné hory) in West Bohemia. This activity became a new source of livelihood for the inhabitants of Jáchymov, after the decline of mining. From the first half of the seventeenth century on, the East Bohemian town of Vamberk also became a centre of lacemaking. The local estate came into the possession of the imperial general Kašpar von Gramb. His wife, Magdalena von Gramb, who came from Flanders, introduced the making of bobbin lace as a component of the coerced labour services local serfs had to carry out for the lord. In the south of Bohemia, there was no consistent lacemaking area. Around the mid-eighteenth century, lacemaking developed in Sedlice u Blatné due to the initiative of Countess Ludmila Černínová. There, too, the making of bobbin lace was a component of the coerced labour services which serfs had to carry out for the lord (Robek et al., 1987: 78). Lacemaking in South Bohemia was important in small mining towns. As soon as silver mining became unprofitable (Hůry, Ratibořské Hory, Rudolfov), miners' wives turned to lacemaking. For example, the small town of Hůrky on the estate of Nová Bystřice recorded that 'in the report from 1722 there were 12 more women making a living by lacemaking' (TK 2, p. 335). The largest number of lacemaking workers in South Bohemia was reported in the small town of Rudolfov, near the city of České Budějovice (Robek et al., 1987: 78).

VII.4. Logging

One of the oldest rural industrial sectors was logging. Woodlands were of great significance within the system of the integrated peasant economy in many European countries, even in the territory of the Pontifical state (Sansa, 2017). There were dense forests in Bohemia, especially in the border areas. Logging was dependent on getting permission from noble landlords who owned most of the forest cover. There were often communal forests pertaining to villages, and in some plentifully forested areas, rich peasants also appeared among the private owners of small pieces of forest. Logging was often a supplementary activity undertaken in areas where arable fields were infertile. On the estate of Orlík it was noted that serfs had previously owed arrears of dues to the landlord which they had paid off by clearing the forests and selling the wood. The local nobility reacted to this newly-emerging situation by radically limiting logging. Pre-established annual limits on logging were supposed to help the renewal of forest cover (TK 2, p. 249). Although rural occupations did not include any woodcutters, in the village of Zahrádka it was noted: 'Full peasant farmers in this village, as in some other villages, sell timber and raft wood, each for 3-6 *Gulden* a year'; in the village of Jetěnice, '2 wood-traders' were recorded among the inmate-lodgers (TK 2, p. 251). A different situation prevailed on the estate of Český Krumlov where logging was one of the coerced labour services owed to the landlord by serfs from certain villages (TK 1, p. 117).

VII.5. Wood trading, transporting, and rafting

In the western part of South Bohemia (the Šumava mountain range, the estates of Orlík and Zvíkov, and the area around the town of Písek), the forest was a proper source of livelihood and income. Peasants transported felled tree trunks on their carts down to the Vltava river. On the estates of Orlík and Zvíkov, peasants owned a lot of woods so they profited not only from transporting timber but also from cutting it down and selling it (BR 28, pp. 464-500). The trouble was that when they reached the river, the logs were bought from them for a 'lousy and low price' by middlemen who organized the construction of wooden rafts and hired the raftsmen. The raftsmen were paid 2 *Gulden* for their trip to Prague but 'they easily spent them on the way and the rest in Prague' (BR 27, pp. 23-24).

Rafting and floating of wood is documented in many places along the river Vltava. In the village of Varvařov on the estate of the same name, 'peasants of this village buy from their noble overlord 20 tree trunks a year and another pile of wood from windfalls. Then they bind the logs together (cottagers buy half the amount) to make rafts and float them down the river to Prague to sell. The same applies to other villages on this lord's estate' (TK 2, p. 297). On the nearby estate of Orlík it was noted in 1654 that 'the serfs have very good opportunities logging on the water' (TK 28, p. 500). In the villages along the banks of the Vltava, raftsmen from both wealthy and poor serf strata were recorded: in the village of Chrást, there were 6 raftsmen – 3 'osedlý' (this was standard unit, in which one *osedlý* was defined as equal to one 'peasant') and 3 day-labourers (TK 2, p. 251). A similar situation was also observed on the estate of Bernatice. In the village of Podolsko, 'the inhabitants make their living mostly by floating wood', while in the village of Staré Sedlo, 'the inhabitants make their living by floating wood, which they also use to build their houses' (TK 2, p. 325).

The river Lužnice, the right-bank tributary of the Vltava, was used for rafting, for instance by serfs from the village of Nuzice on the estate of

Bechyně, where there were '6 inmate-lodgers who make their living by floating wood down to Prague, and their wives by flax-spinning'. Problems arose when wood supplies were depleted, rafting ended, and local inhabitants lost a profitable source of livelihood. For example, on the estate of Týn nad Vltavou, 'the town at one time conducted a wood business and floated salt on rafts but after the forests on the estate were cleared, this activity was conducted by serfs of other estates' (TK 1, p. 155).

In the south-east of Bohemia, too, especially on the estate of Jindřichův Hradec, forests were owned by peasants who cut them down and then transported the wood to the nearby town of Jindřichův Hradec to sell. Their fields were infertile, so cutting and selling wood represented a vital source of income (BR 4, p. 263). Serfs on the estate of Český Krumlov transported and sold wood not only in the nearby estate capital, the town of Český Krumlov, but also in the more distant administrative centre of southern Bohemia, the royal free town of České Budějovice (BR 5, p. 459). In forested areas, the transport of wood, along with its sale, represented an important source of income for serfs.

VII.6. Wood processing

Wood was a livelihood not only for those who cut it, worked it, and arranged for its transport. There was a whole range of other occupations that depended on it. In villages, these mainly consisted of joiners, wheelwrights, carpenters, and shingle-makers. Wood was used for making roofing, farm equipment, and domestic utensils, as in the village of Krasetín on the estate of Český Krumlov: 'There is a total of 8 inmate-lodgers, [of which] 2 earn their livings by making shingles and wooden tools that are needed by the full peasant farmers' (TK 1, p. 125).

In the forests, colliers burnt charcoal for the needs of craftsmen such as blacksmiths and for proto-industrial manufactories such as iron-mills, blast furnaces, and glassworks. Charcoal-fired blast furnaces used oak wood, while iron-mills and blacksmiths' workshops used fir and spruce wood.

One of the by-products of charcoal burning was the production of axle grease. This was a lubricant for revolving parts such as cart wheels. In villages on the forested Czech-Austrian border, such as the villages of Hamr and Klikov on the estate of Chlum u Třeboně, it was noted that 'they make their living by axle grease' (BR 4, pp. 23-24). The noble overlords supported the production of axle grease by allowing their serfs to dig out tree stumps from which they got resin and produced axle grease in manorial or communal village kilns.

Besides the axle grease makers, resin makers, and colliers, other forest producers included ash burners who burnt wood down to ashes. For a very long time, ash was the only material used to make potash, which was an important material for glass production, and was also used in linen manufacturing and to make soap (Woitsch et al., 2003: 107-180; 2019: 11-31).

VII.7. Salt trading and transporting

The proximity of political frontiers provided opportunities for trading activities. The most important was the trade in salt which was brought from Upper Austria (across from the estate of Český Krumlov) or from Bavaria (across from the estate of Vimperk). The salt trade employed serfs from the noble estates of Český Krumlov, Rožmberk, Nové Hrady, České Budějovice, and Vimperk (BR 5, p. 385, 681, 765; BR 7, p. 1237; BR 28, p. 541). The monastery estates of Vyšší Brod and Zlatá Koruna (BR 5, p. 432, 446) also profited from this trade. In the second half of the seventeenth century, carters earned 30 *Kreuzer* for each barrel of salt they transported. This income gave them a good livelihood (BR 5, p. 385, 432). The salt trade was lucrative so it was practised not only by carters from the estates which lay along the so-called Salt Road but also by those from more distant places such as the small towns of Lišov and Stráž nad Nežárkou (BR 6, p. 548, 792). Participation in the salt trade can also be documented for villagers from more distant locations, such as the village of Lidmaň on the estate of Černovice. The impossibility of making a living from infertile soil made villagers travel as far as 130 kilometres to pick up the wares (BR 4, p. 111).

The transporting of salt between the Upper Austrian town of Freistadt and the Bohemian town of České Budejovice was carried out by carters using their own carts. Some of the salt was transported further on ships to Prague along the Vltava river. Like rafting, river transport also employed the poorer strata of the rural population. In the eighteenth century, there was an increase in salt transportation as a result of lords' imposing compulsory carting services on their serfs, which was profitable for those noble landlords who were charged with salt distribution. For example, between 1735 and 1740 an annual average of 88,334.6 quintals of salt was transported into the town of České Budějovice on 13,000-16,000 carts (Kopáček et al., 2005: 356). However, as the transporting of salt became increasingly subject to tolls and charges, this activity ceased to be lucrative. Because the rewards were minimal, rural carters lost interest in undertaking this enterprise (TK 1, p. 139).

VII.8. Transportation of agricultural and textile products

Whereas salt was an import from Upper Austria, South Bohemian carters also exported goods. These mainly consisted of grain and, from the fishpond cultivation areas, fish as well, as in the case of the village of Středmily on the estate of Český Krumlov (Chalupa, 1969: 298). Hop gardens were scattered around the town of Vodňany and South Bohemian hops were in demand in Bavaria; the trade in this crop was concentrated in the town of Volary (BR 27, p. 23). Cabbages were planted in large quantities by farmers in the small town of Hořice in the Bohemian Forest (Czech Šumava) on the estate of Vyšší Brod where there was a large number of weavers, and carters then transported these cabbages to Český Krumlov to sell.

Full peasant farmers from the village of Kobylnice on the estate of Vyšší Brod had only 'humble fields' at their disposal, but 'the nicest of the farmsteads, well provided for and often with five or six carts'. The villagers mostly made their living by 'spinning and linen making', but their ownership of a large number of carts demonstrates that they also profited from the transportation of textile products. Similarly, the inhabitants of the small town of Počátky made their living by spinning, linen-weaving, and woollen-weaving. Their textile wares sold well in Moravia and Lower Austria, and the carters transported back wine to sell (BR 4, p. 187). South Bohemian village carters were continually involved in the transportation of agricultural and textile products.

VII.9. Transporting of miscellaneous goods by carters

Transporting of miscellaneous goods along the roads was carried out by carters. The basic requirement for their occupation was to own draft animals. After the Thirty Years' War, oxen outnumbered horses by one-quarter. Analysis of the Berní rula tax cadaster using the example of the region of Prácheň shows that horses were mostly owned by full peasant farmers (89% of peasants had them), and to a lesser extent by smallholders (7%); only sporadically did cottagers own the occasional horse. Oxen were slightly more widely owned, still mainly by peasants (76% of the total), but also by smallholders (17%), and even by some cottagers (7%). More draft animals were recorded in infertile mountainous areas, as on the estate of Vimperk in the Bohemian Forest (the Šumava mountain range), where many villagers made their living by working as carters (BR 27, pp. 31-32). The main purpose of draft animals (both oxen and horses) was to cultivate the fields and help with the performance of the coerced labour services owed by serfs to the landlord. Carting work represented one of the supplementary activities undertaken by rich villagers. A similar situation is also observed in other European lands, e.g. in the 'prevozništvo' found in Slovenia (Panjek, 2017: 15).

Such activities were particularly advantageous for villages which were not too far from the important roads that were used to transport goods such as salt. The distance of the village from areas where there was a large market for goods such as grain and wood or from the administrative and commercial centres of noble estates was also important. Carters from villages that were located near centres of craft and proto-industrial production profited by transporting local products such as spun yarn, linen fabric, woollen cloth, and cotton textiles. Especially the inhabitants of towns (both full-size towns and small market towns such as Nová Bystřice and Nové Hrady), but also those living in villages located in border areas (e.g. villages on the estate of Landštejn), had plentiful opportunities to carry out carting work. Some estates even included the transportation of such goods as part of the coerced labour services owed by serfs to their landlords, where it was termed 'long-distance carting' (*daleké fůry* in Czech).

VII.10. Iron and steel manufacturing

Unlike textile production, iron and steel manufacturing in the eighteenth-century Czech lands was exclusively an enterprise of the noble estates. Ironworks were established mainly in Central and West Bohemia, although they were also found sporadically in the South Bohemian region. To ensure their operations, the noble lords used day-labourers and coerced labour services from their serfs. The rural population only provided the unskilled work – tree cutting, mining of iron ore, mining and burning of limestone (Novotný, 1983: 17-18). Very large numbers of serfs were involved in transporting the raw materials (Kárníková, 1965: 61-62).

One of the first iron ore furnaces with two iron-mills in the Tábor region was recorded in 1721 in the village of Včelička in the area of Žirovnice on the estate of Černovices (TK 2, p. 373). However, its operation soon ceased because the limited supplies of forest wood became depleted (TK 3, p. 449). In contrast, iron working was initiated on the estate of Nové Hrady by a Dutch entrepreneur who in 1770 started operating a furnace with two iron-mills in the village of Třebíčko (Novotný, 1983: 52). The furnace was located near the forest but far from the iron ore deposits. Although long-distance transport of iron ore employed carters from the villages, the distance the ore had to be transported reduced profitability and limited production in the region.

VII.11. Glass manufacturing

Glass manufacturing operated on early capitalist market principles. A glass foreman was an entrepreneur who produced by covering his overhead costs and at his own risk. He rented a forest from the estate owner or obtained a permit to build a glassworks. He bought the raw materials from the noble overlord or, with the lord's consent, from some other producer who operated on the estate. Glassmakers were freed from the land taxes and from the coerced labour services owed by serfs to landlords. Employees of the glassworks were paid according to how much output they made, so they were interested in making as much glass as possible.

Each glass foreman kept secret the methods he used for melting the glass. In Bohemian glass manufacturing, there were never restrictions similar to guild regulations.

Glass manufacturing represented an important export branch in Bohemia, and 75% of its output was exported abroad (Klíma, 1955: 153-161). The majority of South Bohemian glassworks were located in wooded areas of the Šumava mountain range. From the fourteenth to the seventeenth century, 57 glassworks were established in this region; however, intensive growth did not take place until the eighteenth century when 48 new glassworks arose in this area (Panenková and Fröhlich, 1993). Just as with iron works, glass smelting also involved a huge consumption of wood (Novotný, 1983: 18).

The oldest glassworks in the Šumava mountain range were located in a mountainous area between the towns of Vimperk and Volary (BR 27, p. 24). In the village of Horní Vltavice on the estate of Vimperk, for instance, one peasant was referred to as a foreman at a glassworks that produced mirror glass. He had the assistance of one inmate-lodger and three cottagers who arranged for the transport of wood (BR 28, p. 521; TK 2, p. 269). The same village also recorded one rosary maker. Rosaries were made by stringing glass beads on a cord (TK 2, p. 269).

Important glassworks in South Bohemia were also established in the area of the Novohradské mountains (Freiwald in German). Apart from the production of blown glass, mirror glass, and watch glass, these manufactories were also famous for refining glass products, i.e. for glass cutting, painting, and gilding. The establishment of new glassworks in this area was connected with the colonization of uninhabited mountain and forest areas where logging and glass-making settlements were established (Šmilauer, 1960: 241-242). The glassworks at Nové Hrady were brought into operation between 1743 and 1744 (TK 3, p. 99). In 1783, four glassworks provided evidence of the growth of glass-making on this estate. These glassworks employed 4 foremen, 35 journeymen, 7 apprentices, and 11 assistants. At the same time, they offered employment to an additional 7 glass-grinders, 3 glass-painters, and one glass-cutter. In 1753, on the nearby estate of Chlum u Třeboně, there arose the so-called 'Nová hut' which employed one foreman, 10 journeymen, and 10 assistants (1783). The number of employees fluctuated according to the demand for the products. Two glass furnaces here produced crystal glass and plate glass for domestic consumption (Záloha, 1985: 79-83).

VII.12. Rural crafts in the first half of the eighteenth century

Some poor rural inhabitants and landless persons lived from rural crafts. In the Bohemian countryside, one mainly observed the common crafts needed for agriculture (such as blacksmiths and wheelwrights) or for wood processing (such as carpenters). Other common occupations were connected with clothing (weavers, tailors, hosiers), shoe production (cobblers), and sporadically with food production (butchers and bakers). Other types of crafts were rare in rural areas because most craft products came into the Bohemian countryside from nearby small towns and full-size towns. For example, all the crafts were concentrated in the royal town of České Budějovice and in the small mining town of Rudolfov. As a result, the neighbouring 36 villages which were subject to the overlordship of the royal free towns showed a very minimal number of rural occupations (Grulich, 2013: 138-151), with only two localities having any at all: the village of Vráto had one blacksmith, and the village of Doudleby had four weavers, a carpenter, and a leather worker (TK 1, p. 117). This situation was explicitly confirmed by a report from the town of Lišov on the estate of Hluboká nad Vltavou: 'Crafts in the town only produce for domestic consumption, because all the other earnings go to nearby Budějovice' (TK 1, p. 137).

Crafts in villages were mostly practised by people from the lower strata of rural society. If cottagers and full peasant farmers were recorded as craftsmen, the craft occupation was their supplementary source of livelihood; their priority remained to cultivate the land and raise cattle. Craft activities in South Bohemian rural areas were never a privilege of the wealthy strata. Rural crafts were typically undertaken by inmate-lodgers. For example, in 1748, the estate of Orlík recorded large numbers of craftsmen in this social stratum: 20 tailors, 17 weavers, 16 cobblers, 8 blacksmiths, 4 carpenters, and 3 hosiers. A similar situation was also observable on the estate of Protivín, where there were 32 craftsmen from the stratum of inmate-lodgers, including 11 weavers and 7 blacksmiths (Chalupa, 1969: 306). The degree of specialization and the numbers of rural craftsmen varied regionally depending on local demand.

VII.13. Soldiers – 'away from the village'

The eighteenth century was a period of expansion of the putting-out-system and rapid growth of manufactory production, which took place against the background of a series of military conflicts: the first (1740-1742) and the second (1744-1745) Silesian Wars and the Seven Years' War (1756-1763). The demand for military uniforms was one of the factors that contributed to the growth of textile production.

At the beginning, men were recruited into the army 'voluntarily', and military service was for life. In 1781, Emperor Joseph II introduced compulsory military service for the lowest strata of the male population. Impressing men into the army was replaced by forced recruitment; until 1802, military service was still for life. Military service was compulsory for all men aged 17-40 and for the requirements of the baggage train, even men aged 17-50. However, after either voluntary or compulsory recruitment, if there was no war taking place, soldiers were permitted to stay at home for a few years. Nevertheless, the army still withdrew labour from rural areas of Bohemia. Most such labour was extracted in the form of orphaned males, who comprised almost half of all recruits at the end of the eighteenth century (Černý, 2017: 27).

Due to the lifetime military service obligation, the degree to which recruits returned to rural society was very low. Almost two thirds of soldiers never made it back home. The nobility experienced problems with men who had been released from the army but had lost the habit of manual work and sought an easier source of livelihood. This situation was apparent after the end of the Seven Years' War (1763) when useless soldiers were released from the army. Among them, for example, was Vavřinec Slad who had worked as a servant for nine years before becoming a soldier. After returning from military service, he pretended to be 'sick' and unable to perform hard work. Based on his alleged poor condition, he decided to return to Prague where, by marrying a rich widow, he sought to obtain a butcher's shop (Grulich, 2018: 142-143).

To some men, military service provided an opportunity for social mobility. However, if a released soldier was interested in returning to rural society, how did he proceed? The first step was to get married and start a family. That was often achieved even by those discharged from the army because of injury or disability. The second step was to gain a landholding or practise a craft (Černý, 2017: 32-34). A specific group of veterans consisted of the so-called 'capitulants' (soldiers who volunteered to serve for a longer period than was legally required). In return for the promise of financial reward they served as 'substitutes', e.g. they served in the army in place of sons of magistrates or rich full peasant farmers (Grulich, 2018: 141-142).

VIII. South Bohemia and the theoretical concept of the 'integrated peasant economy'

Why did some categories of Bohemian peasants (particularly smallholders, cottagers, and inmate-lodgers) end up earning income outside agriculture? By no means should we regard them as being passively pushed in this direction. On the contrary, they exercised their own agency in choosing to do these forms of work, in response to the challenges they faced from population growth and the laws governing inheritance in their society.

As mentioned earlier, Bohemian inheritance law provided that the landholding had to be inherited by just one child (usually a son); the other offspring had to look elsewhere for a livelihood, either seeking the opportunity to take over somebody else's holding or experiencing downward social mobility into the poor strata of the village population. As soon as the population losses caused by the Thirty Years' War had been recovered, which happened around 1700, village populations started to grow rapidly. This also meant growth in the numbers of people who were deprived of the possibility of owning a landholding. For them, it was very important to be able to earn a livelihood outside agriculture, based on local opportunities – either by working as day-labourers for wages, setting up as rural craftsmen, producing within the putting-out-system, or taking employment in centralized manufactories.

Local soil quality and climate could also create strong incentives for rural people to undertake non-agricultural activities. Harsh climatic conditions, combined with infertile land, reduced agricultural earnings and increased uncertainty, motivating all strata in the rural population to diversify their risks by seeking opportunities for additional income outside the farm sector. In such infertile agricultural regions, non-agricultural activities were attractive not only to the poorer members of the rural community (smallholders, cottagers, and inmate-lodgers who lacked enough land to subsist entirely from agriculture) but also to better-off peasants. Ownership of draft animals such as horses and oxen meant that peasants could earn extra income by transporting goods as carters.

In this context, it is not possible to ignore the fact that noble overlords in Bohemia tended to permit those non-agricultural activities by their serfs from which they themselves could extort rents, either directly or indirectly. The manorial system used corvée-style coerced labour from serfs to obtain the manpower needed for non-agricultural demesne enterprises such as mining and transport of raw materials in regions with iron and glass manufacturing.

On the basis of the information recorded in the sources analysed (the 1654 'Berní rula' tax cadaster and the 1710-1713 'Theresianum' tax cadaster) it is possible to document the existence in early modern South Bohemia of a system with the characteristic features of an 'integrated peasant economy' (hereinafter IPE). Peasants combined agriculture and market-oriented non-agricultural activities to improve their livelihoods and increase their living standards. Market-oriented activities, in which rural people actively pursued commercial exchange between villages and towns, and between South Bohemia and other regions, including Austria, Bavaria, and Moravia, represented an attractive source of income compared to subsistence agriculture, although its importance relative to agriculture varied according to region and individual circumstances. The IPE, as it operated in early modern South Bohemia, was both dynamic and flexible, adapting to changes over time in the availability of income sources, market conditions, population growth, and family structure.

The activities which peasants undertook to increase their incomes can be observed in all three major sectors of the economy. In the primary sector, peasants in South Bohemia can be observed engaging in agricultural specialization and intensification of cultivation. Depending on soil quality and local climate, they cultivated cereals, root crops, legumes, vegetables, fruit, flax, and hemp. They also intensified animal husbandry by, among other things, increasing the number of horses and oxen which they then used, as did peasants elsewhere in Europe, to offer commercial freight carting. Intensification of forest exploitation in South Bohemia mainly took the form of transporting wood by road and river. Inmate-lodgers also found an important additional source of income by engaging in day-labouring for wages.

In South Bohemia, extension of the cultivated land area was limited by the poor quality of the soil and the harsh climate in submontane and mountainous areas. This gave rise to a pattern whereby infertile land was often used to construct very large ponds which were used to raise fish (especially carp) for commercial sale. Infertile land could also be turned into quarries for raw materials such as stone and sand. These fishponds and quarries were often owned by the noble overlords, which meant that villagers could only earn income by transporting fish, stone, and sand, not by selling them directly.

In the secondary sector, South Bohemian peasants can be observed mainly in activities which transformed primary raw materials into textile products and glass, often oriented towards foreign markets. Rural crafts produced articles for local consumption only. Local production was mainly linked to agriculture, wood processing, and the making of shoes and clothing. As a supplementary source of income in submontane and mountainous areas we observe peasants being considerably involved in the putting-out system, especially in the form of textile proto-industry. In the second half of the eighteenth century, there was a simultaneous implementation of a 'centralized' industrial sector (especially in the form of textile manufactories) and alongside it waged textile work by the rural population. Migrant or itinerant craftsmen first appeared in the specialized glass-making industry, which required skilful and experienced craftsmen. Greater mobility of labour was made possible by the abolition of serfdom in 1781, which made it possible for serfs to move freely without obtaining permission from their overlords.

In the tertiary sector, South Bohemian peasants resembled those in other European regions in transporting goods over short to medium distances. There is plentiful evidence of paid transportation activities being provided by South Bohemian peasants across relatively short distances, for instance in the form of wood transport from rural forests into the towns. The location of this region and its transportation links meant that it played an important role in trade between Bohemia, Moravia, Bavaria, and Upper and Lower Austria. Beyond the borders of the Czech lands, there was considerable demand for Bohemian textile products, glass, corn, hops, and fish. Village carters profited by transporting Alpine salt and Austrian and Moravian wine into Bohemia. Migrant workers from South Bohemia sought employment as day-labourers in neighbouring countries, especially Lower Austria. For South Bohemia, the city of Vienna, as the capital of the entire Habsburg monarchy, was an even greater attractive force than Prague, as the capital of the province of Bohemia (Grulich, 2018: 159-193).

A final component of the integrated peasant economy in South Bohemia was state military service, which uprooted many young men from the rural environment and sent them off to earn a livelihood in military activities for many years. For some individuals this provided an important 'stepping stone' that impelled them towards working outside agriculture, e.g. by taking up a craft after they left the army.

From the point of view of economic and familial structures, the region of South Bohemia displays many features common to other parts of Europe. Even though the Thirty Years' War saw an intensification of the so-called 'second serfdom' in Bohemia, from the second half of the seventeenth century, proto-industrialization gradually set in, at least in certain parts of the country, and this was followed by factory industrialization in the nineteenth century. During this entire period, rural people engaged actively in many economic activities outside agriculture. The concept of the 'integrated peasant economy' (IPE) can thus be appropriately used to characterize the rural economy in Bohemia between the mid-seventeenth and the end of the eighteenth century.

Table 4.1. The Integrated peasant economy checklist: South Bohemia

Activity	Check
Primary sector	
Agricultural specialization	✓
Intensification of cultivation (no fallow, mixed-cropping, …)	✓
Wage day-labour in agriculture and longer-term farmhands on larger farms	✓
Extension/intensification of animal husbandry	✓
Intensification of forest exploitation (in primary sector, but also secondary and tertiary)	✓
Extension of cultivated land (reclamation of commons and woods)	✓
Quarries	
Fishing	✓
Secondary sector	
Transformation of primary resources/products (e.g. wine, cheese, meat products; charcoal, lime)	✓
Rural crafts	✓
Domestic, putting-out system (proto-industry)	✓
Work in 'centralized' industries and plants (manufactures, mining, etc.)	✓
Migrant/mobile craftsmen (e.g. bricklayers)	✓
Wage labour in the industrial sector	
Tertiary sector	
Services in the field of long- and medium-distance trade (draft animal lease, fodder, lodging, inns)	✓
Transport of other people's products and goods over short to medium distances	✓
Trade with own products and goods over short to medium distances	✓
Peddling	✓
Smuggling	
Migrant/mobile workers (dockworkers, etc.)	
Works of trust (estimation of land value, testimonies, etc.)	
Warfare	✓
Looting	✓
Tourism	

Bibliography

Archival sources

Národní archiv Praha, fond České gubenium, spisy manufakturního kolegia, kart. 100, 174, 229, 231, 244, 245.

Published sources

Tereziánský katastr český 1. Rustikál, kraje A-CH (1964), Chalupa, A. et al. (eds), Praha, Archivní správa ministerstva vnitra.

Tereziánský katastr český 2. Rustikál, kraje K-Ž (1966), Chalupa, A. et al. (eds), Praha, Archivní správa ministerstva vnitra.

Tereziánský katastr 3. Dominikál (1970), Burdová, P. et al. (eds), Praha, Archivní správa ministerstva vnitra.

Berní rula 4. Kraj Bechyňský I. (2013a), Čadková, I. and Zahradníková, M. (eds), Praha, Národní archiv.

Berní rula 5. Kraj Bechyňský I. (2013b), Čadková, I. and Zahradníková, M. (eds), Praha, Národní archiv.

Berní rula 6. Kraj Bechyňský II. (2014), Čadková, I. and Zahradníková, M. (eds), Praha, Národní archiv.

Berní rula 7. Kraj Bechyňský III. (2017), Čadková, I. and Zahradníková, M. (eds), Praha, Národní archiv.

Berní rula 27. Kraj Prácheňský I. (1954), Haas, A. (ed.), Praha, Státní pedagogické nakladatelství.

Berní rula 28. Kraj Prácheňský II (1954), Haas, A. (ed.), Praha, Státní pedagogické nakladatelství.

Bibliography

Cerman, M. (1997), 'Proto-industrialisierung und Grundherrschaft. Sozialstruktur, Feudalherrschaft und Textilgewerbe in Nordböhmen (15. bis 17. Jahrhundert)', Ebeling, D. and Mager, W. (eds), *Proto-industrie in der Region. Europäische Gewerbelandchaften vom 16. bis zum 19. Jahrhundert*, Bielefeld, Verlag für Regionalgeschichte, pp. 157-198.

——— (1999), 'Das Projekt Soziale Strukturen in Böhmen, 16.-19. Jahrhundert', *Prager WISOHIM*, 5, pp. 185-203.

——— (2002), 'Soziale Differenzierung, proto-industrielle Entwicklung und Gutsherrschaft in Frýdlant und Liberec, 16.–18. Jahrhundert', Cerman, M. and Zeitlhofer, H. (eds), *Soziale Strukturen in Böhmen. Ein regionaler Vergleich von Wirtschaft und Gesellschaft in Gutsherrschaften, 16.–19. Jahrhundert*, Wien, Verlag für Geschichte und Politik – München, Oldenbourg Wissenschaftsverlag, pp. 174-191.

——— and Luft, R. (2005), *Untertanen, Herrschaft und Staat in Böhmen und im 'Alten Reich'. Sozialgeschichtliche Studien zur Frühen Neuzeit*, München, R. Oldenbourg Verlag.

——— and Ogilvie, S. C. (1994), *Proto-Industrialisierung in Europa: industrielle Produktion vor dem Fabrikzeitalter*, Wien, Verlag für Gesellschaftskritik.

——— and Zeitlhofer, H. (2002), *Soziale Strukturen in Böhmen. Ein regionaler Vergleich von Wirtschaft und Gesellschaft in Gutsherrschaften, 16.–19. Jahrhundert*, Wien, Verlag für Geschichte und Politik – München, Oldenbourg Wissenschaftsverlag.

Černý, V. (2017), 'Odvod branců, délka vojenské služby a návrat vysloužilců do venkovské společnosti. Panství Protivín 1780-1830', Balcarová, J., Kubů, E. and Šouša, J. (eds), *Venkov, rolník a válka v českých zemích a na Slovensku v moderní době*, Praha, Národní zemědělské muzeum, pp. 21-35.

——— (2021), 'Dědicové a jejich sourozenci. Sonda po sňatečnosti mužů a žen ze selských rodin, Protivínsko 1780-1830', *Historická demografie*, 45, 1, pp. 19-66.

Fialová, L. (1996), *Dějiny obyvatelstva českých zemí*, Praha, Mladá fronta.

Fröhlich, J. and Panenková, D. (1993), *Jihočeské sklářství 14.–20. století*, České Budějovice, Jihočeské muzeum.

Grulich, J. (2008), *Populační vývoj a životní cyklus venkovského obyvatelstva na jihu Čech v 16. až 18. století*, České Budějovice, Jihočeská univerzita.

——— (2013), *Migrace městského a vesnického obyvatelstva. Farnost České Budějovice 1750-1824*, České Budějovice, Jihočeská univerzita.

——— (2018), *Migrační strategie. Město, předměstí a vesnice na panství České Budějovice v druhé polovině 18. Století*, České Budějovice, Jihočeská univerzita.

Chalupa, A. (1969), 'Venkovské obyvateltvo v Čechách v tereziánských katastrech (1700-1750)', *Sborník Národního muzeav Praze. Řada A – Historie*, 23, 4-5, pp. 197-378.

Jindra, Z. and Jakubec, I. (2015), *Hospodářský vzestup českých zemí od poloviny 18. století do konce monarchie*, Praha, Karolinum.

Kárníková, L. (1965), *Vývoj obyvatelstva v českých zemích 1754-1914*, Praha, Nakladatelství Československé akademie věd.

Klein, A. and Ogilvie, O. (2016), 'Occupational Structure in the Czech Lands under the Second Serfdom', *Economic History Review*, 69, 2, pp. 493-521.

Klíma, A. (1955), *Manufakturní období v Čechách*, Praha, Nakladatelství Československé akademie věd.

——— (1957), 'Industrial Development in Bohemia 1648-1781', *Past and Present*, 11, 1, pp. 87-99.

——— (1963), 'The Role of Rural Domestic Industry in Bohemia in the Eighteenth Century', *The American Journal of International Law*, 57, 3, pp. 566-587.

——— (1979), 'Agrarian Class Structure and Economic Development in Pre-Industrial Bohemia', *Past and Present*, 85, 1, pp. 49-67.

——— (1991), 'Hausindustrie, Manufaktur und Frühindustrialisierung in Böhmen', Klíma, A. (ed.), *Economy, Industry and Society in Bohemia 17th–19th Centuries*, Praha, Karolinum, pp. 71-83.
Kopáček, J. (2006), *Encyklopedie Českých Budějovic*, České Budějovice, Statutární město České Budějovice a Nebe s.r.o.
Kriedte, P., Medick, H. and Schlumbohm, J. (1977), *Industrialisierung vor der Industrialisierung. Gewerbliche Warenproduktion auf dem Land in der Formationsperiode des Kapitalismus*, Göttingen, Vandenhoeck & Ruprecht.
———, ——— and ——— (1998), 'Eine Forschungslandschaft in Bewegung. Die Proto-Industrialisierung am Ende des 20. Jahrhunderts', *Jahrbuch für Wirtschaftsgeschichte*, 39, 2, pp. 9-20.
Levine, D. (1984), *Proletarianization and Family History*, Orlando, Academic Press.
Machačová, J. and Matějček, J. (2010), *Nástin sociálního vývoje českých zemí 1781-1914*, Praha, Karolinum.
Marfany, J. (2012), *Land, Proto-Industry and Population in Catalonia, c. 1680-1829: An Alternative Transition to Capitalism?* London, Routledge.
Martínek, Z. (2000), *Etnografický atlas Čech, Moravy a Slezska III. Řemeslná, domácká a manufakturní výroba a obchod v Čechcách v letech 1752-1756*, Praha, Etnologický ústav Akademie věd České republiky.
Matušíková, L. and Ogilvie, S. (2006), 'Bohemia after the Thirty Years War: Historical Sources Deposited in the National Archives in Prague', *Naše rodina*, 18, 1, pp. 1-6.
Maur, E. (1985), 'Vrchnost a poddaní za třicetileté války', *Folia historica bohemica*, 8, pp. 241-264.
Medick, H. (1976), 'The proto-industrial family economy: the structural function of household and family during the transition from peasant society to industrial capitalism', *Social History*, 1, pp. 291-315.
——— (1996), *Weben und Überleben in Laichingen 1650-1900. Lokalgeschichte als allgemeine Geschichte*, Göttingen, Vandenhoeck & Ruprecht.
Mendels, F. F. (1981), *Industrialization and population pressure in eighteenth-century Flanders*, New York, Arno press.
——— (1972). 'Proto-Industrialization: The First Phase of the Industrialization Process', *Journal of Economic History*, 32, pp. 241-261.
Mikulec, J. (1993), *Poddanská otázka v barokních Čechách*, Praha, Historický ústav.
Myška, M. (1979), 'Pre-Industrial Iron-Making in the Czech Lands: the Labour Force and Production Relations *c.* 1350 – *c.* 1840', *Past and Present*, 82, pp. 44-72.
——— (1984), 'K charakteristice výrobních vztahů a forem v předení lnu ve slezsko-moravské "proto-industriální oblasti" v 16. až v polovině 18. století', *Časopis Slezského muzea*, 33, pp. 253-270.
——— (1994a), 'Proto-industrializace. Čtvrtstoletá bilance jednoho historiografického paradigmatu', *Český časopis historický*, 92, pp. 759-774.

——— (1994b), 'Proto-Industrialisierung in Böhmen, Mähren und Schlesien', M. Cerman, M. and Ogilvie, S. C. (eds), *Proto-Industrialisierung in Europa: industrielle Produktion vor dem Fabrikzeitalter*, Wien, Verlag für Gesellschaftskritik, pp. 177-189.

Nekvapil Jirásková, Š. (2015), 'Proto-industrializace a možnosti studia populačního vývoje v oblasti severovýchodních Čech', *Český časopis historický*, 113, pp. 27-49.

——— (2019), *Proto-industriální společnost. Populační chování a životní strategie venkovského obyvatelstva severovýchodních Čech v 18. a 19. století*, Pardubice, Univerzita Pardubice.

Novotný, K. (1983), 'Rozmístění manufakturní výroby v Čechách kolem r. 1790', *Hospodářské dějiny*, 11, pp. 5-94.

Ogilvie, S. C. (1993), 'Proto-industrialization in Europe', *Continuity and Change*, 8, 2, pp. 159-179.

——— (1997), *State corporatism and proto-industry. The Württemberg Black Forest, 1580-1797*, Cambridge, Cambridge University Press.

——— (2002), 'Zur Ökonomischen Welt der Untertanen in Böhmen. Eine Fallstudie zur Herrschaft Frýdlant', Cerman, M. and Zeitlhofer, H. (eds), *Soziale Strukturen in Böhmen. Ein regionaler Vergleich von Wirtschaft und Gesellschaft in Gutsherrschaften, 16.–19. Jahrhundert*, Wien, Verlag für Geschichte und Politik – München, Oldenbourg Wissenschaftsverlag, pp. 145-173.

——— (2005), 'Communities and the "second serfdom" in early modern Bohemia', *Past and Present*, 187, pp. 69-119.

Panjek, A. (2011), 'Not demesne but money: lord and peasant economies in early modern western Slovenia', *The Agricultural History Review*, 59, 2, pp. 293-311.

——— (2017), 'The Integrated Peasant Economy as a Concept in Progress', Panjek, A., Larsson, J. and Mocarelli, L. (eds), *Integrated Peasant Economy in a Comparative Perspective. Alps, Scandinavia and Beyond*, Koper, University of Primorska Press, pp. 11-49.

Procházka, V. (1963), *Česká poddanská nemovitost v pozemkových knihách 16. a 18. Století*, Praha, Nakladatelství Československé akademie věd.

Purš, J. (1965), 'Struktur und Dynamik der industriellen Entwicklung in Böhmen im letzten Viertel des 18. Jahrhunderts (Schluß)', *Jahrbuch für Wirtschaftsgeschichte*, 6, 1, pp. 160-196, 6, 2, pp. 103-124.

Robek, A. (eds) (1987), *Jihočeská vlastivěda. Řada A – Národopis*, České Budějovice, Jihočeské nakladatelství.

Sansa, R. (2017), 'Woodlands as a Source of Income Integration in Peasant Economies: the Pontifical State (18th-19th Centuries)', A. Panjek, J. Larsson and L. Mocarelli (eds), *Integrated Peasant Economy in a Comparative Perspective. Alps, Scandinavia and Beyond*. Koper, University of Primorska Press, pp. 191-204.

Schlumbohm, J. (1994), *Lebensläufe, Familien, Höfe. Die Bauern und Heuerleute des Osnabrückischen Kirchspiels Belm in proto-industrieller Zeit, 1650-1860*, Göttingen, Vandenhoeck & Ruprecht.

Šmilauer, V. (1960), *Osídlení Čech ve světle místních jmen*, Praha, Nakladatelství Československé akademie věd.

Tilly, Ch. and Tilly, R. (1971), 'Agenda for European Economic History in the 1970s', *Journal of Economic History*, 31, pp. 184-198.

Velková, A. (2009), *Krutá vrchnost, ubozí poddaní? Proměny venkovské rodiny a společnosti v 18. a první polovině 19. století na příkladu západočeského panství Šťáhlavy*, Praha, Historický ústav.

Wrigley, E. A. and Schofield, R. S. (1989), *The Population History of England 1541-1871*, Cambridge, Cambridge University Press.

Woitsch, J. (2003), *Zapomenutá potaš. Draslaři a draslářství v 18. a 19. století*, Praha, Etnologický ústav Akademie věd České republiky.

——— (eds) (2019), *Prague historical ethnology in the beginning of the third millennium*, Pelhřimov, Nová tiskána Pelhřimov.

Záloha, J. (1985), 'Naše znalosti o dějinách skláren v někdejším budějovickém kraji', *Jihočeský sborník historický*, 54, pp. 78-85.

Zeitlhofer, H. (2014), *Besitzwechsel und sozialer Wandel. Lebensläufe und soziaoökonomische Entwicklungen im südlichen Böhmerwald 1640-1840*, Wien – Köln – Weimar, Böhlau Verlag.

INES BEGUŠ &
ALEKSANDER PANJEK

5. At the Roots of the Integrated Peasant Economy Concept

Early Modern Western and Central Slovenia

I. Introduction

Central and western Slovenia, comprising the duchy of Carniola and the county of Gorica (Gorizia), represents the area where the integrated peasant economy concept originated. The integrated peasant economy comprises all on-farm and off-farm marked-related activities, which integrate that part of the agricultural income of a holding, which is used for self-consumption. Together, self-produced and self-consumed agricultural income and market-oriented engagements belonging to the primary, secondary and tertiary sectors, form the whole of the integrated peasant economy. In the first part, a brief excursion into Slovenian historiography on the theme is presented. In the second part, we present some data on the fragmentation of farms and on the foundation of cottages, which are used as a proxy of the extent of self-insufficient holdings. In the third part, empirical information on the diverse ways of income integration are presented. The region had different institutional regulations concerning farm status, heritage, and land market rules and practices. In presenting income integration practices, we distinguish between three areas, based on environmental characteristics: the Alps, the karstic highlands, and the lower hills and lowlands. Notwithstanding natural and institutional differences, as well as local specificities in resources, production, and opportunities, peasant income integration activities appear to have been the common rule. The term 'peasant' is used in its most general sense, including all categories and social strata of the farming population. Specific groups (e.g. smallholders, cottagers, lodgers etc.) are expressly mentioned when necessary.

Integrated Peasant Economy in Central and Eastern Europe, ed. by Aleksander Panjek, Rural History in Europe, 18 (Turnhout: Brepols, 2024), pp. 115–141
BREPOLS ✠ PUBLISHERS 10.1484/M.RURHE-EB.5.142466

II. 'Additional' activities: peasant income integration in older Slovenian historiography

The fact that peasants engaged in activities other than agriculture is one of the most evident features in Slovenian early modern agrarian history. In many, if not most, of the works by Slovenian historians dating back to the second half of the twentieth century and dealing with the history of either agriculture, industry, or trade, the involvement of peasant figures keeps emerging. Nonetheless, the topic has not often represented the central focus of articles or monographs and one has to dig a lot into local histories, too. Moreover, Slovenian historiography did not engage in the proto-industry research wave, but continued using the term *Verlagssystem* (*založništvo*) instead, and did not adopt pluri-activity either, but spoke of 'non-agrarian' and 'additional' activities. Despite these limitations, a large amount of evidence has been gathered on the diffusion of peasant income integration practices. This feature is acknowledged also in a recent general history of Slovenia: 'The specificity of the peasants in the Slovene area was more in the fact that they – as pack-horse and cart drivers, but also as middlemen-traders and craftsmen – combined their work on the farms with non-agricultural economy' (Štih-Simoniti, 2010: 154).

The area that received the most scholarly attention related to peasant non-agrarian activities was central-western Slovenia, mostly coinciding with the duchy of Carniola. The region, and indeed the whole of present-day Slovenia, was a transit area on medium and long-distance trade routes between Pannonia and the Balkans on the one side and northern Italy and the Adriatic Sea on the other. Indeed, peasant trade and transport were considered the most outstanding activities and received the most attention (Table 1). Nonetheless, the involvement of the peasant population in industrial activities such as iron and textile, to mention only two of them for the moment, was detected and studied, as well.

When dealing with types of peasant income integration, Slovenian historians mostly defined them as 'additional activities'. The reason why so many peasants engaged in them was mainly identified in the need to find money to pay increasing dues to landlords and taxes to the state, and in the demographic growth which caused the fragmentation of the medieval family-sized holdings named *hube*, transforming them into smallholdings in some areas, along with the growth of social groups with little land such as cottagers (*kajžarji*) and with barely any land (*podružniki*, *gostači*). In brief, the main reason why the different categories of peasant population engaged in 'additional' activities was identified in the necessity – because they had not enough land to make a living solely from on-farm agriculture. This condition was determined by rising monetary demands by overlords and the parallel growth of the population, perceived as some kind of fate.

Table 5.1. Types, characters, and chronology of peasant trade and transport in Slovenian scholarship, based on Gestrin, Grafenauer, and Šorn

I. EXPANSIVE PHASE: MID-13th – MID-14th CENTURY	II. EXPANSIVE PHASE: MID-15th – END-16th CENTURY	III. EXPANSIVE PHASE: MID – LATE 18th CENTURY
1. With own products	4. With goods of professional (urban) merchants	7. Cart-transport
2. On behalf of tradesmen	5. With goods of other peasants	
3. For *corvées* service	6. Smuggling	
Short distance, to borough and town markets.	*Longer distance, interregional and international (also by sea); to local ironworks.*	*Export through sea-ports; economic policy measures.*

Note: The types and characters of peasant trade in each phase are present in the later phases, too.
Source: Panjek, 2017: 17.

Demographic growth would have resulted in the expansion of the cottages, which were mostly not self-sufficient on their agricultural produce.

Truth be told, we may also find more nuanced interpretations. Among the different possible examples, Bogo Grafenauer may be cited, stating that during the sixteenth century, which was a phase of economic development, besides a majority of poor income integrators, there was 'a less numerous group of peasants who acquired considerable wealth through trading and rose above the average of their fellow villagers' (Grafenauer, 1974: 133-134). 'Economic opportunities offered many possibilities' for geographical and social mobility, and 'the sons of peasant subjects would actually go where they wanted to go'. They did not take over their fathers' farms but preferred to establish a cottage, seeking their living mainly in non-agrarian activities (Grafenauer, 1973: 27, 29). Along the trade routes, villages composed mostly of cottagers developed.

These are clear recognitions that through non-agrarian activities, peasants were able to improve their material conditions and standard of living, raise their social position and, not least, consciously strived for this. Moreover, they were able to make choices in the economic domain and implement them. The fact is that Slovenian historians never openly addressed and consequently did not solve this apparent contradiction in interpretations. In the narratives, income integration practices resulting

Table 5.2. Yearly volume of peasant trade and transport in Slovenian lands between the early 14th and the early 17th centuries, as estimated by F. Gestrin (per household by A. Panjek)

Period	Yearly quantity (tons)	Yearly quantity per peasant household (tons)
Early 14th century	18,500	0.2
Late 15th century	67,200	0.5
16th and early 17th centuries	92,400	0.6

Source: Panjek, 2017: 17.

from economic and demographic coercion coexisted with recognitions of peasant agency whose driving force was the desire and the ability to improve living standards. The former was the main stream while the latter was a side rivulet of interpretation, which could run in parallel even within the very same text by the same author.

When dealing with the early modern peasant economy in general and with peasant income sources in particular, quantifications are a hard task and a risky business. Ferdo Gestrin, who dedicated a large part of his research to the history of trade and mobility, advanced a quantification of the amount of goods transported by peasants in the Slovenian regions (Carniola, Littoral, but also parts of Styria and Carinthia) between the late Middle Ages and the early modern period. Jože Šorn, the main author in industrial history in Slovenia so far, advanced a quantification of the shares of industrial production for the market in Carniola in the second half of the eighteenth century, distinguishing between different modes of production. For the sake of brevity, we present them in the form of tables (Tables 2 and 3) with the warning that they are only estimates, although by esteemed scholars. Both display a rather large impact of the peasant involvement in the secondary and tertiary sectors. As far as industry is concerned, one should keep in mind that peasants were also largely present as a work force in centralized plants (Table 3).

III. Farm fragmentation and holdings with little land as a proxy of the integrated peasant economy

The diffusion of smallholdings can be understood as an indicator of a situation in which smallholder households were not able to fully meet their nutritional needs based on their own agricultural produce. Consequently,

Table 5.3. Shares of industrial production for the market in Carniola 1760-1775, as estimated by J. Šorn (without the Idrija quicksilver mine and plant)

Form of production	Share of gross domestic product (%)
Peasant production (partly included in proto-industrial networks)	29
Craft (including rural craftsmen and proto-industrial networks)	25
Centralized plants in light industry	25
Centralized plants in heavy industry (mines and iron works)	21
Total	**100**

Source: Šorn, 1984: 62-63.

smallholdings may represent a proxy of the diffusion of income integration practices. Since better-off peasants would engage in market and non-agrarian activities, too, the share of small farms tends to indicate the lower threshold of how widespread income integration actually was. On the other hand, what small actually means and what size of holdings grants self-sufficiency depends on several factors, such as the quantity and quality of soil, the environmental conditions, the size of the family and, not least, the cultivation techniques.

Western Slovenia is mostly made of Alpine mountains and valleys, as well as karstic, hilly highlands (mostly between 300 and 1,000 meters a.s.l.). Arable land is rather scarce, flat fertile lowlands are of limited extension. In principle, we may consider that only the family-sized farms of medieval origin, the *hube*, were able to sustain a peasant family. Over time, in most of western Slovenia the majority of these old farm units did not remain intact, since they were fragmented into smaller holdings through inheritance divisions and sales. In parallel, the land market and dowries offered the possibility of enlarging the holdings, including to cottagers. Since by the late Middle Ages all most suitable terrains were colonized, later on new holdings were cottages (*kajža, košanija, rut*) or even smaller units with a garden and the right to use the commons (*podružniki*), while lodgers (*gostači*) with virtually no land lived as tenants in the houses of better-off peasants. Areas where farm division was allowed or practiced, prevailed over those where farm indivisibility was the rule. As a result of these trends, by the eighteenth century smallholdings strongly prevailed over larger and self-sufficient ones. It goes without saying that in mountain areas holdings might include large amounts of grassland, which represented an important asset, but in the case where we focus on arable land, scarcity ruled. For this reason, many peasants were not able to feed their families with their own grain production the whole year long.

In fact, contemporary sources explicitly depict this situation. According to Ferdo Gestrin (1991), as early as 1552 the provincial estates of the Duchy claimed that in Carniola and the Karst (central and south-western Slovenia) in particular, the peasants could not remain on their farms if they were not active in trade and transport activities. In the next century, in his monumental description of the Duchy of Carniola, published in 1689 after decades-long field researches, J.W. Valvasor mentioned the peasants' need to obtain incomes from outside their farms as one of the striking economic and social characteristics of the region.

As far as agricultural techniques are concerned, it is worth noting that relevant measures were taken by the peasant population to increase productivity. Firstly, there is the generalized practice of obtaining two crops per year. Two examples may suffice, the first regarding the whole of Carniola in the second half of the seventeenth century, while the second is a declaration by Jernej Celič, the owner of a large farm and community head in Zakojca in the upper Soča valley (Alps, county of Gorica), in 1745.

Cultivated fields yield two harvests each year. Because if wheat or rye is harvested, it is immediately ploughed and afterwards buckwheat seeds are sown again [...]. And likewise, after the harvest of barley, broad beans, lentils, peas and other crops of this type, buckwheat is sown. Even after hemp or flax or millet or something else. In this way, the crop is harvested twice on one field; which does not happen in other countries, namely in neighbouring ones (Valvasor, 2009-2013: 166).

Since the farm is located in the mountains, the second crop is uncertain, so that sometimes a little buckwheat is grown, but mostly turnips and carrots are grown, which sometimes would not meet the domestic needs (Panjek, 2018: 35).

The second type of intensification may be traced on the Karst. By connecting regional data on the sowing quantity of grain per surface unit (286 litres per ha) and on the amount of grain needed to feed a person (0.8 litres a day) with the data on grain reserves and on the extension of arable land in the probate inventory of Marko Gabrovec (1766), it is possible to conclude that most probably there was no fallow, but a continuous cropping sequence was used. Another important result relates to the carrying capacity of farms on the Karst in the mid-eighteenth century. Gabrovec possessed a holding with around one hectare of arable land and in his probate inventory he was defined as a 'middle-sized peasant'. With the net grain produce listed in the inventory, his 'middle-sized' farm of about one hectare could sustain 2.2 adults over the year (Panjek, 2018: 33-35).

Table 5.4. Number of peasant households on hube and cottages subject to the Rihemberk manor (Karst, Gorica county) in 1502 and 1624

	Hube		Cottages	Total households	
	Official units	Actual households		All	Cottages %
1502	265	239	33	272	12.1
1624	249	498	524	1,022	51.3
Index (1502=100)	94	208	1,589	376	

Source: Panjek, 2022b.

The parallel processes of farm fragmentation and of new smallholding foundation in this area are evident from the data concerning the Rihemberk manor. During the sixteenth and the first decades of the next century, the number of peasant households subject to the manor almost quadrupled. Besides the divisions of the old *hube*, it was a dizzying increase in the number of cottages that contributed for the most part to the growth. By 1624, half of the households lived on holdings with little soil (Table 4). This indicates the proportions of the extension and intensification of both agrarian and non-agrarian activities on the part of the peasantry, which were the condition to feed such a rapidly growing amount of households.

As already mentioned, the sixteenth century was a period of economic expansion in the region. The demographic growth and the multiplication of households provided with little land at the time must be understood as a proactive response of the rural population by catching arising opportunities, particularly in market-related activities (from wine growing and animal husbandry in the primary sector to transport in the tertiary). In the same area (Karst), the same mechanism was disclosed in the eighteenth century as a reaction to growing opportunities offered by the newly established free-port in Trieste: the peasant population grew, but selectively in the villages more suitable to exploit the advantages. Moreover, such demographic growth depended to a large extent on immigrants from more distant rural areas, that is, people who decided to move to catch the opportunities (Kalc, 2017).

The path towards the fragmentation of holdings may be registered also in the Alps, as in the manor of Bela Peč in Upper Carniola. Even without counting the places, units, and households directly connected with iron forges, which cannot with certainty be connected with a peasant status, several *hube* had two or three co-owners (Table 5). In 1636, this was the case of 17 *huben* with brothers and of 20 with non-brothers as co-owners

Table 5.5. Farm division and household growth: the manor of Bela Peč (Alps, Upper Carniola)

Year	*Hube*		*Rut*		Small cottagers*
	No.	Owners	No.	Owners	
1498	61	68	13	13	?
1636	61	102	15	21	162

Source: Panjek, 2022a on data from Mlinar, 2018.

*Small cottagers = *podružniki*, *Untersassen*: landless persons/families/holdings.

(61%). Some of these were conducted in co-ownership, but many were divided into separate real-life holdings. Even the *rut* farms, more recently founded through forest reclamation (forest cottages), were co-owned, mostly by brothers (same family name).

In the Alpine area, farm indivisibility was also present, as is the case of the large Škofja Loka manor in Upper Carniola. But even in this case, we may notice a relevant growth in the number of households between the late Middle Ages and the mid-eighteenth century. While the number of old (indivisible) *hube* stayed extremely stable through the centuries, the expansion was carried out by founding new holdings of different dimensions and categories: fractions of *hube*, cottages and lodger households (in declining order of soil landholdings). In the eighteenth century, these represented nearly 70 percent of all households (Table 6). Only for the around 30 percent of households living on whole farms may we assume that they surely enjoyed a reliable food self-sufficiency. These data reveal two important traits of the agrarian structure characterized by the indivisibility of farms coupled with the single-heir inheritance system. This was socially sustainable, because in the mountains there still was room for expanding the number of holdings founded by non-heirs, and economically viable, because additional households could be founded (cottages, lodgers) counting on income integration practices, both in the agrarian and non-agrarian sectors, besides the intensification of agricultural techniques.

IV. Dues in money as an indicator of the peasants' market activities

The existence and the extent of dues which peasant subjects had to pay to their landlords in money is a sign of market-related activities. The landlords in early modern western and central Slovenia favoured receiving

Table 5.6. Absence of farm fragmentation and household growth: the Škofja Loka manor (Alps, Upper Carniola)

Year	Whole *huben* or more	Fraction of *huben*	Cottagers and lodgers	Households
1318	1,126 + 28 p	0	0	1,126
1501	1,016 + 46 p	97	63	1,176
1754	1,129 + 0 p	1,164	1,380	*2,795
	30.7%	31.7%	37.6%	

Source: Panjek, 2022a on data from Blaznik, 1973.
P = *pustota*, an abandoned farm.

*Census, prob. including several lodgers (*gostači*) within the *hube*-households (this explains the lower number compared to the sum of the holdings from the manorial land register).

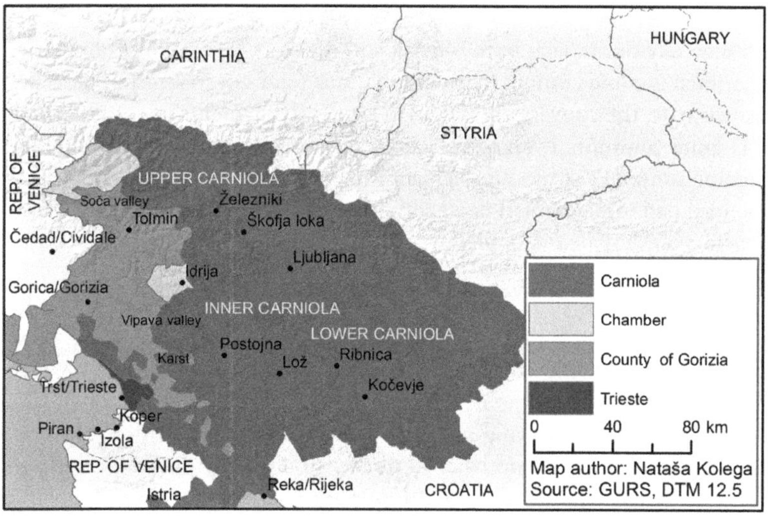

Map 5.1. Regions, provinces and areas of Early Modern western Slovenia

consistent parts of their rents in money instead. Rents in money already prevailed at the end of the fifteenth century (Bizjak, 2017) and this trait remained a distinctive character even in the sixteenth century, when the rising value of crops because of inflation would suggest a different choice, and also later on. Depending on the manors, the average landlords' rent-income in money amounted to about half of their value (Table 7). It is indeed rather difficult to define exact data on this, because of the sources

Table 5.7. Rent structure across manors (Karst and Alps), percent values

Manor	Money	Kind (partly in money)	Labour services (partly in money)	Total
Senožeče 1615	55.2	41.5	3.3	100
Schwarzenegg 1618	24.0	62.6	13.4	100
Socerb 1620	66.8	31.0	2.2	100
Duino 1637	51.3	32.3	16.4	100
Reifenberg 1624	22.7	59.0	18.2	100
Vipava 1624	26.8	62.5	10.8	100
Tolmin 1633	68.7	22.3	9.1	100
Average share	**45.1**	**44.5**	**10.4**	**100**

Source: Panjek, 2011: 298.

we may rely on. In fact, both official land registers (*urbar*) and summaries of annual income compiled by commissions tend not to register, or to underestimate, the conversion of dues in kind into payments in money, which was quite common. Even *corvée* labour duties were converted. The annual income summary of the Vipava manor in 1624 mentions, for example, that the lord had implemented new ploughing services, amounting to fourteen days a year, but peasants preferred to pay in money rather than services (Panjek, 2011).

Two main sets of reasons for the conspicuous rents in money can be identified. The first is that during the early modern period, a growing share of landlords' income originated from their public functions, for which they would increase various fees, which were to be paid in money. The second is that the growing share of peasant households with little land, such as cottagers, gave no basis to extract noteworthy dues in kind from them, since they simply did not produce enough crops for that. Similarly, a significant part of the peasants who owned bigger farms were not self-sufficient based on their own crop produce, because these farms tended to be divided and fragmented. In such conditions, if lords would have raised dues in kind over a certain limit, they could have easily disrupted the economic balance of peasant households and consequently undermined the peasants' solvency.

In these circumstances, the resource from which manorial lords could most benefit was the peasants' trading activities, rather than an enlarged demesne economy, which indeed did not develop. Since many peasant holdings were not self-sufficient, it was not viable to force them to work on a demesne, given that they had to integrate their income in other ways before that. Lords could demand money instead, without breaching the agricultural subsistence basis of their peasants. As for the peasants, paying in money had its advantages, since it did not further diminish their self-sufficiency, while incomes in money from market-related activities were more flexible than those from agriculture.

To conclude, if peasants were able to pay a significant share of their dues in money and even preferred them to those in kind or in labour, they must have had access to money – and the only place to find money was the market.

V. Income integration practices in Carniola and the county of Gorica

In this part we will take a closer look at the types of economic activities with which the peasant population integrated their agricultural income. Before that, an explanation is due about the occupations which have not been included in the analysis. Since a large number of historical works mention the combining of agriculture with non-agricultural activities and many mention individual non-agricultural occupations in which peasants were engaged, it is not possible to cover every author and work. It is likewise impossible to discuss all non-agricultural activities, as they were so abundant in the early modern period. Hence, this chapter mostly discusses those that were particularly widespread and established in a specific area. A specific clarification concerns information about some professions (e.g. miller, cooper, ironworker), for which it remains unclear whether the authors write about specialized profiles or about peasants who combined agricultural activities with such activities. Such examples are not discussed in this paper.

The analysis encompasses about one half of present-day Slovenia, namely the central and western Slovenian provinces and regions, that is, mainly the duchy of Carniola and the County of Gorica (Görz, Gorizia), which stretched more to the west along the border to Venetian Friuli. The presentation is divided into three parts. In the first the activities present in the Alpine area (Upper Carniola and upper Soča Valley) are addressed, the second treats the karstic highlands (the Karst proper, Inner Carniola and the Trnovo forest highland), while the third is dedicated to the lower hills and lowlands of Lower Carniola.

V.1. The Alpine area

In Upper Carniola (*Gorenjska*) the activities with which peasants integrated their income from agricultural activities were quite diverse. In the second half of the seventeenth century, Valvasor mentions many pack-animal drivers 'who transport goods to and from with horses; and many miners, and many weavers and merchants who ensure their subsistence and business by doing all sorts of work'. In the village of Bitnje, the majority of the inhabitants were 'sieve makers, who weave screens for sieves out of horsehair [...] these same peasants are also breeding many beautiful horses, which are mostly taken to Italy to graze and are sold there'. Almost every village in Upper Carniola produced fabric made of flax and wool (*mezzalana*) for sale. People would trade in wool and sheep cheeses, black and red leather, and even scorpions, which chemists used to make scorpion oil. Valvasor mentions the extraction and processing of iron as two important industries. In the village of Bohinjska Bistrica, he recorded 'a lot of miners that dug iron ore or found other ways to subsist in the mining activity' (Valvasor, 2009-2013: 110, 117-118).

In Upper Carniola, the iron industry or blacksmithing developed as early as the Middle Ages. At first, peasants extracted and smelted the ore by themselves, from which they then made products for domestic use (Blaznik, 1959: 93; Mohorič, 1955: 25-26; Gašperšič, 1959: 5). When ironworkers and blacksmiths from nearby provinces (Carinthia and Friuli) started moving there, the local craft of iron extraction began to develop into a more modernized iron industry. In certain areas, ironworkers had 'several *huba* of land with pastures and Alpine meadows, where they produced food for the ironworks settlement of miners, smelters, and blacksmiths, and forests, where they burnt charcoal and collected pit props' (Mohorič, 1969: 30). In the village of Železniki, ironworks employed peasants and day labourers as prospectors, ore diggers, charcoal burners, carriers, and plant workers (Mohorič, 1954: 96; Blaznik, 1973: 88; Mohorič, 1969: 39). In the sixteenth century, in certain areas of Upper Carniola the development of the iron industry also brought about a fast increase in the number of cottagers and landless lodgers. Gašperšič mentions that the boom in ironworks beneath the Jelovica mountain plateau was the main reason behind the appearance of cottagers in this area (Gašperšič, 1959: 98). In areas with ironworks, cottagers worked mainly as ironworkers or charcoal burners, while in other parts of the region many cottagers were engaged in crafts, rural trade, and transport (Blaznik, 1973: 201).

In addition to the iron industry, linen manufacture was rather widespread in this area. The linen trade was already quite lively in the fifteenth century and was used by its main producers – peasants, and by professional merchants. In the sixteenth century, the domestic system was already established in linen manufacture, sieve-making, and the iron industry in the villages surrounding the town of Kranj (Žontar, 1982: 161). According to Žontar, in the Škofja Loka manor in the eighteenth century 'almost every peasant produced linen, for almost every house owned a loom'; the putting-out system was also widely established in

Table 5.8. Craftsmen in the Škofja Loka manorial jurisdiction in the mid-18th c. (Alps, Upper Carniola)

Crafts	Škofja Loka town		Countryside			Total
	House owners	Lodgers	Whole farmers	Cottagers	Lodgers	
Weavers	15	6	7	187	203	418
Innkeepers and wine taverns	30	3	47	6		86
Shoemakers	3	6		23	52	84
Tailors	1	6		30	41	78
Sieve makers			1	47	22	70
Carpenters	3			18	44	65
Bricklayers		1		13	36	50
Blacksmiths*	15			10	4	29
Barrel makers	1	4		12	2	19
Leather workers	6			13		19
Locksmiths	6	3		3		12
Spinning-wheel makers				6	5	11
Bakers	9	1				10
Other crafts (<10)	46	16		18	17	97
Total	**135**	**46**	**55**	**386**	**426**	**1,048**
Percentage	12.9	4.4	5.2	36.8	40.6	100.0
Percentage town & country	17.3		82.7			

Source: data from Blaznik, 1973: 284.

*Without the iron-making locality of Železniki.

hosiery production (Gestrin, 1965: 194; Žontar, 1956; Blaznik, 1973: 289; Šorn, 1984: 87-88, 98; Čepič et al., 1979: 339).

In addition to the already mentioned crafts, in Upper Carniola, the following may be mentioned: tailoring, carpentry, masonry, coopery, inn-keeping, and the milling industry, which were mainly run by cottagers and landless peasants (Blaznik, 1973: 280-284; Hodnik, 1995a: 34, 36; Mihelič, 1999: 659). The presence of crafts in the Škofja Loka manor area was much larger in the countryside than in the small-town centre, and most of the people registered as practicing a craft were lodgers and cottagers (Table 8).

Transport also developed to a great extent. Valenčič noted that in this area the transport activity of peasants mostly consisted in 'selling the products of the local iron and linen industries. It was also partly connected with peasant trade. The carriers of iron products to Trieste and Italy returned with cargoes of wine, most certainly not for their own needs but for selling' (Valenčič, 1985: 251). This means peasants would transport the products of the ironworks to the Adriatic Sea or to the Republic of Venice, covering a distance of one hundred kilometres or more; with the earnings they would buy wine and resell it once back in the Alpine valleys. Apart from this, they transported linen, wine, and livestock to Gorica and the towns of Venetian Friuli. They bought the livestock in Hungary, reared it on their farms and then sold it to the Republic of Venice via the Tolmin region (Blaznik, 1973: 223; Gašperšič, 1960: 152; Gestrin, 1965). Also significant was the transport activity which the peasants performed for the needs of ironworks. Closely connected with the iron industry were, e.g., the carriers who transported ore and charcoal to the ironworks in Železniki, and iron products from there to their final destinations (Blaznik, 1973: 180). The ironworks beneath the Jelovica plateau mostly transported their products via the Soča valley in county of Gorica to the border-town of Gorica itself, to Udine in Venetian Friuli, or to the Adriatic sea-ports (Devin, Trieste, and Rijeka). Apart from working in them, peasants also did the greater part of the transport of products and half-products of the Upper Carniolan textile and iron industries, which were partly meant for export and partly for the small north Adriatic shipyards (Pahor, 1978; Pahor, 1979).

Along the upper Soča Valley, within the County of Gorica, the peasants of Bovec and Tolmin would transport wine, livestock, meat products, and cheese. They were also the main suppliers to the town of Gorizia and sold their products and livestock across the border, to the Venetian town of Cividale. 'The mountains of Tolmin, Kanal, Bovec [...] produce the butter which supplies the province; the rest is transported by the ones from Bovec and Tolmin mainly in the Venetian territory.' Another marketed product from the primary sector was honey, of which, around 1775, 'about 100,000 pounds [50 tons] was produced' and being in 'excess of the needs of the province' was 'exported to Salzburg and Carinthia' (Baselli, 1775: 175). Wine was the 'wealth of the County of Gorica' (Panjek, 2015: 60), whose principal market was over the Alps, in Carinthia. The sweet wines of Gorica and Trieste (*rebula, prosek; ribolla, prosecco*) were supplied to Carinthia by Carinthian carriers, innkeepers, merchants and, not least, local transporters – the latter were mostly peasants. Carinthia and the region of Gorizia also exchanged wine for iron (Panjek, 2015: 59-79; Gomiršek, 2007: 59). In a description from 1775, an officer wrote that not having enough soil for their nutrition, in the upper Soča valley 'those of Bovec and Tolmin mainly deal with the spinning of flax and the processing of various wooden tools, and then again with other small crafts for which they are also called *crameri*' (*kramarji, Krämer*), and with producing charcoal (Baselli, 1775: 177).

For the rest, there is no information on the involvement of the peasant population in the timber production and flotation in the Soča river valley, which developed from the sixteenth century onward in particular, but by analogy with other places we may assume they should have been involved as labour force (the woods were partly state owned and partly landlord owned).

V.2. The karstic highlands

In this part we address areas at different altitudes and with different conditions for agriculture, stretching from the northern shores of the Adriatic Sea (the Karst proper) towards the inland until the Alps. Their common feature is karstic terrains, which offer scarce arable soil and wide pastures, in the case where it is not covered with dense forests.

The Trnovo forest plateau is an example of the latter. In this area, peasants and cottagers would exploit the royal forests for grazing sheep and goats, and for mowing. In the village of Lokve they would, in addition to pasture, engage in activities connected with forestry, such as woodcutting, charcoal burning, carpentry, and the transport of timber. The already mentioned report from 1775 stated that 'the inhabitants of the imperial-royal forests [Trnovo forest] live on the supply of wood for construction and firewood from which they earn from 14 to 15,000 guilders a year; they also dedicate themselves to cutting those wooden sticks used to bind books, which have a considerable sale not only in the province, but also in the Kingdom of Naples' (Baselli, 1775: 177).

Demand for wood and charcoal from the highlands was created by the industries in the nearby small town of Ajdovščina, where iron and copperworks were present, albeit fluctuating, from the sixteenth century at least (Beguš, 2020: 164-167). The peasant population of the surroundings worked in these plants alongside the townspeople. The area had a highly developed wood trade, which was connected mostly with the towns of Udine, Gorizia, and Trieste. As peasant-foresters, the inhabitants of Trnovo forest earned much of their income from felling and selling wood to Gorizia (Panjek, 2015. 110-111; Kolenc, 2012: 206). In the eighteenth century, the craft of glassmaking developed and the locals also took part in it, besides the wooden pail-making which was mostly practised by men in winter time (Kolenc, 2011: 97-99; Kolenc, 2012: 131). Forest wood was also exploited by the locals for making woodenware to sell (Panjek 2015, 107).

The only large industrial plants in the area were, since the sixteenth century, the mercury mines and plant in Idrija, on the highlands, which were among the biggest in the world. This mine employed peasant lads for wage labour and contract work as diggers, ore smelters and as pumpers of water from the mine (Verbič, 1952-1953: 534, 538). The transport of mercury, which implied journeys of several dozen kilometres, was carried out by peasants from Idrija itself and the neighbouring manors (Verbič, 1963: 98). In the first two centuries of the mine's operation, the leading manufacturers and suppliers of clay pots for ore smelting were peasant potters from the area of Škofja Loka. These pots were manufactured solely for the needs of the mine, which indicates a form of the putting-out system (Verbič, 1963: 99; Blaznik, 1973: 222; Kavčič, 2010: 144; Panjek, 2015: 108). It would seem that the smuggling of mercury ore was inevitable; it was mainly carried out by pedlars subject to the manors of Idrija, Tolmin, and Škofja Loka, who came to Idrija under the pretence that they were bringing provisions in exchange for lace, which they purchased from the female lace makers of Idrija. The tradition of making Idrija lace, which was carried out by peasant women and girls, dates back to the sixteenth century. These lace makers purchased linen yarn and linen fabric in Škofja Loka in exchange for lace (Verbič, 1969: 157; Hodnik, 1995a; Hodnik, 1995b; Terpin, 2007: 84).

In the lowland surroundings of the town of Gorica as well as in the nearby Vipava valley and the Karst, sericulture developed as an industrial activity, for which wood was an important energy source. This industry is composed of a long series of successive phases from the cultivation of the mulberry trees as fodder for the silkworms, through silkworm breeding and the subsequent production stages of the yarn up to the final fabric. Mulberry leaf production was widespread among the peasants. Silkworm rearing was mostly carried out by the 'poor inhabitants of villages' (Žontar, 1957: 16). Some of the succeeding phases were also carried out in the countryside in the form of the domestic system, although the production of semi-finished products was greater than that of finished ones. At the beginning of the eighteenth century, before the mercantilist development policies started, in the county of Gorica about 9,000 kg of silk cocoons were produced yearly; altogether there were seven manual spinneries in the towns of Gorica and Cormons, while about thirty looms were scattered in the villages (Panjek, 2015: 105). Later in the century, after state-promoted centralized silk spinneries were founded, peasants engaged even more in silkworm breeding and also sent their children to work in the manufacture (Žontar, 1957: 54-55, 70, 76).

Inner Carniola and the Karst lay along the main transit route that connected Ljubljana with the Adriatic coast and with Gorica by the border with the Republic of Venice. This was a segment on which nearly all of the trade traffic transited between the Pannonian and Balkan regions and the Italian states. It may therefore not be a surprise that probably the most important non-agrarian activities of peasants in this area were trade and transport, smuggling included. Peasant trade in and transport of salt, wine, and olive oil was conducted from the Adriatic coastal towns towards the interior of the provinces of Carniola, Styria and all the way to Croatia. In the opposite direction, towards the littoral towns, peasant trade and transport brought 'all kinds of cereals and flour, livestock and meat products, cheese and fat, hides and leather, home-made cloth and linen, honey and wax, wood and wooden products, and other products of the cottage industry' (Gestrin, 1965: 42). Peasants transported their own cereals or someone else's, which they had bought at markets, or transported and sold products for landlords under corvée labour. Voje established that the most sizeable cottager settlements were located along the Ljubljana – Trieste route, which indicates the presence of transport activities. However, he inferred that often cottagers were used as wage carriers for large-farm peasants, who owned the horses (Voje, 1952-1953: 661). By the second half of the eighteenth century, when the port-city of Trieste had grown lively enough and the trade traffic had grown accordingly, opportunities grew as well, and peasants exploited them in a sector that was traditional to them, that is, transport and related services: 'A part of this population also benefits from its proximity to the royal regional and commercial roads; in fact, the residents derive large profits from the loads and passengers who pass through them' (Baselli, 1775: 177).

According to entries in the rules of the Ljubljana market of 1571, inhabitants of the Vipava Valley (and Trieste) were among the leading sellers of fruit, either their own or of other producers, at the Ljubljana market (Valenčič,1980: 321). Wine was another important article produced, sold, and transported by the peasant population of the area closer to the coast (Vipava valley, Karst, and Goriška Brda/Collio), with renowned white sorts at the time being *vipavec, rebula* and *prosek* (the originary prosecco), which were very sought-after in Carinthia, Carniola, and even in Vienna (Panjek, 2002: 181-219). Viticulture expanded strongly in this area during the sixteenth century precisely because of the market perspectives of the wines. The production and sale of wine and fruit were therefore important activities throughout the early modern period. In 1775, the population of the Vipava valley was said to live 'not only on its ordinary income but also on the trade of fruit, laurel, rosemary, sage, and other herbs, sold to the inhabitants of Carniola, who do not have them'. The inhabitants of the Karst would 'distil both a little coal and the grape-pomace, and they trade a small variety of foodstuffs which they buy in Trieste and resell at a profit' in the county of Gorica and in Carniola. They produced and sold honey and wax, as well (Baselli, 1775: 175, 177).

In the more forested parts of Inner Carniola and the Karst, wood represented a relatively important resource for peasant income integration.

The simplest item was firewood; the production of limestone required more preparation, as did timber for construction. But the most interesting type of use of this resource for income integration is probably the one that Valvasor already noticed in the seventeenth century, that is, that many of the inhabitants in this area made a living from the wood they transported to the sea, where they made 'all sorts of things out of it that large ships needed' (Valvasor, 2009-2013: 263-265). In fact, the peasants did not simply supply the raw timber, but were able to produce specific forms and semi-finished products for the shipyards. This activity gained in relevance after the port-city of Trieste started developing during the eighteenth century and afterwards. A nobleman from Trieste in 1724 stated as follows:

> Who can be more skilled in the forest than the peasant who was born in it, who never does any other activity than cutting, whether for home repairs, for wagons and other needs. In addition, since the Trieste harbour has existed, there has always been a small shipyard [...] and it is not known that any other wood was used than that brought by the peasants [...]. For this reason, there are always people among them who are well skilled in this profession, so that from among my subjects, who are really few in number, I can myself list over 20 who have always devoted themselves to making all kinds of wood for any kind of ship that can be found here in Trieste and nearby. [...] On this basis, it can be understood that true knowledge of wood is absolutely to be sought by the peasant. (Babudieri, 1986: 52-54)

Peasants in the area were skilled enough to choose the trees and branches with the right curves needed for shipbuilding, and were even able to transport trunks for mainmasts of huge dimensions. The longer ones could reach 50 metres, but largest ever, that even endured in local oral tradition, was a 'monster' that measured 64 metres. The whole composition, including four pairs of horses, reached 78 metres in length and was transported for about 80 kilometres from the village of Rakitna in Inner Carniola to a Trieste shipyard in 1894 (Pahor, 1976: 106; Pahor, 1977: 37-39; Pahor, 1981).

A curious activity took place in the forests of Inner Carniola, where peasants trapped dormice. According to the natural scientist Franz Anton Steinberg (1758), this activity generated great profit for peasants: 'Dormouse pelts are generating a very good profit; they sell them to furriers, who dress them and sew them into quadrangular sheets, and sell them in large quantities [...] they also send them to foreign lands. The local countryfolk send them to Holland, together with scorpion oil and other small goods, from where they are sold as far away as India. Because dormice are very fatty, peasants dissolve the fat and consume their meat with cabbage and turnips' (Baš, 1981-1983: 44).

An activity with which peasants integrated their income and was widespread from the Alps to the sea, was smuggling. It included especially livestock (particularly cattle), wine, cereals, fat, and cheese, depending on the area. In most cases the final destination was the Republic of Venice (Gestrin, 1963: 78-79; Gestrin, 1965: 81-82; Gestrin, 1991: 277; Vilfan, 1963: 2-4; Panjek, 2002: 151-172).

V.3. Lower Carniola

A well-known activity of the peasant population in Lower Carniola is the production and sale of woodenware, which is attested at the earliest from 1492, when Emperor Frederick III granted a privilege to the subjects of two areas, Kočevje and Ribnica, allowing them to take their livestock, linen and anything else they could rear and produce by themselves to Croatia and other lands. The aim was to help restore the villages in the area that had been ruined by Ottoman raids. This privilege became the foundation for local peddling (Otorepec, 1982: 83; Gradišnik, 2012: 13). In the sixteenth century, the trade in wooden products had become so widespread that the authorities wanted to tax it. In time, it expanded into several, more specialized industries, such as pail-making, spoon-making, pot-making, etc. (Trošt, 1950-1951: 36-37). As described by Valvasor, 'all of the inhabitants of the Kočevje plain make boxes, plane wooden plates and bowls, make spoons, sifters, and sieves; they make all kinds of wooden products and transport them' (Valvasor, 2009-2013: 218-219). Woodenware makers also sold their products as pedlars, at the latest by the second half of the seventeenth century, 'both in their province and abroad'. The raw material was provided by the vast forests of Snežnik and Kočevje. The peasants beneath the mountain Snežnik had an easement to use commercial wood for selling and trading in wooden products. Just as the Kočevje peasants were granted a privilege to sell wooden products, so were the peasants beneath Snežnik granted the aforementioned right in order to recover economically from the Ottoman raids of the sixteenth century (Kačičnik Gabrič, 2004: 48-49).

Apart from the woodenware craft, Valvasor mentioned that some villages specialized in one or more activities. For example, in the village of Šmartno, there were 'many pack-horse drivers and different kinds of craftsmen, especially tanners who made black leather. The village of Perišče is named after the laundresses (*perice*), women who bleached the laundry. Women would go to Ljubljana every week to collect dirty linen and wash it. They would also bleach a lot of linen fabric and linen yarn'. In the valley of Ribnica in the same region of Kočevje, there are also 'many potters and those who make sifters, hoops, bowls, plates, pails and plane other woodenware, and carpenters, who transport and sell their products at home as well as abroad' (Valvasor, 2009-2013: 180-181, 218-219).

An important peasant activity in the area was transport. On different routes, goods were transported to Ljubljana, Inner Carniola and the Karst, and to the Adriatic Sea (both in the direction of Rijeka and Trieste). An important transport connection ran through Novo Mesto from Ljubljana towards the Croatian city of Zagreb (Gestrin, 1991: 105-106; Kosi, 1998: 235); subjects from White Carniola and the Kočevje area joined the peasant trade towards the town of Rijeka (Gestrin, 1972: 57). Goods were not transported only by land. In fact, peasants also rafted cargo on the Sava River, that is, 'all of the merchandise from Croatia, and some of the merchandise from Styria and Lower Carniola, towards Ljubljana' (Valvasor, 2009-2013: 158). Boating 'was for most boatmen a side job, which they performed when they did not have to work on their own farm or in a manor' (Umek, 1999: 276). Peasants would therefore integrate their income from agriculture with income from trade and boating.

Within the borders of the Višnja Gora manorial court (*Landgericht*), they would also integrate it with income from the lease of tollhouses. In the sixteenth and seventeenth century, the rural, 'smaller tollhouses were generally leased by peasants', whereas in the small town of Litija they were leased by its inhabitants and magistrates (Golec, 1995: 84). Like most of the previously described regions, Lower Carniola was a wine-growing region, too. Peasants would work the vineyards either as subjects or as tenants of 'mountain vineyards', for which they paid in kind or in money. It can therefore be assumed that they also traded in wine. As the population began to expand in the sixteenth century, new social groups of the rural population were formed, i.e. cottagers and lodgers, who 'live at the homes of other peasants, and trade in linen and other items' (Vilfan, 1952: 112; Granda, 2005: 287).

VI. Concluding remarks

Early modern western and central Slovenia represents the area where, based on empirical evidence in historical literature and from research in the last couple of decades, the concept of the integrated peasant economy was developed and, as shown, it applies well to it. Both land-poor and well-off villagers engaged in on-farm and off-farm market-oriented activities. Their aim may have been sustenance or the improvement of the living standard. Engaging in these activities was not simply an unavoidable need, but also a choice and a matter of economic agency. The latter is especially true in the more economically dynamic periods, when opportunities were larger and it was simpler and attractive to make a good living on a small holding. When opportunities shrank, they sought for alternative engagements, while the fragmented holdings, inherited by the predecessors living in times of expansion, might become too tight, transforming the choice to integrate in a must.

To conclude, we will categorize by economic sectors the activities in which the peasant population was engaged besides self-consumption farming, and apply the integrated peasant economy checklist. Among the activities that fall within the primary sector and are characterized by being market oriented, denote intensification, or both, have been traced viticulture, fruit and mulberry tree growing, silk-worm breeding, animal husbandry for marketing, and forest exploitation for wood and timber production for sale in construction and shipbuilding. The reclamation of forested areas and clearing of woods, which were implemented throughout the early modern period (Panjek, 2015: 85-117), were meant for the acquisition of new pastureland and the expansion of animal husbandry. Forested surfaces were also cleared by peasants for the needs of viticulture, both in the Vipava valley and in Lower Carniola. In the eighteenth century in the Snežnik manor (Inner Carniola), peasants were involved in seasonal migrant work, by going 'to Croatia in the summer to mow the grass and in the winter to thresh' (Valenčič, 1985: 254). Farmhands in agriculture were present especially in Upper Carniola, while wage labour in agriculture was widespread, although we have not mentioned it earlier. The same goes for stone quarries and sea fishing in the Karst.

As peasant activities in the secondary sector which consist of processing raw materials to produce finished and semi-finished products within rural crafts, we can note charcoal, lime, woodenware, sieves, wine, meat, cheese, leather, scorpion oil, and dormouse pelts. Activities within the domain of the domestic and putting-out system were present in Upper and Lower Carniola in particular, where there were also small and larger centralized plants with mines involved in the extraction and processing of ore, plants for the production of iron products and semi-finished products, mercury, glass, and weaving facilities. Wage work of peasant family members in modern industries appeared in the eighteenth century in the iron plants in Upper Carniola, in the quicksilver plant in Idrija, and in plants in the Gorica county (Ajdovščina and Gorica town surroundings). Migrant and mobile craftsmen have not yet been identified with certainty.

In the domain of the tertiary sector the activities we spotted include peasant trade with their own and other's goods as well as transport over short, medium, and long distance, even across state borders. Especially in the eighteenth century, when better roads were constructed which allowed a wide use of carts and carriages, this opened additional opportunities for the lease of draught animals as well as for lodging of transporters and passengers by peasant innkeepers along the roads. We may well add long distance rafting on rivers, the Sava in particular. Transport and carrier services, which were mostly connected with the main transport routes from the hinterland towards the sea and from the area of Gorizia towards

Venetian and Inner Austrian provinces, likewise belong to the tertiary sector. Let us also mention peddling in Inner and Lower Carniola, in the Idrija area and in the upper Soča valley in the Alps (the *kramar*). Smuggling was widespread in all provinces, particularly around the coastal towns and along the border with the Republic of Venice. This sector also includes the services of female commuting workers, such as the laundresses in Lower Carniola, who went to Ljubljana on a weekly basis to wash and bleach linen. Mobile dock workers of peasant origin became numerous in Trieste during the eighteenth century (Kalc, 2017). Works of trust are best studied in the Karst, where the peasant land market was well developed and institutionalized. The estimators, who belonged to the village elites, were well paid for the measurement and valuation of the plots and buildings on sale (Panjek, 2023). The Karst and Inner Carniola represent the first area on a world scale where cave tourism appeared and already in the seventeenth and eighteenth centuries the first guides who led visitors underground were local peasants (Kavrečič, 2017). So, tourism represented a possible source of income integration very early, too.

From the range of peasant economic activities one can infer their considerable diversity and density. However, it would be difficult to determine which activity was the most widespread and which the least, which provided the greatest part of income and which was the most marginal. Nevertheless, it can be said that most tertiary activities (trade, transport, and smuggling) were represented and highly present in all areas of early modern western and central Slovenia. On the other hand, some of the activities were locally specific, such as female lace makers in Idrija, silkworm breeding in a part of the County of Gorica, or scorpion oil in Inner Carniola. As Table 9 shows, almost all of the activities listed in the integrated peasant economy checklist were present in early modern western and central Slovenia.

Funding

This research was carried out within the project *Concepts of peasant economy: a theoretical and empirical comparative approach (15th-20th c.)*, financed by the Slovenian Research and Innovation Agency (ARIS).

Table 5.9. The integrated peasant economy in Carniola and the county of Gorica (16th-18th c.)

ACTIVITY	CHECK
Primary sector	
Agricultural specialization	✓
Intensification of cultivation (no fallow, mixed-cropping, etc.)	✓
Wage day-labour in agriculture and longer-term farmhands on larger farms	✓
Extension/intensification of animal husbandry	✓
Intensification of forest exploitation (through primary sector activities, but also secondary and tertiary)	✓
Extension of cultivated land (reclamation of commons and woods)	✓
Quarries	✓
Fishing	✓
Secondary sector	
Transformation of primary resources/products (e.g. wine, cheese, meat products; charcoal, lime)	✓
Rural crafts	✓
Domestic, putting-out system (proto-industry)	✓
Work in 'centralized' industries and plants (manufactures, mining, etc.)	✓
Migrant/mobile craftsmen (e.g. bricklayers)	
Wage labour in the industrial sector	✓
Tertiary sector	
Services in the field of long and medium distance trade (draft animal lease, fodder, lodging and food – inns, etc.)	✓
Transport of other people's products and goods over short to medium distances	✓
Trade with own products and goods over short to medium distances	✓
Peddling	✓
Smuggling	✓
Migrant/mobile workers (dock-workers, etc.)	✓
Works of trust (estimation of land value, testimonies, etc.)	✓
Tourism	✓

Bibliography

Babudieri, F. (1986), *Squeri e cantieri a Trieste e nella regione Giulia dal Settecento agli inizi del Novecento*, Trieste.

Baš, A. (1981-1983), 'Polšji lov na Slovenskem', *Traditiones, zbornik inštituta za slovensko narodopisje*, 10-12, pp. 35-60.

Baselli, G. P. (1775), 'Descrizione delle contee di Gorizia e Gradisca'. In: Cavazza, S., Iancis, P. and Porcedda, D. (eds), *Istoria della Contea di Gorizia di Carlo Morelli*, 5, *Studi e documenti*, Gorizia 2003, pp. 172-216.

Beguš, I. (2020), 'Dolga zgodovina industrije v Ajdovščini: osredotočeni obrati ob Hublju (oris od 16. do začetka 20. stoletja)', Lazar, I., Panjek, A. and Vinkler, J. (eds), *Mikro in makro: pristopi in prispevki k humanističnim vedam ob dvajsetletnici UP Fakultete za humanistične študije*, 1, Koper. pp. 163-186.

Bizjak, M. (2017), 'Integrated peasant economy in Medieval Slovenia: a preliminary study', Panjek, A., Larsson, J. and Mocarelli, L. (eds), *Integrated peasant economy in a comparative perspective: Alps, Scandinavia and beyond*, Koper, pp. 83-93.

Blaznik, P. (1959), 'O podeželski obrti na loškem ozemlju do začetka 16. stoletja'. *Loški razgledi*, 6, pp. 91-97.

——— (1973), *Škofja Loka in loško gospostvo (973-1803)*, Škofja Loka.

Čepič, Z. (1979), *Zgodovina Slovencev*, Ljubljana.

Gašperšič, J. (1959), 'Gorenjsko železarstvo v XIV. in XV. stoletju', *Kronika: časopis za slovensko krajevno zgodovino*, 7, 1, pp. 5-10.

——— (1960), 'Ferdinandejski rudarski red za fužine pod Jelovico', *Kronika: časopis za slovensko krajevno zgodovino*, 8, 3, pp. 149-158.

Gestrin, F. (1963), 'Trgovina slovenskega zaledja s primorskimi mesti od XIII. do konca XVI. stoletja', *Kronika: časopis za slovensko krajevno zgodovino*, 11, 2, pp. 73-85.

——— (1965), *Trgovina slovenskega zaledja s primorskimi mesti od 13. do konca 16. stoletja*. Ljubljana.

——— (1991), *Slovenske dežele in zgodnji kapitalizem*. Ljubljana.

Golec, B. (1995), 'Trgovski promet na širšem območju Višnje gore do konca 18. stoletja v luči deželskosodnih in mestnih mitnic', *Zgodovinski časopis*, 49, 1, pp.75-98.

Gomiršek, T. (2007), *Rebula nekoč in danes*. Nova Gorica.

Gradišnik, M. (2012), 'Obdobje petnajstega in šestnajstega stoletja – med novo vero, božjo šibo in krošnjarjenjem', Gradišnik, M. and Židov, N., *Križem svajt so se podal pa sujo ruobo ponujal: pregled ribniškega krošnjarjenja od patenta leta 1492 do danes*, Ribnica, pp. 8-15.

Grafenauer, B. (1973), 'Položaj kmeta in kmečki upori od 15. do 19. stoletja', *Mednarodni kulturnozgodovinski simpozij Modinci*, 5, Maribor, pp. 19-36.

——— (1974), *Boj za staro pravdo v 15. in 16. stoletju na Slovenskem: slovenski kmečki upor 1515 in hrvaško-slovenski kmečki upor 1572/73 s posebnim ozirom na razvoj programa slovenskih puntarjev med 1473 in 1573*. Ljubljana.

Granda, S. (2005), 'K zgodovini cvička', Mihelič, D. (ed.), *Ad fontes. Otorepčev zbornik*, Ljubljana, pp. 281-301.

Hodnik, M. (1995a), 'Kraja živosrebrne rude in kaznovanje tatov iz loškega gospostva', *Loški razgledi*, 42, pp. 31-37.

——— (1995b), 'Tihotapci živosrebrove rude v 18. stoletju'. *Idrijski razgledi*, 40, pp. 22-27.

Kačičnik Gabrič, A. (2004), *O kmečkih dolgovih nekoliko drugače: problem servitutnih pravic na posestvu Snežnik*. Ljubljana.

Kalc, A. (2017), 'Peasant population and income integration: the case of the Trieste port-town hinterland (Karst, 16th-20th centuries)', Panjek, A., Larsson, J. and Mocarelli, L. (eds), *Integrated peasant economy in a comparative perspective: Alps, Scandinavia and beyond*, Koper, pp. 205-227.

Kavčič, I. (2010), 'Petsto dvajset let vezi med Idrijo in Škofjo Loko'. *Loški razgledi*, 57, pp. 135-147.

Kavrečič, P. (2017), 'Tourism as a source of non-agricultural rural income: the case of the Karst (16th-19th centuries)', Panjek, A., Larsson, J. and Mocarelli, L. (eds), *Integrated peasant economy in a comparative perspective: Alps, Scandinavia and beyond*, Koper, pp. 259-281.

Kolenc, P. (2011), 'Med glažutarji na robu Trnovskega gozda: razvoj steklarske obrti med Gorenjo Trebušo, Lazno in Lokvami v letih od 1722 do 1825/30', *Goriški letnik: zbornik Goriškega muzeja*, 35, pp. 95-125.

——— (2012), 'V osrčju brezmejnega gozda. Raba, izkoriščanje in gospodarjenje s Trnovskim gozdom od naselitve do konca 19. stoletja', *Kronika: časopis za slovensko krajevno zgodovino*, 60, 2, pp. 203-220.

Kosi, M. (1998), *Potujoči srednji vek. Cesta, popotnik in promet na Slovenskem med antiko in 16. stoletjem*. Ljubljana.

Mihelič, D. (1999), 'Zgodovina sodarske obrti na Slovenskem', Rajšp V. and Bruckmüller, E., *Vilfanov zbornik: pravo, zgodovina, narod*, Ljubljana, pp. 659-679.

Mlinar, J. (2018), *Urbarji belopeškega gospostva*, Ljubljana.

Mohorič, I. (1954), 'Zgodovina plavža v Železnikih'. *Kronika: časopis za slovensko krajevno zgodovino*, 2, 2, pp. 95-100.

——— (1955), 'Zgodovina fužin ob Bistrici pri Kamniku'. *Kronika: časopis za slovensko krajevno zgodovino*, 3, 1-2, pp. 25-32.

——— (1969), *Dva tisoč let železarstva na Gorenjskem*, 1, Ljubljana.

Otorepec, B. (1982), 'Doneski k zgodovini Ribnice in okolice v srednjem veku'. *Kronika: časopis za slovensko krajevno zgodovino*, 30, 2, pp. 79-87.

Pahor, M. (1976), 'Kraška vas Povir, primer simbioze med kopnim in morjem', *Goriški letnik: zbornik Goriškega muzeja*, 3, pp. 95-122.

——— (1977), 'Senožeče – slovenska pomorska postojanka na kopnem', *Slovensko morje in zaledje*, 1, pp. 21-79.

——— (1978), 'Vloga furmanstva pri rekrutiranju prostovoljnega kadra avstrijske mornarice', *Časopis za zgodovino in narodopisje*, 1, pp. 92-99.

——— (1979), 'Vloga gorenjsko-koroške prometne pahljače pri rekrutiranju pomorskega kadra v preteklosti', *Kronika: časopis za slovensko krajevno zgodovino*, 1, pp. 30-42.

——— and Hajnal, I. (1981), 'Po sledeh nekega jambora', *Informator*, 22, 3, pp. 43-49.

Panjek, A. (2002). *Terra di confine. Agricolture e traffici tra le Alpi e l'Adriatico: la contea di Gorizia nel Seicento*. Mariano del Friuli.

——— (2011), 'Not demesne but money: lord and peasant economies in early modern western Slovenia', *Agricultural history review*, 59, 2, pp. 293-311.

——— (2015), *Vzhodno od Benetk, slovenski obmejni prostor: gospodarstvo, družba, prebivalstvo in naravni viri v zgodnjem novem veku*. Koper.

——— (2017), 'The integrated peasant economy as a concept in progress', Panjek, A., Larsson, J. and Mocarelli, L. (eds), *Integrated peasant economy in a comparative perspective: Alps, Scandinavia and beyond*, Koper, pp. 11-49.

——— (2018), 'Kruh naredi človeka: kdo je kdaj sit na primorskem podeželju v 17. in 18. Stoletju', Šorn, M. (ed.), *Lakote in pomanjkanje: slovenski primer*. Ljubljana, pp. 25-41.

——— (2022a), 'Land will tear us apart: family-farm division and real estate market in Slovenia (sixteenth to eighteenth centuries)', *The history of the family*, 27, 1, pp. 54-81.

——— (2022b), 'Demografska eksplozija med Vipavo in Krasom v 16. stoletju: poskus kvantifikacije in periodizacije (gospostvo Rihemberk)', *Goriški letnik: zbornik Goriškega muzeja*, 46, in print.

——— (2023) 'Črna leta in rdeče številke Ivana Černeta, župana v Tomaju sredi 18. stoletja: o dolžniško-upniških razmerjih na podeželju', *Zgodovinski časopis*, 77, 1, in print.

Šorn, J. (1984), *Začetki industrije na Slovenskem*. Maribor.

Štih, P. and Simoniti, V. (2010), *Na stičišču svetov. Slovenska zgodovina od prazgodovinskih kultur do konca 18. stoletja*, Ljubljana.

Terpin, M. (2007), 'Marina Melhiorca – pomočnica tatov: proces proti tolpi tatov in tihotapcev 1729-1731', *Idrijski razgledi*, 52, 2, pp. 84-99.

Trošt, J. (1950-1951), 'Ribniška suha roba v lesni domači obrti', *Slovenski etnograf*, 3-4, pp. 28-67.

Umek, E. (1999), 'Promet po Savi in Ljubljanici', Mihelič, D. (ed.), *Gestrinov zbornik*, Ljubljana, pp. 271-278.

Valenčič, V. (1980), 'Sadjarstvo', Blaznik, P. et al. (eds), *Gospodarska in družbena zgodovina Slovencev. Zgodovina agrarnih panog*, 1, *Agrarno gospodarstvo*. Ljubljana.

——— (1985), 'Tovorništvo na Kranjskem', *Zgodovinski časopis*, 35, 3, pp. 243-277.
Valvasor, J. V. (2009-2013). *Čast in slava vojvodine Kranjske*, 2, Ljubljana (facsimile translation, original 1689).
Verbič, M. (1952-1953), 'Idrijski delavec v 16. stoletju', *Zgodovinski časopis*, 6-7, *Kosov zbornik*, pp. 531-551.
——— (1963), 'Gospodarski stiki Loke z Idrijo v 16. in 17. stoletju', *Loški razgledi*, 10, pp. 97-103.
——— (1969), 'O začetkih slovenskega čipkarstva s posebnim ozirom na Idrijo', *Kronika: časopis za slovensko krajevno zgodovino*, 17, 3, pp. 157-160.
Vilfan, S. (1952), 'Od vinskega hrama do bajte: prispevki k zgodovini bajtarstva in gostaštva v dolenjskih vinogradih', *Slovenski etnograf*, 5, pp. 107-142.
——— (1963), 'K zgodovini kmečkega kupčevanja s soljo: gospodarsko-pravne podlage povesti o Martinu Krpanu', *Kronika: časopis za slovensko krajevno zgodovino*, 11, 1, pp. 1-12.
Voje, I. (1952-1953), 'Kajžarstvo v logaškem gospostvu', *Zgodovinski časopis*, 6-7, *Kosov zbornik*, pp. 650-662.
Žontar, J. (1956), 'Platnarstvo in sitarstvo v loškem gospostvu v 18. stoletju', *Loški razgledi*, 3, pp. 89-102.
——— (1957), *Svilogojstvo in svilarstvo na Slovenskem od 16. do 20. stoletja*, Ljubljana.
——— (1982), *Zgodovina mesta Kranja*, Ljubljana.

MILOŠ IVANOVIĆ

6. Diversity of the Peasant Economy in Medieval Serbia (Thirteenth to Fifteenth Century)

I. Introduction

A Serbian manuscript from the seventeenth or eighteenth century,[1] written by an unnamed author and belonging to the genre of 'questions and answers', contains the description of a well-known medieval trifunctional scheme of society. According to that pattern, the duty of a farmer was to feed the priest and the soldier (Novaković, 1904: 527; Ćirković, 1994: 223). Thus, this scheme foresaw the role of a peasant as a food producer. However, the medieval reality was not so simple either in Europe or in Serbia.

The aim of this research is to show that the peasant population was not limited to the production for their own subsistence and meeting the needs of the privileged classes. Furthermore, the intention is to point out that a part of the peasants was market-oriented and that they could take on various activities to improve their living standard. Therefore, I believe that the concept of the integrated peasant economy (IPE) is applicable to the objectives of this paper. According to this concept, peasants combine agricultural and market-oriented activities to make a living and/or raise their living standard. Further, all economic activities which provided income to peasants belonged to three economic sectors. The primary-sector activities include agricultural specialization, intensification of cultivation, animal husbandry, forest exploitation, extension of cultivated land, wage/day labour in agriculture, work in quarries, and fishing. The production of cheese, wine, meat products, charcoal and lime, rural crafts, the putting-out system (proto-industry), work in manufacturing and mining, mobile craftsmen, and wage labour in industry belong to the secondary sector.

1 Stojanović, 1901: 190. It is likely that this manuscript reproduced an older one (Mavromatis, 1991: 72).

Integrated Peasant Economy in Central and Eastern Europe, ed. by Aleksander Panjek, Rural History in Europe, 18 (Turnhout: Brepols, 2024), pp. 143–168
BREPOLS PUBLISHERS 10.1484/M.RURHE-EB.5.142467

Finally, the tertiary group of activities includes transport services, trafficking of own products, peddling, smuggling, mobile workers, works of trust such as the estimation of land value, and tourism (Panjek, 2017: 20-25, 39, 42-44). Moreover, peasants did not passively adapt to external conditions and pressures, but were active participants in the wider environment of production and consumption. The system was dynamic and flexible, which means that single activities could be adopted, increased, decreased or abandoned (Panjek, 2017: 25, 36, 43).

It should be stressed that this research will essentially cover only the period from the late twelfth to the mid-fifteenth century due to the lack of sources. Namely, for the earlier period, there are no preserved charters (*povelje*) of Serbian rulers (Stanojević, 1937: 1), or other relevant sources for the topic of this paper.[2] It is necessary to note that this research does not refer to the nobility who lived in the villages. However, some petty nobles will be mentioned because of their origin and the fact that they performed physical work.

The charters are the main source for the activities of the rural population of medieval Serbia. Their regulations contain the list of work obligations that the dependent peasants owed to the rulers and their masters (Ćirković-Mihaljčić, 1999: 530). At the same time, these sources sometimes testify that peasants produced not only for themselves and the needs of their lords. The other sources, primarily Ragusan archival documents, contain information that peasants sold a part of their products on the market. Important information for the fifteenth century is provided also by Ottoman sources.

According to the preserved sources, a part of the peasant population in Serbia from the thirteenth to fifteenth century practiced many different activities from the three above-described sectors. It should be underlined that it is impossible to determine the exact percentage of the population engaged in market activities. In addition, the volume of their agricultural production remains unknown (Ćirković-Kovačević-Kojić, 1997: 45). Thus, the preserved data do not allow us to estimate the income that the peasant population earned by performing non-agricultural works. It should also be mentioned that the production and incomes of the medieval Serbian rural population have not been comprehensively researched in historiography. Therefore, this research must rely on the books and papers that treat of individual aspects of the peasant economy.[3]

2 The Serbian charters were written testimonies of an act of legal nature. Their emergence was a consequence of business or legal relation of rulers, nobles and church dignitaries with institutions or individuals (Ćirković-Mihaljčić, 1999: 529-530).

3 Miloš Blagojević researched agronomy in medieval Serbia in detail (Blagojević, 2004). Stojan Novaković's old study (Novaković, 1965, third edition; the first edition was published in 1891) dedicated to the village did not focus on the issues that are the subject of this paper.

It should be noted that the Serbian state from the thirteenth to the fifteenth century has changed its territorial scope. That was a consequence of its internal development and relations with its neighbours. In the north, the Serbian state did not cross the Danube and Sava rivers, where it bordered with the Hungarian Kingdom. The main direction of Serbia's expansion was to the south, where it occupied Byzantine territories, among which Macedonia remained in its borders for the longest time. The influence of Byzantium was great, considering that Orthodox Christianity was accepted in Serbia. In the late fourteenth century, the Ottoman Empire began to endanger Serbian areas from the south and east. Finally, Serbia had very intensive ties with the West, especially economic ones, due to the control over the southern part of the eastern Adriatic coast (Blagojević 1983: 68-88, 101-106, 110-122).

In the following pages, the obligations of the rural population in favour of the lords and the ruler will be presented first, and then their various activities directed towards the market. The impact of urban development on the rural economy will be particularly dealt with. An important place in the analysis will be given to the armed activities of the peasants. Finally, the Ottoman sources will be used to provide an insight in the obligations and income of the rural population at the end of the observed period.

II. Work obligations and incomes of the rural population in medieval Serbia during the 13th and 14th century

The rural population of medieval Serbia consisted of several different categories of inhabitants who differed in their rights and obligations. The most important source for this topic is the charters of Serbian rulers. All preserved extant documents regulated the position of the peasants on the possessions of monasteries. However, similar stipulations probably applied to the estates of the ruler and the nobles, as well (Blagojević, 2004: 310-319).

First, it should be noted that not all peasants had a permanent place of residence. Thus, the monk Simeon assigned 170 *Vlachs* to the Chilandar monastery in 1198. They are not listed as belonging to any settlement (Trifunović-Bjelogrlić-Brajović, 1986: 49, 55, 57). The term *Vlachs* designated the population primarily engaged in cattle breeding. Most of them were nomadic to some extent, but some of the Vlachs lived sedentarily and cultivated possessions of the lords (Ćirković-Mihaljčić, 1999: 86-87; Isailović, 2017: 28; Blagojević 1979: 150). On the other hand, there were several categories of sedentary population. The charter of King Vladislav Nemanjić (1234-1243) for the monastery of Saint Mary in Bistrica mentions *meropsi* and *sokalnici*. The stipulations of the charter clearly testify that *meropsi* were primarily engaged in agricultural works. In addition, they had to make beer, and give firewood, lamb fur, and ropes for the benefit of the monastery. Also, they had an obligation to fish for the needs of the monastery, King, and Archbishop during festivities (Mošin-Ćirković-Sindik, 2011: 167). The *sokalnici* had fewer agrarian obligations than *meropsi*, but they had to perform construction work for the monastery and to travel on horseback by order of the abbot. All the dependent peasants were supposed to give to the monastery a tenth of honey production. Finally, both categories of peasants and priests had to provide food when the King, a noble, or guest were staying on the possessions of the monastery (Mošin-Ćirković-Sindik, 2011: 167). It should be stressed that King Vladislav issued this charter, since the older documents of his father and grandfather were lost (Mošin-Ćirković-Sindik, 2011: 166). This fact indicates that similar regulations concerning peasants were in force even at the end of the twelfth century (Blagojević, 1979: 135-139). The text of this charter clearly shows that the peasant population was not exclusively focused on agricultural work at that time. However, in listing only the obligations of the rural population, the source does not show how they handled potential surpluses of products.

More detailed information on the obligations of the dependent population is contained in the charter of King Milutin (1282-1321) for the monastery of Banjska from late 1315 or early 1316 (Bubalo, 2016: 23-25). Although this document is about eighty years younger than the previous one, it is clear that some of its provisions are of older origin (Blagojević, 1979: 142, 154). The position of the dependent population was regulated by the *Law on Churchmen* and the *Law on Vlachs* in that charter. The first *Law* mentions the obligations of *meropsi*, *sokalnici*, *majstorije* (craftsmen), *rataji* (farmers), priests, and servants (*otroks*). The work obligations of *meropsi* in the *Law on Churchmen* were similar to those in the charter for the Bistrica monastery. The only significant difference was that the *meropsi* of Banjska had to cultivate vineyards. The other categories of peasants had the same duty, including priests (Mošin-Ćirković-Sindik, 2011: 464). All the subjects mentioned in the charter, with the exception of priests, had to give every fifth hive a year to the monastery (Mošin-Ćirković-Sindik, 2011: 465). The status and obligations of the *sokalnici* were more clearly defined in this charter. Thus, one provision of the *Law on Churchmen* determines that *sokalnici* must receive food from the monastery when they went on the road with the abbot or monk. If they went alone, *sokalnici* had to feed themselves (Mošin-Ćirković-Sindik, 2011: 464). It follows from this regulation that they could travel for the sake of their jobs, regardless of the monastery. Another provision of the same *Law* provided that *sokalnici* should transport a certain amount of grain and wine each year, from wherever the abbot ordered it (Mošin-Ćirković-Sindik, 2011: 465). They performed this transport activity thanks to the fact that they owned horses.

According to the charter, a *sokalnik* could get a horse from the monastery after marriage. In that way, he took over duties in accordance with his status. The duty of a *sokalnik* to participate in extinguishing fires can also be connected with the possession of horses, since such a situation required a swift reaction. The *sokalnici* of the Banjska monastery also had an obligation to repair churches, dining rooms, and royal palaces (Mošin-Ćirković-Sindik, 2011: 464; Trijić, 2002-2003: 10-11, 15-17, 19). The specific position of the *sokalnici* is reflected not only in the non-agricultural works they performed, but also in the personal relationship they established with the master by travelling with him (Trijić, 2002-2003: 22). In addition, the possibility of travel gave them the opportunity to make contacts with people outside their households and communities. These contacts could have significance for their potential trading activities.

The craftsmen (*majstorije*) were mentioned as a special category of dependent peasants in this charter. The *Law on Churchmen* ordered that blacksmiths, carpenters, tailors, tanners, saddlers, potters, masons, and goldsmiths had to plough and mow hay like *sokalnici*. Further, they had to hand over all their handcrafts to the monastery. In the case the craftsmen ruined a product, they had to compensate for it at their own expense (Mošin-Ćirković-Sindik, 2011: 464-465). The obligation to hand over craft products was not precisely defined. These products were probably made from raw materials provided by the monastery. On the other hand, it is certain that craftsmen did not produce only for the Banjska monastery. Namely, it is clear that they could only compensate the monastery for damage or faulty production if using material acquired by their own sources and therefore through that other part of production. The proportion between these two parts of production cannot be determined, but the monastery received at least a tenth of all their products (Fostikov, 2016: 202). The last stipulation of the *Law* notes that the monastery had ten leather tailors, six bootmakers and two potters (Mošin-Ćirković-Sindik, 2011: 465). Particularly important was the regulation according to which if a craftsman had several sons, only one should inherit his father's occupation. The others were to be agricultural workers (Mošin-Ćirković-Sindik, 2011: 465). This stipulation shows that the position of craftsmen was privileged in comparison to the peasants without non-agricultural obligations (Fostikov, 2016: 202). Some examples indicate that this provision was not consistently respected, but its importance cannot be ignored (Fostikov, 2016: 203).

The charter of King Milutin for the monastery of Saint George near Skopje from 1299/1300[4] stipulates that peasants had to give the monastery

4 Historian Srđan Pirivatrić determined that these were actually two charters, the first of which was most likely issued in 1298, while the second was published in 1299/1300. See: Pirivatrić, 2015: 208, 212-213. This fact is not of major importance for this paper.

a quarter of the yield if they wished to cultivate its land (Mošin-Ćirković-Sindik, 2011: 327; Blagojević, 2004: 183). This distribution of yields in the case of land leases was common (Blagojević, 2004: 182-192). There were rare cases where the lessees had to give the landowner a third of the harvest (Šekularac, 1987: 205; Blagojević, 2004: 185-186, 189). If a farmer leased oxen or took seeds for sowing, the same distribution of yields applied (Blagojević, 2004: 211-251). Finally, the same principle seems to have applied when peasants used other resources of their lords. The stipulations of the above-mentioned charter for the Saint George monastery emphasize that the fee for the use of monastic hunting grounds, fishponds, gardens, and forests amounted to a quarter of the catch, fruits, and felled trees (Mošin-Ćirković-Sindik, 2011: 327; Blagojević, 2004: 183-184). This charter therefore demonstrates that peasants used to lease different means of production and rights to use natural assets. Unfortunately, it is impossible to determine to what extent the lease of the lord's goods was driven by the need for subsistence, and to what extent it was an attempt to acquire surplus.

King Milutin assigned 496 Vlachs to the Banjska monastery, who were grouped in nine pastoral settlements (*katuns*)[5] (Mošin-Ćirković-Sindik, 2011: 465; Filipović, 1963: 47, 67-68). The *Law on Vlachs* determined that they had to give the monastery a sheep with a lamb and another barren sheep. Further, all the Vlachs had to give the monastery two lambskins per year. Like *sokalnici,* they also had transport obligations. Their duty was to transport grain, wine, cheese, and salt. Some of the Vlachs were obliged to mow hay three days during the year (Mošin-Ćirković-Sindik, 2011: 467-468). This *Law* distinguished two categories of Vlachs who differed in some of their obligations. Thus, *Vlachs soldiers* were supposed to guard horses, while *ćelatori* were supposed to take care of the sheep and shear their wool. In the case of dangerous situations, all the Vlachs had to take care of the sheep. The *ćelatori,* who were among the poorer Vlachs (Blagojević, 1979: 152-154; Ćirković-Mihaljčić, 1999: 751), had to process the monastery wool. The duty of the *Vlachs soldiers* was to give finished fabric (Mošin-Ćirković-Sindik, 2011: 468). The Vlachs were also obliged to pay their owners for the use of the pastures (Milojević 1880: 56; Ćirković-Mihaljčić, 1999: 87, 736-737). It needs to be mentioned that sedentary Vlachs had to do some agricultural works, but to a much lesser extent than other peasants (Mošin-Ćirković-Sindik, 2011: 328; Blagojević 1979: 150-151).

Various sources of information show that Vlachs were able to generate income through livestock, transportation services, trade, and crafts. It is well known that they played a key role in the caravan trade between

5 A *katun* could be a permanent or mobile settlement: Ćirković-Mihaljičić, 1999: 286; Novaković, 1960: 47.

Ragusa (Dubrovnik) and the territories of Serbia and Bosnia (Dinić, 1937: 119-120). The Ragusan merchants remunerated their services with money, except in the case of transporting salt. Then, they got a half of the transported salt, regardless of the length of the trip. The price of the transport of other goods depended on the season, the type of merchandise, security of trade routes, the reputation of the caravan leader, and other factors (Dinić, 1937: 136-137; Jireček, 1959: 200-202). The archival documents testify that the merchants and craftsmen bought livestock products directly from the Vlachs, certainly since the late thirteenth century. The most important products of this trade were cheese, furs, lambskin, and sheepskin (Čremošnik, 1932: 123, 132, 145; Ćuk, 2019: 106-108; Kovačević-Kojić, 1983: 79). From the early fourteenth century, the Vlachs themselves more often sold wool, cattle and especially horses and mares in Ragusa (Čremošnik, 1932: 125; Kovačević-Kojić,1983: 79; Dinić-Knežević, 1982: 10). The information presented seems to indicate that surplus products first appeared in animal husbandry. As a result, livestock products more easily become objects of trade than typical agricultural products such as grain. It must be borne in mind that this information refers to trade with coastal areas. Therefore, it can be said that the high transport costs affected trade between Serbia and the Adriatic coast (Ćirković-Kovačević-Kojić, 1997: 39-40).

Furthermore, the participation of the Vlachs in trade was increasing from the mid-fourteenth century. Some of them created trading companies together with Ragusan merchants and the fact that some of them borrowed large sums of money means that they entered into large business ventures (Kovačević-Kojić, 1983: 80-84). These incomes were certainly significant for their better economic position. An indirect testimony is provided by a stipulation of the *Law on Churchmen* which forbade dependent peasants (in the original, *Serbs*) to marry the Vlachs. If a farmer did so, he had to return to his father's status. The exception was made only in the case of farmers who had lived longer among the Vlachs, but they had to be *ćelatori* (Mošin-Ćirković-Sindik, 2011: 464; Šarkić, 2010: 42; Filipović, 1963: 75). This provision indicates that dependent peasants tried to pass to the status of the Vlachs, since their obligations were more bearable (Fliliović, 1963: 75; Šarkić, 2010: 42), and that the ruler wanted to prevent reduction in the numbers of farmers (Taranovski, 2002: 78-79; Šarkić, 2010: 42).

The charters from the next decades contain basically the same information on the dependent population in medieval Serbia. However, some regulations provide more details about their income and status. The charters of King Stefan III (1321-1331) for the Dečani monastery from 1330 and 1331 regulated that if Vlachs brought more salt than they were supposed to give to the monastery, a half of that surplus belonged to them (Grković, 2004: 78; Milojević, 1880: 63).[6] Therefore, it can be seen that the distribution was the same as in the case of dealing with the merchants. The same documents provided that the Vlachs who took care of monastery mares were to receive a monthly subsistence from the monastery. The shepherds who looked after the sheep received a sheep with a lamb per hundred sheep and a monthly subsistence (Grković, 2004: 78; Milojević, 1880: 62; Blagojević, 1979: 154-156). The regulations of two of Stefan Dušan's charters provided that the shepherds in charge of mares had the right to receive foals for their service (Mišić-Subotin-Golubović, 2003: 111; Marjanović-Dušanić, 2005: 73; Blagojević, 1979: 156-157).

That the status of the Vlachs was privileged is confirmed by the provisions about marriages within the charters for the Dečani monastery. Thus, peasants were forbidden to marry Vlach women. In the case that happened, the woman was supposed to have the status of *meropsi* after the marriage (Grković, 2004: 78; Milojević, 1880: 62). On the other hand, the third charter for the same monastery issued by King Stefan Dušan between May 1343 and December 1345[7] ordered that if a peasant married a Vlach, he would be a *ćelator*, also after the marriage (Milojević, 1880: 134). This was a similar regulation as in the charter for the Banjska monastery. On the estates of the Dečani monastery, the ratio between the number of the Vlach houses and other peasant houses was 1:8 (Novaković, 1965: 49).

The principle of dividing production in half is also found in the charter of King Stefan Dušan by which he grants the Church of Saint Nicholas in Vranje to the Chilandar monastery, issued in the period between 1343 and 1345 (Marjanović-Dušanić, 2005: 69, 80). Namely, the poorer Vlachs who processed a larger amount of wool than prescribed would share half of that additional amount with the monastery (Marjanović-Dušanić, 2005: 73). This stipulation shows that the principle of dividing the surplus product in two equal parts between lords and the dependent population was usual. The same pattern applied when the Vlachs took wool from the Ragusans to make coarse wool cloth (Dinić-Knežević, 1983: 86-87; Dinić-Knežević, 1982: 12-16). In addition, the Vlachs sold the same kind of cloth in Ragusa that they produced themselves (Dinić-Knežević, 1983: 87; Dinić-Knežević, 1982: 11-12). It can be assumed that a similar custom applied to surpluses of other products. Some farming families were also engaged in silkworm breeding. Two peasants had to hand over 6000 silk cocoons a year to the Dečani monastery (Grković, 2004: 76; Jireček-Radonić, 1952: 156; Ćuk, 1981: 17). An unknown number of peasants from the region of Donji Pilot were supposed to give 100,000

---

6 For dating of these charters see: Blagojević, 1970: 79-81; Blagojević, 1989: 25-26.

7 For dating see: Blagojević, 1970: 81-86.

silk cocoons or 100 perpers[8] to the monastery of the Holy Archangels near Prizren (Mišić-Subotin-Golubović 2003: 99; Jireček-Radonić, 1952: 156; Ćuk, 1981: 17). The fact that the giving in-kind could be replaced by money clearly indicates that peasants produced silk cocoons for the market. Floss silk from Prizren was exported to Ragusa and through there to Venice (Ćuk, 1981: 18-24; Han, 1972: 165-166). The possibility that they produced silk fabrics themselves cannot be ruled out, since one weaver from the vicinity of Prizren is known (Mišić-Subotin-Golubović, 2003: 90; Ćuk, 1981: 17).

The regulations on the dependent peasants were simplified during the reign of King and Emperor Stefan Dušan (1331-1335). Thus, the first part of *Dušan's Code* from 1349 stipulated that the *meropsi* should work two days a week for the lord. In addition, they had to mow hay one day a year and also work one day a year in a vineyard for their master. The lord took from them the tax which belonged to the ruler (Bubalo, 2010: 88, 173). Accordingly, it is considered that the dependent peasants worked for their masters for a third of the year. Such a regulation did not substantially change the position of the dependent peasants, but did not elaborate the character of their obligation to the lord (Blagojević, 2004: 306-323). Similar provisions on work obligations of dependent peasants are also contained in some of Stefan Dušan's charters (Mišić-Subotin-Golubović, 2003: 110-111; Mišić, 2012: 66, 74). It is important to stress that after Dušan's reign, there is no mention of other categories of dependent peasants such as *sokalnici* and *craftsmen* (Blagojević, 2004: 395; Trijić, 2002-2003: 27-28; Fostikov, 2016: 204). This suggests that the aim was to equalize members of different categories and to abolish the privileges that some of them had (Trijić, 2002-2003: 27-28). In this way the lords were given the right to determine for themselves how they would use the part of the peasant labour force that belonged to them (Blagojević, 2004: 395).

This does not mean, however, that the position of individual craftsmen was not special. The obligations of some craftsmen were measured by the number of products they needed to make for the master. Emperor Stefan Dušan determined that two blacksmiths give forty horseshoes a year to his endowment, the monastery of the Holy Archangels near Prizren (Mišić-Subotin-Golubović, 2003: 113; Fostikov, 2016: 38). Also, three brothers were obliged to give three fox skins per year to the same monastery (Mišić-Subotin-Golubović, 2003: 113, 143; Fostikov, 2016: 170-171). Indeed, perhaps these craftsmen lived in the town of Prizren (Fostikov, 2016: 224). In addition, it is known that there were craftsmen with special privileges. Thus, the monastery of the Holy Archangels received five masons with their sons and brothers, whom Emperor Stefan Dušan moved from Pnuća

8 The term 'perpera' meant a unit of account consisting of 12 silver coins (Ćirković-Mihaljčić, 1999: 441).

near Ras, the former Serbian capital (Mišić-Subotin-Golubović, 2003: 110; Fostikov, 2016: 98, 108-110). These masons got fields, meadows, a mill on the river and a vineyard as hereditary possessions. Since they had the obligation to build, these craftsmen were released from most of the other duties that the dependent peasants had (Mišić-Subotin-Golubović, 2003: 110; Fostikov, 2016: 109, 196). It should be said that the masons are mentioned as tied to one village in the charter for the monastery of Banjska (Mošin-Ćirković-Sindik, 2011: 462; Fostikov, 2016: 108-110, 196), but it is not clear whether they had similar privileges as masons of the Holy Archangels. The second and third charters for the Dečani monastery contain important information about craftsmen. King Stefan III stated that master builder (*protomajstor*) Georgije, together with his brothers, decorated numerous churches in the Serbian state. After that they performed numerous construction works for the monastery of Dečani. Since they decided to live on the estates of the monastery, the King gave them a village for their merits. There are indications that King Stefan Dušan assigned them another village (Milojević, 1880: 58-59, 128-129; Fostikov, 2016: 84, 94, 105-106, 111, 241, 247). The term *protomajstor* meant the leader and supervisor of craftsmen. Georgije received this title from the ruler (Fostikov, 2013: 64, Fostikov, 2016: 106). Thanks to the possession of the village, it can be said that they became petty nobles (Fostikov, 2013: 57). Unfortunately, it is not possible to determine the total annual production and income of all these craftsmen.

Peasants with special obligations, such as craftsmen, are mentioned even after the reign of Stefan Dušan. The evidence is provided by the charter of Emperor Uroš (1355-1371) from 1363 on the exchange of possessions between two prominent nobles, *knez* Vojislav and *čelnik* Musa. The district (*župa*) of the town of Brvenik which was given to *čelnik* Musa included, among other settlements, thirteen court villages with special duties. Their inhabitants were the ruler's grooms, hunters, chamberlains, cooks, goldsmiths, laundry makers, and servants under the supervision of the court manager (Šuica, 2003: 144-145; Solovjev, 1928: 29-37). Two of these villages appear to have belonged to individual craftsmen. That would mean that they became petty nobles (Solovjev, 1928: 33-35). It is probable that they got these villages at some point from the ruler. Further, it is interesting that the charter mentions the goldsmith's village, although *Dušan's Code* forbade the work of goldsmiths in villages (Bubalo, 2010: 111-112, 213-214). Presumably, the term in this regulation referred to a coin smith, and not all goldsmiths (Fostikov, 2016: 63). At this point, it is worth mentioning some other categories of dependent peasants with special duties. The sources testify that there were people who took care of the ruler's dogs and falcons. These peasants also cultivated land, but due to their special obligations, they were exempted from certain taxes (Bubalo, 2010: 116-117; 220-221; Mišić, 1995: 57-58).

The presented information shows that the charters of Serbian rulers state the obligations of the rural population, but do not provide information on the property of peasants. Indirectly, that impression can be gained on the basis of another source. Namely, the preserved Byzantine cadastre of the Serbian monastery of Chilandar from 1300 clearly shows that peasants differed in the property they owned.[9] Their data refer to the region of the river Struma and the Thessaloniki area (Mošin, 1939: 193-205; Ćirković-Mihaljčić, 1999: 572-573). These regions were then under Byzantine rule, but they were located in the neighbourhood of Serbia. Therefore, it can be assumed that the situation was similar in some Serbian areas. The mentioned cadastre testifies that peasants paid taxes of differing amounts depending on how much property they held. Some of them had, in addition to land, a certain number of animals (horses, sheep, pigs, and cattle), vineyards, and fruit trees (Mošin, 1939: 205-217).

III. The impact of urban development on the peasant economy

The development of urban settlements in medieval Serbia was also an important factor for the peasant economy. The mining towns which formed from the mid-thirteenth century onwards had a special significance. First, mines and mining plants needed a large number of workers. On the other hand, peasants were able to place a part of their produce on the city market (Ćirković-Kovačević-Kojić, 1997: 41-42). The charter of King Milutin for the Commune of Ragusa from 1302 testifies that the Ragusans bought meat and honey in Serbia (Mošin-Ćirković-Sindik, 2011: 345; Ćuk, 2019: 105). An important product of beekeeping was also wax. Huge quantities of this product were exported from Serbia (Ćirković-Mihaljčić, 1999: 103-104; Mišić, 2009: 17; Kovačević-Kojić, 1971: 143-152). It remains unknown how much economic benefit beekeepers had from these exports.

The *Novo Brdo Legal Code* from 1412 offers information on the relationship between peasants and the city. At the time the *Code* was passed, Novo Brdo was the biggest city in the Serbian state and one of the most important European silver mines.[10] The provisions of the *Code* testify that peasants from the surrounding area sold cattle and wine in the town (Radojčić, 1962: 51, 53). It can be further assumed that they also sold grain, fruits, wood, and animal skins. They paid a tax for the goods sold

9 The original document, written in Greek in November 1300, has not been preserved; only its translation into Serbian Church Slavonic from the time of Emperor Stefan Dušan has been preserved: Ostrogorski, 1948: 215-216; Mošin, 1939: 193-201.

10 For more information about Novo Brdo in first half of the fifteenth century see: Dinić, 1962: 46-67, 72-95.

(Radojčić, 1962: 51-55). One Ragusan document testifies that the people from the vicinity of Srebrenica brought foodstuffs to that mining town (Kovačević-Kojić, 1978: 191, 199; Kovačević-Kojić, 2010: 55-58). The prices of products in Novo Brdo were defined by the *Code* and the decisions of city authorities (Radojčić, 1962: 52-55). The research showed that almost everywhere in Europe, urbanization encouraged the development of agriculture (Pinilla, 2009: 14-17).

Some workers in the mines of Novo Brdo lived in the villages around the town, as evidenced by the indebtedness book of Ragusan merchant Mihailo Lukarević from the fourth decade of the fifteenth century (Dinić, 1957: 40, 41, 45, 50, 65, 68, 75; Dinić, 1962: 33-36, 84-85). Some mining smelters were donated to the monasteries by Serbian nobles in the fifteenth century were also located in villages (Pavlikianov, 2018: 106, 108, 110, 172; Stojanović, 1890: 34).[11] The workers in these plants certainly came from the countryside.

The villages on the Adriatic coast in the Serbian state (the region of Zeta) were economically dependent on the old town centres. Peasants made money by selling meat, skins, wine, wood, homemade wool cloth, cordage, earthen pots, and similar items in towns. It is important to note that Adriatic towns tried to direct the economy of the surrounding villages, sometimes by force. For example, these towns strove to ban peasants from planting new vineyards. This was the reason why peasants were dissatisfied with the attitude of the city nobles towards them, especially at the time of the Venetian domination of this region.[12] They therefore sided with Venetian opponents during the wars (Božić, 1979a: 102-103).

In addition to the towns, it is certain that peasants were commercially active at fairs (Serbian term *panađuri*), organized near churches and monasteries that were often located in villages. These were temporary markets organized to mark Christian holidays. The fairs lasted between one and fifteen days (Ćirković-Mihaljčić, 1999: 488-489; Bojanin, 2005: 137-145). Only those fairs whose revenues were allocated to churches and monasteries are known (Živković, 1992: 92; Koprivica, 2014: 148-149; Mladenović, 2003: 54, 83, 94; Bojanin, 2005: 139-141). The church of Saint George near Skopje had a monopoly on the sale of bread, wine, and meat during the fair (Mošin-Ćirković-Sindik, 2011: 319-320; Bojanin, 2005: 144-145). It can be assumed that other fair owners had similar privileges (Ćirković-Mihaljčić, 1999: 489; Bojanin, 2005: 145). This regulation diminished the possibility for peasants to earn income at such gatherings. Undoubtedly, other goods were also sold at fairs, but we lack more information. King Stefan Uroš III stipulated that everyone could

11 Lukarević's book also mentions some smelters: Dinić, 1957: 39, 40, 50, 54, 76, 79, 81, 85, 88.

12 Venice began to acquire possessions in this area from the end of the fourteenth century. The Republic occupied all coastal towns in this region until 1443 (Božić, 1970: 150).

come to the fair of the Prizren episcopate, no matter how much he owed to someone (Mišić, 2009: 17; Ćirković-Mihaljčić, 1999: 489; Bojanin, 2005: 142). The data from the charters clearly testify that foreign merchants also visited Serbian fairs (Mošin-Ćirković-Sindik, 2011: 328; Mišić, 2009: 17; Ćirković-Mihaljčić, 1999: 489). Finally, it should be mentioned that certain settlements had the status of marketplaces (Serbian term *trg*). This was an open-type settlement, without fortifications, where trade usually took place once a week (Krstić, 2007: 96). This characteristic distinguished it from the fairs, where the trade activity was temporary (Ćirković-Mihaljčić, 1999: 489). The Serbian rulers also assigned marketplaces to their endowments (Mošin-Ćirković-Sindik, 2011: 69, 82, 91, 462; Mladenović, 2003: 18, 53, 93, 181; Krstić, 2007: 96-97). At the beginning of the fourteenth century, the Serbian king had a monopoly on the sale of his meat in the marketplaces (Mošin-Ćirković-Sindik, 2011: 345; Ćirković-Mihaljčić, 1999: 489).

IV. Peasants as soldiers and robbers

The system of obligations of the dependent population changed in Serbian territories in the late fourteenth century due to the strong Ottoman pressure. First of all, there was an increase in cash fees (Ivanović, 2019: 391-394). In addition, dependent peasants and Vlachs were burdened with military service. The charters of Despot Stefan Lazarević (1402-1427) from 1417 and 1427 indicate that people on the monastery estates had to take part in different types of military actions, from the local level to situations where the ruler led the army or when he sent auxiliary troops to the Ottomans (Laskaris, 1935-1936: 180; Mladenović, 2007: 260; Veselinović, 2006: 165-166, 192-193). The most difficult form of military service was called *zamanica* because no one was exempted from this obligation according to a charter from 1458 (Rački, 1867; Veselinović, 2006: 190). The Serbian sources do not provide more detailed information on the military duties of the dependent population, but the Turkish regulations shed more light. Namely, the Ottoman legal provision from the *qanun* for the *Sancak* of Smederevo from 1536 points out that in the past, the Vlachs had to send one warrior with a pack horse for every five houses in the case of the Sultan's campaign or service at the borders (Bojanić, 1974: 47; Bojanić, 1962: 242; Veselinović, 2006: 168, 190). Further, the same regulation stipulates that every Vlach house should give one warrior with a pack horse or infantryman as *zamanica* in the case of urgent tasks in the border areas. (Bojanić, 1974: 47; Bojanić, 1962: 242, 244; Veselinović, 2006: 190-191). The Vlachs had to support themselves during these campaigns (Bojanić, 1974: 47; Veselinović, 2006: 191-192). Since the Slavic term *zamanica* is used, it is clear that the Ottomans took over this institution from the former Serbian medieval state with no changes (Bojanić, 1962: 244; Veselinović, 2006: 191). In such a way the conqueror adopted the institution which was created for resistance and started using it to his advantage.

The Turkish laws do not mention other categories of peasants as participants in military actions. There are indications that *zamanica* in some cases involved the recruitment of all men capable of carrying weapons (Veselinović, 2006: 191-192). The *zamanica* as a kind of recruitment was more often used in the border regions (Veselinović, 2006: 191-192). It seems that the military service of the Vlachs in the Serbian state was limited to one month during the year (Bojanić, 1974: 13; Bojanić, 1971: 258, 263). Military obligations were undoubtedly very difficult for the dependent population because they drew them away from their primary jobs. However, they could benefit from a successful action by gaining a share in the spoils. The dependent population also had the obligation to build, renew, and defend fortifications (Mladenović, 2007: 254, 296, 362, 372; Stojanović, 1890: 32-33; Ćirković-Mihaljčić, 1999: 125-126). These duties were difficult for peasants and could not bring them income.

However, warfare was one of the main occupations and an important source of income for the rural population in some areas. The region of Zeta (a coastal Adriatic province) was a distinctive case as there were many warrior companies in the fifteenth century. These communities were created as state power was weakening in the second half of the fourteenth century. Many previously dependent peasants managed to become independent (Božić, 1979b: 156-157). The warrior companies were organized on the model of the Vlach communities. It also seems that the Vlachs were a significant element of these military organizations (Božić, 1979b: 158-160). The prominent peasant-warriors became the holders of rights that once belonged to the ruler or lords. Therefore, it can be said that they had the status of petty nobles (Božić, 1979b: 161; Božić, 1979c: 137). Some of these warriors had dependent peasants (Ljubić, 1886: 226; Božić, 1979c: 137-138), although it is certain that there could not be many of them due to scarce arable land. Hence it is clear that the members of these noble families had to do most of the agricultural work. They differed from the dependant peasants because these warriors could be elected to office in their community (Božić, 1979c: 138). The core of the small companies was the family or fraternity of petty nobles around whom friends and followers gathered. They went to war or plunder at the call of their commander. Usually, these companies grouped into wider communities (Božić, 1979b: 161, 172-173). During the fifteenth century, these companies were in the service of the noble family of Balšić, Serbian Despots, or, on the other side, Venice (Božić, 1979b: 157, 162-171). Also, the Commune of Ragusa hired them when it waged war (Stojanović, 1929: 486-487; Božić, 1979b: 163-164; Škrivanić, 1954: 91-93). A preserved contract from November 1403 testifies to the conditions under which warriors from Zeta fought as mercenaries. Grubac Dapčić from Luštica undertook to bring to Ragusa fifty warriors from his region. The Ragusans were obliged to give them a monthly salary and take care of the renewal of their weapons and their treatment. They had the right to keep 80% of the loot and received rewards for each captured or killed enemy soldier. If any of them was captured, he was to be exchanged for a prisoner of the other side (Stojanović, 1929: 486-487; Škrivanić, 1954: 91-92). Finally, warrior companies also engaged in looting. Sometimes several companies teamed up for a robbery (Stojanović, 1929: 386-387; Božić, 1979b: 170-171).

Looting was an important source of income for the rural population. This is especially true for the inhabitants in the neighbourhood of Ragusa. The oldest preserved Ragusan documents about this phenomenon date from the last decades of the thirteenth century. These acts testify that peasants and Vlachs from the Serbian territory stole money, goods, and cattle from the Ragusans (Čremošnik, 1932: 123, 143, 145, 151, 158, 162). The regulations of the second part of *Dušan's Code* from 1353/1354 seem to indicate that the problem of theft and robbery was very widespread in the Serbian state. Emperor Stefan Dušan prescribed a severe punishment with the intention of eradicating such offenses. The village in which the thief or brigand was found was to be punished by displacement of its population. Further, the same regulation stipulates that thieves were to be punished by blindness, and brigands by hanging. The lord of the village where the thief or brigand was found had to compensate for all the damage they did and, in addition, he had to be punished as a thief or brigand. The same responsibility was foreseen for the headmen of the Vlach settlements (Bubalo, 2010: 105-106, 204-205; Solovjev, 1980: 293-295).

Several provisions of *Dušan's Code* are dedicated to security of trade routes, which was especially important for traders. The villages were obliged to organize guards around deserted hills and had to compensate for any damage (Bubalo, 2010: 109, 210). *Dušan's Code* also imposed an obligation on villages to provide overnight lodging for traders. If this did not happen, the village and its lord and headman would have to compensate for the damage that the merchants suffered as a result (Bubalo, 2010: 109, 210). It should be clarified that the term 'village' was probably used in these regulations to denote a community of villagers. These provisions emphasized the collective responsibility of the villagers (Ćirković, 1997: 344-346). The effectiveness of these measures cannot be assessed due to the lack of sources. Looting and banditry were certainly not eradicated. The Ottoman pressure on the Serbian lands, which began in the late fourteenth century, worsened the situation in this respect.

V. Work obligations and incomes of Serbian peasants after the establishment of Ottoman rule

The Serbian medieval state finally fell under Ottoman rule in 1459 (Spremić, 1994: 544-545). The Ottoman *defters* (register books) created in the first decades after the conquest of the Serbian lands can be used to some extent as an important source about the state of the economy before the establishment of Turkish rule. This type of sources contains lists of the adult males in the villages and towns with information about their legal status, obligations, landed estates and privileges according to the economic and social class to which they belonged (B. Lewis-Ch. Pellat-J Schacht, 1991: 81-82). The data from these sources confirm that agriculture was by far the most important activity in the Serbian areas. Peasants mostly grew cereals, but there were regions with developed viticulture and beekeeping. The breeding of cattle, sheep, and pigs was also important for the Serbian rural population (Novaković, 2001: 91-96; Miljković-Bojanić, 2004: 83-96; Stojaković, 1987: 13). Judging by the *defters* information, a small number of craftsmen lived in villages. The most numerous were blacksmiths, potters, and those who made clothes and shoes. In some villages there were fulling mills for cloth processing. However, it is certain that craftsmen were also engaged in agriculture, just as a number of farmers performed some craft jobs (Rašević, 2001: 443-447; Miljković-Bojanić, 2004: 90, 96-98). Probably, most of their craft products were used for household needs (Faroqhi, 1977: 185). Some craftsmen engaged in the maintenance of the surrounding fortresses. In exchange for their service, they received tax relief (Stojaković, 1987: 256; Miljković-Bojanić, 2004: 98-99, 261, 265). Priests were also numerous in the area of the former Serbian state, but they did not have a special fiscal status (Miljković-Bojanić, 2004: 287-290; Rašević, 2001: 445).

The exact production is difficult to determine, but it is clear that there were product surpluses.[13] However, trade was a secondary activity for peasants in the Balkans. They produced primarily for their own needs and to pay taxes to the Ottoman state and *sipahis* (Faroqhi, 1977: 163-164).[14] Thus, the taxes collected by Ottoman authorities testify that wine production was large in the area of Kosovo in the late fifteenth century (Beldiceanu, 1964: 231, 236-240; Bojanić, 1983: 117-126; Hrabak, 1974: 53-54). Wine production was also significant in the Braničevo area in the northeast of the *Sancak* of Smederevo (Miljković-Bojanić, 2004: 89, 92). An Ottoman defter from 1455 indicates that the main source of wealth of villages in the south of the former Serbian state was vineyards, not

---

13 For more information, see: Faroqhi, 1977: 192-195.

14 Sipahis were Ottoman provincial cavalrymen remunerated through military fiefs (*timars*). See: Ágoston-Masters, 2009: 16, 20, 619.

cereals (Hrabak, 1974: 42-43). A regulation for the town of Niš from 1498 indicates the sale of horses, cattle, sheep, cow skins, and wood in this settlement (Bojanić, 1974: 14). There is no doubt that peasants managed to produce certain surpluses of cereals that were sold in towns (Beldiceanu, 1964: 211, 221, 237). For a later period, there is information that the Venetians in the Balkans asked for permission to buy grain directly from the producers (Faroqhi, 1979: 132).

A large number of families in the *Sancak* of Smederevo had the status of the Vlachs. They enjoyed substantial tax breaks in exchange for military service. The Turkish laws (*qanuns*), unlike Serbian ones, released the Vlachs from transport obligations. At this time, the Vlachs were already engaged in farming, in addition to cattle breeding, and became tied to the land (Bojanić, 1974: 12-13, 15; Miljković-Bojanić, 2004: 227-237). Their military service was limited to one month a year. That restriction was later lifted (Bojanić, 1974: 13; Bojanić, 1971: 263). At that time, about 40% of all inhabitants of the mentioned *Sancak* had the status of the Vlachs (Miljković-Bojanić, 2004: 193, 196). Unlike them, the Vlachs from the region of Sjenica had to take care of road safety and performed the transport service (Šabanović, 1964: 8; Bojanić, 1987: 100-111). There was also another privileged group of the rural population with military obligations. These were *voynuks,* who were free peasants. They performed their service on horses. Some of them were grooms and chamberlains (Đurđev, 1947: 87-101; Miljković-Bojanić, 2004: 241-244; Inaldžik, 1952-1953: 46-49). The institution of *voynuks* also existed in medieval Balkan states (Đurđev, 1947: 76-87). There were only around 300 of them in the *Sancak* of Smederevo in 1476 (Miljković-Bojanić, 2004: 244-247). The peasants who raised falcons and hawks for the needs of the Ottoman governor (*pasha*) also had certain privileges (Stojaković, 1987: 257-259; Miljković-Bojanić, 2004: 266-267). All the aforementioned categories of the population had a similar position in the Serbian state in the last decades of the fifteenth century. Evidence is provided by an Ottoman *qanun* that mentions the *Despot's qanun* for the Vlachs (Bojanić, 1974: 32, 140).[15] However, the number of people with the status of Vlachs in the Serbian state during the fifteenth century cannot be estimated. It is known that the Turks settled the Vlachs after they occupied the Serbian state in 1459 (Bojanić, 1971: 256; Đurđev, 1984: 18-27; Miljković-Bojanić, 2004: 229-230). Finally, the Vlachs certainly had a greater opportunity to earn from spoils during the Ottoman actions, which were often offensive.

---

15 Dušanka Bojanić thought that it was about Despot Stefan Lazarević (Bojanić, 1974: 140).

VI. Conclusions

The information presented shows that the peasant population participated in many economic activities in medieval Serbia. However, agricultural works and production remained the primary income source for the largest part of the rural population until the end of the existence of the Serbian state in the Middle Ages. According to a rough estimate, at most 5% of the population worked outside the agricultural sector (Ćirković-Mihaljčić, 1999: 215). The Ottoman defter for the region of the Branković family (southern part of the Serbian state in the fifteenth century) from 1455 seems to confirm this hypothesis (Hadžibegić-Handžić-Kovačević, 1972: 3-347; Rašević, 2001: 444, table V.8). Nonetheless, it is clear that most of these peasants combined agricultural works with other activities (Ćirković-Mihaljčić, 1999: 215). However, the situation was not the same in all areas of the medieval Serbian state. The geographic circumstances had a significant impact on the choice of occupation of the rural population. In the case of scarce arable land, peasants turned to activities such as transport service, warfare, and looting. On the other hand, the development of mining required the engagement of a lot of workers in that sector, which was very profitable. The information from a Turkish source from 1530/1531 testifies that more than 5700 men worked in the mines of Novo Brdo, Janjevo, Priština, Belasica, Koporić, Gornja Trepča, and Donja Trepča. Consequently, it is estimated that between 10,000 and 20,000 people could work in all mines in the territory of the former Serbian state (Ćuk-Kovačević-Ćirković, 2002: 207, 209). Some of these workers certainly lived in villages. Also, it can be assumed that there were examples where one member of a peasant family worked in the mine, while the rest of the family was doing agricultural work. It is difficult to estimate to what extent the performance of non-agricultural activities improved the economic standard of the peasantry. A part of the Vlachs certainly earned significant income from trade and transport. The most successful among them became the citizens of Ragusa, who thus changed their earlier status (Jireček, 1959: 198, 203; Kovačević-Kojić, 1983: 81). The rest of the rural population probably participated only in small local trade. Also, a smaller number of peasants could increase their income by engaging in crafts. Undoubtedly, the original closed character of the rural economy was changed due to more intensive connections with towns whose existence enabled peasants to place their product surpluses.

The concept of an integrated peasant economy proved useful for examining the work activities of the rural population in medieval Serbia. Thanks to this approach, the relevant sources were viewed from a different perspective. Some information about peasants' work obligations also suggests that they produced not only for the lords, but also for the market. That the system of the integrated peasant economy was dynamic and adaptive

Table 6.1. Integrated peasant economy checklist: Medieval Serbia

ACTIVITY	CHECK
Primary sector	
Agricultural specialization	✓
Intensification of cultivation (no fallow, mixed-cropping, …)	✓
Wage day-labour in agriculture and longer-term farmhands on larger farms	
Extension/intensification of animal husbandry	✓
Intensification of forest exploitation (in primary sector, but also secondary and tertiary)	✓
Extension of cultivated land (reclamation of commons and woods)	
Quarries	
Fishing	✓
Secondary sector	
Transformation of primary resources/products (e.g. wine, cheese, meat products; charcoal, lime)	✓
Rural crafts	✓
Domestic, putting-out system (proto-industry)	✓
Work in 'centralizd' industries and plants (manufactures, mining, etc.)	✓
Migrant/mobile craftsmen (e.g. bricklayers)	✓
Wage labour in the industrial sector	
Tertiary sector	
Services in the field of long and medium distance trade (draft animal lease, fodder, lodging, inns)	✓
Transport of other people's products and goods over short to medium distances	✓
Trade with own products and goods over short to medium distances	✓
Peddling	✓
Smuggling	
Migrant/mobile workers (dock-workers, etc.)	
Works of trust (estimation of land value, testimonies, etc.)	
Warfare	✓
Looting	✓
Tourism	

seems to be confirmed by the present state of research. For example, due to the political situation, a part of the rural population resorted to warfare as a source of income. The peasants from Zeta showed a personal initiative by succeeding in becoming independent and forming warrior companies. This illustrates that peasants could be active subjects, not only under external influences. However, the lack of relevant sources for the medieval period made it impossible to answer some questions. Therefore, the ratio of income from various activities remains unknown. Everyone had to set aside a third of their time for the lord, but many factors influenced the amount of peasant production during the rest of the time. It can only be said with certainty that it also varied depending on the region and specific conditions in a certain period of time. Additional analyses of Ottoman sources could provide significant data on the subject. Finally, it would be worth exploring the history of the Serbian peasantry from the point of view of the above-mentioned concept, until the mid-twentieth century, when mass industrialization took place.

Bibliography

Ágoston, A. and Masters, B. (eds) (2009), *Encylopedia of the Ottoman Empire*, New York, Facts On File.

Beldiceanu, N. (eds) (1964), *Les actes des premiers sultans conserves dans les manuscrits turcs de la Bibliothèque nationale a Paris. II Règlements miniers, 1390-1512*, Paris-La Haye, De Gruyter Mouton.

Blagojević, M. (1989), 'Čelnici manastira Dečana', Đurić, V. (ed.), *Dečani i vizantijska umetnost sredinom XIV veka*, Beograd, Srpska akademija nauka i umetnosti – NIRO 'Jedinstvo' Priština, pp. 21-34.

——— (1970), 'Kada je kralj Dušan potvrdio Dečansku hrisovolju', *Istorijski časopis*, 16-17, pp. 79-96.

——— (1979), 'Zakon svetoga Simeona i svetoga Save', Đurić, V. (eds), *Sava Nemanjić – Sveti Sava: istorija i predanje*, Beograd, Srpska akademija nauka i umetnosti, pp. 129-166.

——— (1983), 'Pregled istorijske geografije srednjovekovne Srbije', *Zbornik Istorijskog muzeja Srbije*, 20, pp. 45-126.

——— (2004), *Zemljoradnja u srednjovekovnoj Srbiji*, Beograd, Službeni list SCG.

Bojanić-Lukač, D. (1962), 'Ko je učestvovao u zamaničnoj vojsci?', *Vesnik Vojnog muzeja*, 6-7, pp. 240-244.

Bojanić, D. (1983), 'O Novobrdskoj gospoštini', *Istorijski časopis*, 29-30, pp. 117-127.

——— (eds) (1974), *Turski zakoni i zakonski propisi iz XV i XVI veka za Smedrevsku, Kruševačku i Vidinsku oblast*, Beograd, Istorijski institut.

——— (1987), 'Šta znače podaci o sjeničkim Vlasima u popisu iz 1455. godine', *Istorijski časopis*, 34, pp. 97-112.

——— (1971), 'Vlasi u severnoj Srbiji i njihovi prvi kanuni', *Istorijski časopis*, 18, pp. 255-269.

Bojanin, S. (2005), *Zabave i svetkovine u srednjovekovnoj Srbiji: od kraja XII do kraja XV veka*, Beograd, Istorijski institut.

Božić, I. (1979a), 'Grad i selo na Zetskom primorju u XV veku', Božić, I., *Nemirno Pomorje XV veka*, Beograd, Srpska književna zadruga, pp. 95-104.

——— (1979b), 'Uloga i organizacija ratničkih družina u Zeti XV veka', Božić, I., *Nemirno Pomorje XV veka*, Beograd, Srpska književna zadruga, pp. 156-173.

——— (1979c), 'Paštrovići', Božić, I., *Nemirno Pomorje XV veka*, Beograd, Srpska književna zadruga, pp. 105-149.

——— (1970), 'Zeta u Despotovini', *Istorija Crne Gore. Knj. 2, Od kraja XII do kraja XV vijeka. Tom. 2, Crna Gora u doba oblasnih gospodara*, Titograd, Redakcija za istoriju Crne Gore.

Bubalo, Đ. (ed.) (2010), *Dušanov zakonik*, Beograd, Zavod za udžbenike.

——— (2016), 'Nekoliko zapažanja o povelji kralja Milutina za manastir Banjsku', LJ. Maksimović, Lj. And Vukašinović, V. (eds), *Manastir Studenica – 700 godina Kraljeve crkve*, Beograd, Srpska akademija nauka i umetnosti, pp. 19-33.
Čremošnik, G. (ed.) (1932), *Kancelarijski i notarski spisi 1278-1301*, I., Beograd, Srpska kraljevska akademija.
Ćirković, S. and Mihaljčić, R. (eds) (1999), *Leksikon srpskog srednjeg veka*, Beograd, Knowledge.
——— and Kovačević-Kojić, D. (1997), 'Naturalna privreda i tržišna proizvodnja između XIII i XV stoleća', Ćirković, S., *Rabotnici, vojnici, duhovnici: društva srednjovekovnog Balkana*, Beograd, Equilibrium, pp. 37-46.
——— (1994), 'Počeci socijalne hijerarhije u Srba', *Godišnjak za društvenu istoriju*, 3, pp. 223-235.
——— (1997), 'Seoska opština kod Srba u srednjem veku', Ćirković, S., *Rabotnici, vojnici, duhovnici: društva srednjovekovnog Balkana*, Beograd, Equilibrium, pp. 341-348.
———, Kovačević-Kojić, D. and Ćuk, R. (2002), *Staro srpsko rudarstvo*, Beograd–Novi Sad, Vukova zadužbina – Prometej.
Ćuk, R. (2019), 'Izvoz stoke i stočarskih proizvoda iz Srbije u Veneciju u XIII i XIV veku', Ćuk, R., *Srbija i mediteranski svet u poznom srednjem veku: odabrani radovi Ruže Ćuk*, Beograd, Istorijski institut, pp. 103-110.
——— (1981), 'Izvoz svile iz Dubrovnika u Veneciju u XIV veku', *Istorijski časopis*, 28, pp. 17-25.
Dinić, M. (1937), 'Dubrovačka srednjevekovna karavanska trgovina', *Jugoslovenski istorijski časopis*, 3, pp. 119-146.
——— (ed.) (1957), *Iz dubrovačkog arhiva*, knj. I, Beograd, Naučno delo.
——— (1962), *Za istoriju rudarstva u srednjovekovnoj Srbiji i Bosni* II, Beograd, Naučno delo.
Dinić-Knežević, D (1982), *Tkanine u privredi srednjovekovnog Dubrovnika*, Beograd, Srpska akademija nauka i umetnosti.
——— (1983), 'Učešće Vlaha u preradi vune i prevozu sukna u XIV i XV veku', *Radovi Akademije nauka i umjetnosti Bosne i Hercegovine*, 73, pp. 85-92.
Đurđev, B. (1984), 'O naseljavanju Vlaha stočara u sjevernu Srbiju u drugoj polovini XV veka', *Godišnjak društva istoričara Bosne i Hercegovine*, XXXV, pp. 9-35.
——— (1947), 'O vojnucima (sa osvrtom na razvoj turskog feudalizma i na pitanje turskog agaluka)', *Glasnik Zemaljskog muzeja u Sarajevu*, II, pp. 75-137.
Faroqhi, S. (1977), 'Rural Society in Anatolia and the Balkans During the Sixteenth Century, I', *Turcica*, IX, pp. 161-195.
——— (1979), 'Rural Society in Anatolia and the Balkans During the Sixteenth Century, II', *Turcica*, XI, pp. 103-153.

Filipović, M. (2013), 'Struktura i organizacija srednjovekovnog katuna', Filipović, M. (ed.), *Simpozijum o srednjovekovnom katunu održan 24. i 25. novembra 1961. g.*, Sarajevo, Naučno društvo SR Bosne i Hercegovine, pp. 45-112.

Fostikov, A. (2013), 'Zanatstvo srednjovekovne Srbije u svetlu tri povelje iz 14. veka', *Beogradski istorijski glasnik*, 4, pp. 51-69.

——— (2016), *Zanatstvo u srednjovekovnoj Srbiji*, Beograd (PhD thesis).

Grković, M. (2004), *Prva hrisovulja manastira Dečani. The First Charter of the Dečani Monastery*, A. Mayor, R. A. (trans.), Beograd, Centar za očuvanje nasleđa Kosova i Metohije – MNEMOSYNE – Srpski pravoslavni manastir Visoki Dečani – Muzej u Prištini (sa izmeštenim sedištem) – Arhiv Srbije.

Hadžibegić, H., Handžić, H., and Kovačević, E. (eds) (1972), *Oblast Brankovića: Opširni katastarski popis iz 1455. Godine*, Sarajevo, Orijentalni institut u Sarajevu.

Hrabak, B. (1974), 'Poljoprivredna proizvodnja Kosova i susednih krajeva sredinom XV veka', *Glas SANU*, CCLXL, *Odeljenje istorijskih nauka*, knj. 1, pp. 33-73.

Inaldžik, H. (1952-1953), 'Od Stefana Dušana do Osmanskog carstva. Hrišćanske spahije u Rumeliji u XV vijeku i njihovo porijeklo', *Prilozi za orijentalnu filologiju i istoriju jugoslovenskih naroda pod turskom vladavinom*, 3-4, pp. 23-54.

Isailović, N. (2017), 'Legislation Concerning the Vlachs of the Balkans Before and After Ottoman Conquest: An Overview', Rudić, S. and Alsantaş, S. (eds), *State and Society in the Balkans Before and After Establishment of Ottoman Rule*, Belgrade, Institute of History Belgrade – Yunus Emre Enstitüsü – Turkish Cultural Centre Belgrade, pp. 25-42.

Ivanović, M. (2019), 'Militarization of the Serbian State under Ottoman Pressure', *Hungarian Historical Review*, 8, pp. 390-410.

Jireček, K. (1959), 'Vlasi i Mavrovlasi u dubrovačkim spomenicima', Jireček, K., *Zbornik Konstantina Jirečeka I*, Beograd, Srpska akademija nauka, pp. 191-204.

——— and Radonić, J. (1952), *Istorija Srba. Knj. 2, Kulturna istorija*, Beograd, Naučna knjiga.

Koprivica, M. (2014), 'Hrisovulja kralja Stefana Dušana Htetovskom manastiru', *Stari srpski arhiv*, 13, pp. 143-179.

Kovačević-Kojić, D. (1978), *Gradska naselja srednjovjekovne bosanske države*, Sarajevo, Veselin Masleša.

——— (1971). 'O izvozu voska iz srednjovjekovne Srbije i Bosne preko Dubrovnika', *Istorijski časopis*, 18, pp. 143-153.

——— (2010), *Srednjovjekovna Srebrenica XIV–XV vijek*, Beograd, Srpska akademija nauka i umetnosti.

——— (1983), 'Učešće Vlaha u trgovinskoj razmjeni tokom XIV i XV vijeka', *Radovi Akademije nauka i umjetnosti Bosne i Hercegovine*, 73, pp. 79-84.

Krstić, A. (2007), 'Srednjovekovni trgovi i osmanski pazari u Braničevu – kontinuitet i promene', Mišić, S. (ed.), *Moravska Srbija. Istorija–kultura–umetnost*, Kruševac, Istorijski arhiv Kruševac – Odeljenje za istoriju Filozofskog fakulteta u Beogradu, pp. 95-113.

Laskaris, M. (1935-1936), 'Actes serbes de Vatopedi', *Byzantinoslavica*, 6, pp. 166-185.

Lewis, B., Pellat, Ch. and Schacht, J. (eds) (1991), *The Encyclopaedia of Islam. New edition*, Volume II, C–G, Leiden, Brill.

Ljubić, S. (ed.) (1886), *Listine o odnošajih između južnoga slavenstva i Mletačke republike*, knj. VIII, Zagreb, Jugoslavenska akademija znanosti i umjetnosti.

Marjanović-Dušanić, S. (2005), 'Povelja kralja Stefana Dušana o poklanjanju crkve Svetog Nikole u Vranju manastiru Hilandar', *Stari srpski arhiv*, 4, pp. 69-85.

Mavromatis, L. (1991), 'O ideji monarhije u srednjovekovnoj Srbiji', Đurić, V. J. (ed.), *Arhiepiskop Danilo II i njegovo doba*, Beograd, Srpska akademija nauka i umetnosti, pp. 69-74.

Milojević, M. (1880), *Dečanske hrisovulje*, Glasnik Srpskog učenog društva XII.

Miljković-Bojanić, E. (2004), *Smederevski sandžak 1476-1560: zemlja, naselja, stanovništvo*, Beograd, Istorijski institut.

Mišić, S. (2012), 'Hrisovulje cara Stefana Dušana o Svetom Petru Koriškom sa sabora u Krupištima', *Stari srpski arhiv*, 11, pp. 59-90.

——— (2009), 'Hrisovulja kralja Stefana Uroša III Prizrenskoj episkopiji', *Stari srpski arhiv*, 8, pp. 11-36.

——— (1995), 'Lov u srednjovekovnoj Srbiji', *Istorijski glasnik*, 1-2, pp. 51-66.

——— and Subotin-Golubović, T. (2003), *Svetoarhanđelovska hrisovulja*, Beograd, Istorijski institut.

Mladenović, A. (ed.) (2003), *Povelje kneza Lazara: tekst, komentari, snimci*, Beograd, Čigoja štampa.

——— (ed.) (2007), *Povelje i pisma despota Stefana: tekst, komentari, snimci*. Beograd, Čigoja štampa.

Mošin, V. (1939), 'Akti iz svetogorskih arhiva', *Spomenik Srpske kraljevske akademije*, 91, pp. 153-260.

———, Ćirković, S. and Sindik, D. (2011) (eds), *Zbornik srednjovekovnih ćiriličkih povelja i pisama Srbije, Bosne i Dubrovnika*, knj. 1, 1186-1321, Beograd, Istorijski institut Beograd.

Novaković, R. (2001), 'II. Istorijsko-geografske prilike', Macura, M. (ed.), *Naselja i stanovništvo oblasti Brankovića 1455. godine*, Beograd, Srpska akademija nauka i umetnosti, pp. 47-100.

Novaković, S. (1904), *Primeri književnosti i jezika staroga i srpsko-slovenskoga*, Beograd, Kraljevska srpska državna štamparija.

——— (1965), *Selo*, Beograd, Srpska književna zadruga.

Ostrogorski, G. (1948), 'Vizantiskie piscovie knigi', *Byzantinoslavica*, 9, pp. 203-306.

Panjek, A. (2017), 'Integrated Peasant Economy as a Concept in Progress', Panjek, A., Larsson, J. and Mocarelli, L. (eds), *Integrated Peasant Economy in a Comparative Perspective: Alps, Scandinavia and Beyond*, Koper, Založba Univerze na Primorskem, pp. 11-49.

Pavlikianov, C. (2018), *Medieval Slavic Acts from Mount Athos 1230-1734. Critical Edition and Commentary of the Texts*, Sofia, 'St. Kliment Ohridski' University Press.

Pinilla, V. (2009), 'The impact of markets in the management of rural land', Pinilla, V. (ed.), *Markets and Agricultural Change in Europe from the 13th to the 20th Century*, Turnhout, Brepols, pp. 11-36.

Pirivatrić, S. (2015), 'Hronologija prvih vladarskih akata kralja Milutina izdatih posle osvajanja Skoplja', Miljković, B. and Dželebdžić, D. (eds), *Περίβολος I. Zbornik u čast Mirjane Živojinović*, Beograd, Vizantološki institut SANU – Zadužbina svetog manastira Hilandara, pp. 205-213.

Rački, F. (1867), 'Prilozi za sbriku srbskih i hrvatskih listina', *Rad Jugoslavenske akademije znanosti i umjetnosti*, 1, pp. 124-163.

Radojčić, N. (1962), *Zakon o rudnicima despota Stefana Lazarevića*, Beograd, Naučno delo.

Rašević, M. (2001), 'Demografske prilike i stanovništvo', Macura, M. (ed.), *Naselja i stanovništvo oblasti Brankovića 1455. Godine*, Beograd, Srpska akademija nauka i umetnosti, pp. 407-469.

Solovjev, A. (1928), 'Jedna srpska župa za vreme carstva', *Glasnik skopskog naučnog društva*, 3, pp. 25-43.

——— (1980), *Zakonik cara Stefana Dušana 1349. i 1354. Godine*, Beograd, Srpska akademija nauka i umetnosti.

Spremić, M. (1994), *Despot Đurađ Branković i njegovo doba*, Beograd, Srpska književna zadruga.

Stojaković, M. (ed.) (1987), *Braničevski tefter. Poimenični popis pokrajine Braničevo iz 1467. Godine*, Beograd, Istorijski institut.

Stanojević, S. (1937), *Istorija srpskog naroda u srednjem veku. 1. Izvori i istoriografija*. Knj. 1, *O izvorima*, Beograd, Srpska kraljevska akademija.

Stojanović, Lj. (1901), *Katalog rukopisa i štampanih knjiga: zbirka Srpske kraljevske akademije*. Beograd, Srpska kraljevska akademija.

——— (1890), 'Stari srpski hrisovulji, akti, biografije, letopisi, tipici, pomenici, zapisi i dr.', *Spomenik Srpske kraljevske akademije*, 3.

——— (ed.) (1929), *Stare srpske povelje i pisma* I–1, Beograd – Sremski Karlovci, Srpska kraljevska akademija.

Šabanović, H. (ed.) (1964), *Krajište Isa-bega Ishakovića. Zbirni katastarski popis iz 1455. godine: uvod, turski tekst, prevod i komentari*, Sarajevo, Orijentalni institut.

Šarkić, S. (2010), 'Pravni položaj Vlaha i otroka u srednjovekovnoj Srbiji', *Zbornik radova Pravnog fakulteta u Novom Sadu*, 3, pp. 37-51.

Šekularac, B. (ed.) (1987), *Dukljansko-zetske povelje*, Titograd, Istorijski institut SR Crne Gore.

Škrivanić, G. (1954), 'O najamničkoj vojsci u srednjovekovnoj Srbiji', *Vojnoistorijski glasnik*, 5, pp. 80-94.

Šuica, M. (2003), 'Povelja cara Uroša o zameni poseda između kneza Vojislava i čelnika Muse', *Stari srpski arhiv*, 2, pp. 143-166.

Taranovski, T. (2002), *Istorija srpskog prava u nemanjićkoj državi*, Beograd, Lirika.

Trijić, V. (2002-2003), 'O sokalnicima', *Prilozi za književnost, jezik, istoriju i folklor*, LXVIII–LXIX, 1-4, pp. 3-28.

Trifunović, Đ., Bjelogrlić, V. and Špadijer, I. (1986), 'Hilandarska osnivačka povelja svetoga Simeona i svetoga Save', *Osam vekova Studenice. Zbornik radova*, Beograd, Sveti arhijerejski sinod Srpske pravoslavne crkve, pp. 49-60.

Veselinović, A. (2006), *Država srpskih despota*, Beograd, Zavod za udžbenike i nastavna sredstva.

Živković, B. (ed.) (1992), *Gračanička povelja*, Beograd, Sveti arhijerejski sinod Srpske pravoslavne crkve.

PHILIPPE GELEZ

7. The Autarky of Peasantry in Ottoman Bosnia (1463-1878), Between Myth and Reality

I. Introduction

Most of the territory of present-day Bosnia and Herzegovina was conquered by the Ottomans between 1465 and 1525, with some areas being dominated as early as 1455 and others around 1590. Here, a distinction has to be made between Bosnia in the north and Herzegovina in the south; at the time this chapter deals with, these two regions, united under the official name of 'Bosnian *eyalet*' (province), included areas that were separated from them only in the nineteenth century: the right bank of the Lower Drina and the Sandjak (parts of today's Serbia), and southern Herzegovina (now part of Montenegro). Present-day Dalmatia and Slavonia, which belonged to the *eyalet* at the time of its greatest expansion (1550-1700), will be considered here only at the margin.

The delimitation of Herzegovina poses a number of thorny questions; Tropolje is sometimes considered part of it, as well as a small part of Stari Vlah. As for the Sandjak, whose historical continuity is less marked than that of the other areas, it was divided between Bosnia and Herzegovina until 1878.

The economic life of Bosnia-Herzegovina was entirely dominated by agriculture and pastoralism from the early Middle Ages until the 1890s, when the first modern industries appeared. At the end of the nineteenth century, more than 85% of the population were still farmers. Despite a large number of detailed contributions (e.g. Hrabak, 2003-2010; Taslidža, 2011; Salihović, 2014), neither this agro-pastoral economy in general, nor the peasant economy in particular has been the subject of a comprehensive monographic presentation (partial synthesis in Tomasevich, 1955; Mirković, 1958; Palairet, 1997: 135-142). For the Ottoman period, there are scattered considerations for which Marxism often represents the theoretical basis: the aim was to show that the end of this period corresponded to a transition between feudalism and capitalism (different

Integrated Peasant Economy in Central and Eastern Europe, ed. by Aleksander Panjek, Rural History in Europe, 18 (Turnhout: Brepols, 2024), pp. 169–202
BREPOLS PUBLISHERS 10.1484/M.RURHE-EB.5.142468

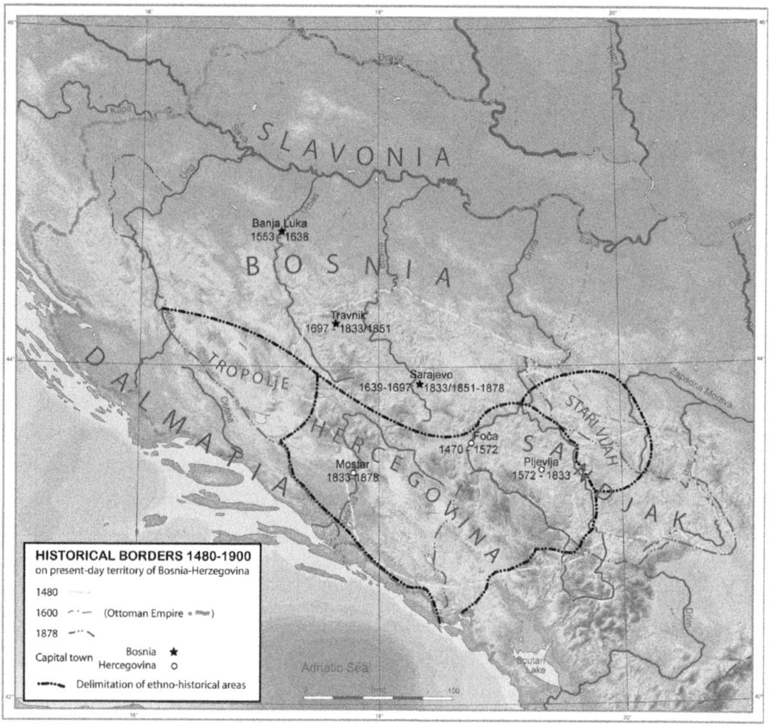

Map 7.1. Historical borders
Author: Ph. Gelez

methodological contributions in Nikašinović, 1901; Bičanić, 1936; Berić, 1994). The majority of rural historians, preoccupied with land ownership and the status of peasants, are very interested in production but only touch at the margin peasant pluriactivity and the question of exchange. Among the Ottomanists themselves, the analysis focuses on the vagaries of monetarization of economic exchanges from the eighteenth century onwards, but explanations remain very general (particularly in Avdo Sućeska).

In this panorama, only two titles stand out, the first for intelligibility, the second for originality. In 1959, in the *History of the Peoples of Yugoslavia*, the Ottomanists Hamdija Kreševljaković (1888-1959) and Nedim Filipović (1915-1984) depicted the peasant economy in Ottoman Bosnia and Herzegovina, giving some clues as to how it worked. Although they were influenced by Marxist ideology, they did not really adopt the feudalist reading that Marxism applies to economic history (Coll., *Historija naroda Jugoslavije* 1959). Subsequent research has validated many of their assertions, but it leads to a redefinition of how peasantry was linked to the market. Some fifty years later, Vlado Smoljan (1926-2008) questioned the economic functioning of Ottoman Herzegovina, pointing out the lack of structural organization and consequent poverty; as he was not a historian, he lacked many elements to refine his thinking (Smoljan, 2006; in the same vein, Krkić, 2000).

This dearth of research is obviously due to the quasi-absence of narrative or quantitative sources on peasant life; although the Ottoman period is much better documented than the Middle Ages, even a close reading of Ottoman tax rolls and the archives of the Adriatic coast cities (Ragusa, Split, Zadar) does not lead to satisfactory conclusions on diversity of peasant economics because these sources mainly depict agriculture (and, on the margins, stock raising) and do not mention any other activity than fiscally valuable ones. Although there is a very large literature relying on tax roles to describe agricultural activities in Ottoman Bosnia, it will not be used here since the purpose of this chapter is precisely to define what existed alongside these activities. At the end of the period (1850-1918), consular correspondence, statistics generated by the Austro-Hungarian administration, and ethnographic documents offer better views; however, these cannot be generalized too quickly to the time before 1850.

In practice, the reality of villages and families remains beyond the historian's reach; this article therefore proposes to observe the IPE (integrated peasant economy) signs at the macro-economic level in order to gradually induce its dynamics at the regional and then at the local level, as manifestations of it become increasingly scarce. From a reflection on the marketing of the surplus, we will thus move from one step to the next to a description of pluriactivity and income integration among the peasantry. This seems to be a logical consequence of the natural conditions of this mountainous region but shall not be generalized to the whole of Ottoman Bosnia and Herzegovina.

II. Foreign trade: marketing a surplus?

Over more than four centuries, the foreign trade of the Bosnian *eyalet* slowly shifted from the south to the north. Driven by global factors as well as by competition between Ragusa and the provincial traders in the eighteenth century, this transformation had important consequences for the way the peasant economy was organized.

II.1. International destinations

The foreign trade of Ottoman Bosnia and Herzegovina gives us strong clues about the peasant economy in general. On the Dalmatian coast, due to the administration of the cities under Venetian influence, but also due to distrust towards Ottomans, people and goods from the empire were closely monitored. This was also the case in the Habsburg Empire. In contrast, trade within the Ottoman Empire is less known, as the movement of goods was not so closely monitored.

II.1.1. Trade with Europe

Since the Middle Ages (at least the twelfth century), Bosnia and Herzegovina have been producing raw materials or semi-processed goods for the Adriatic coast, which a harsh climate made dependent on the hinterland (Živković, 1986: 187-194; Kovačević-Kojić, 1987). Although trading towards the north (present-day Croatia and the Belgrade region) possibly existed as early as the fifteenth century, no trace of it has been preserved; the Sava River, whose northern bank was at that time lined with marshes, seems to have acted as a natural barrier that was difficult to cross for a very long time (there is, for example, only one important Roman road crossing the river).

The main trade from south-eastern Bosnia and Herzegovina to the Republic of Ragusa (Dubrovnik) was hardly disturbed by the commencement of the Ottoman conquest and, despite the hazards, did not dry up until the nineteenth century (Hrabak, passim; Vinaver, 1960; Moroni, 2011). Flow of goods was relatively important; Ragusa was a place of consumption but also of transit for Bosnian commodities, which were shipped to Puglia or northern Italy (Hrabak, passim; Traljić, 1971), or even further (Hrabak, 2009 (VI): 394-427; Houssaye Michienzi, 2015). Small quantities could be transported overland directly to the city gates; however, the bulk of it was traded in the Neretva estuary (Drijeva and then Gabela i.e. Neretva; Ploče) and conveyed by boat.

During the sixteenth century, Venetian Split became a competitor to Ragusa. Elevated to the rank of a Levant Port by the Serenissima in 1579, the city developed an active policy to attract merchants from the Bosnian *eyalet*, so that by the end of the century it was in the footsteps of Ragusa. Of course, this activity benefitted its neighbouring towns of Trogir, Šibenik, and Skradin, as well as Makarska, but most of the goods were forwarded to Venice or, as for Ragusa, to Florence and Ancona. In the seventeenth century, the Republic of St. Blaise was defeated, and its trade declined significantly after the earthquake of 1667.

The city of Zadar, also Venetian, had direct commercial relations with the Bosnian *eyalet*, which supplied it with the goods that its poor natural environment could not offer in sufficient quantities; as in Neretva i.e. Ploče for Ragusa and as in Split, there was an *emin*, a sort of Ottoman consul, who ensured the smooth running of commercial affairs between the city and Bosnia. Like Ragusa and Split, Zadar was also a Levant port; herds of oxen were exported from here to Venice (Traljić, 1965; Mayhew, 2008; Fabijanec, 2011).

Trading was affected by wars and epidemics, which in return impacted the *eyalet* peasant economy. When diplomatic tensions arose, the Ottoman authorities issued bans on the exit of goods (*yasak*). On the other hand, quarantines and lazarettos were set up in the sixteenth century to contain epidemics from the Ottoman East. With the outbreak of the Candia War in 1645, trade came to a complete halt with Split and reoriented to Dubrovnik, but to a much lesser extent (Carter, 1970: 387). It resumed for a short decade in the mid-1670s, before the Holy League War ruined this new beginning in 1682: war and its evils, famine, depopulation, financial crisis, and ruin of towns and cities (including the burning of Sarajevo in 1697) combined to deal a fatal blow to this whole early period of trade (Hrabak, 2008 (V): 188-202; Sućeska, 1984; Pelidija, 1997).

The Peace of Karlowitz (1699) and, even more so, the Treaty of Passarowitz (1719) slowly ushered in a new era, which accentuated the slow commercial northward movement of the Bosnian *eyalet*. Split and its Venetian counterparts faded in favour of Austrian Trieste, proclaimed a free port by Vienna in 1719, which took a large share of the foreign trade of Bosnia and Herzegovina (Erceg, 1972; 1986). Split did not recover from the fall of Venice (1797) and in the nineteenth century, the city only attracted goods from the hinterland for its own consumption (Zaplata, 1933; 1935; Ivić, 2019: 123). The French occupation of Dalmatia (1805) and the creation of the Illyrian Provinces (1809-1813) only confirmed Trieste's position as the main transit point for Bosnian and, more broadly, Ottoman goods to Italy and France (Do Paço, 2019; Scandola, 2020: 389).

Armed conflicts blocked these export routes less than in the past. On the other hand, sanitary restrictions were tightened with the Treaty of Passarowitz due to the retreat of the borders into the hinterland: lazarettos were now set up along the border, and trade took place in small batches in secure places called *rastels*. These were vast, open-air palisaded trading and sale areas where contact between people was prohibited. There were about ten of them; salt, wheat, and livestock were traded there. Maria Theresa made this new arrangement official in 1770 under the name of Cordon Sanitaire, and similar measures were taken by Venice (Panzac, 1986; Radojčić, 2004; Slukan Altić, 2006; Skenderović, 2015).

In the decades following the Congress of Vienna (1815), the Bosnian province turned ever more decisively towards the Austrian capital via Croatia, without abandoning Trieste; Bosnian goods could be found in Central Europe and as far as Leipzig (Tepić, 1972-1973: 85-87). Osijek, Sisak, and Karlovac were established as places of exchange (Zaplata, 1933: 79, 82). Austrian trade with the Levant was in deficit at the beginning of the century, but the situation was rebalanced following the Congress of Berlin, when Bosnia-Herzegovina became a kind of Austro-Hungarian protectorate; trade flows to the Adriatic then dried up and turned to Central Europe. They passed through Brod and Brčko, on the Sava (Vrbanus-Skenderović, 2016).

II.1.2. Serbia and the rest of the Ottoman Empire

Although they are more confused than for the Adriatic coast or Austria, important trade movements also existed between the Bosnian *eyalet* and the rest of Rumelia (the European part of the Ottoman Empire).[1] First of all, with its neighbours: it is likely that in the sixteenth century, trade with Smederevo was important; after 1600, Belgrade rose in power and supplanted this city, commercially speaking (Katić-Popović, 2013). In the following decades, Banja Luka asserted itself as a shipping place to Belgrade, Skopje, and Thessaloniki (Hrabak, 2003 (I): 280-306, 348-386). Constantinople may also have been an outlet for some Bosnian products, such as fur garments, but relative to Constantinople, the *eyalet* was a secondary trading area as the main traffic went through the Belgrade-Skopje road (called *carigradska džada* or *carigradski drum*).

In the nineteenth century, major merchants from Sarajevo participated in Uzuncovo international fair, Bulgaria, which took place throughout September and was attended by more than 50,000 people; from there, their clerks would spend the winter in Constantinople to place the rest of their goods. They also had partners on the road, in Pazardžik and Plovdiv (Tepić, 1972-1973: 78-82).

These flows used not only land routes – from Sarajevo to Salonika and, from Skopje, to Constantinople – but also river routes: navigable along the entire stretch of Bosnia proper, the Sava River was lined with ports, and small boats travelled up the Drina River to Zvornik (Tepić, 1972-1973: 79; Uzunović, 2010: 80).

II.2. Export production

Apart from a few specific products, Ottoman Bosnia and Herzegovina constantly exported the same items for five or six centuries, despite the hazards of the Ottoman conquest, the wars of the seventeenth century, or the epizootic diseases (last episode between 1862 and 1878).

The main commodities came from pastoral activities: cheese, tallow, hides, skins, furs, raw wool, and coarse woollen blankets, to which were added wax and honey. Until the seventeenth century, Herzegovina specialized in exporting beaver, ermine, and wolf skins (Fabijanec, 2007: 125),

---

1 Characteristically, Behija Zlatar hardly mentions it in her article on Sarajevo trade in the sixteenth century (1988). Trade with the Near East was anecdotal and mainly import-related. At the end of the 1760s, there is evidence of a wealthy Egyptian trader in Sarajevo bringing in arms from Cairo; however, he died as early as 1770 (Čar-Drnda, 2008: 34-41).

while from the nineteenth century onwards, northern Bosnia exported large quantities of pigs to the Military Frontier. Cordovan (goat skins) which were processed in Sarajevo, where tanneries developed in the sixteenth century, was transported to Split and Ragusa. Cattle and sheep were also transported, but it is more difficult to trace them before the nineteenth century as they were less often the subject of written contracts; many herds actually came from neighbouring *sancak* and were only transiting through Bosnia from Serbia or Rumelia to the Adriatic coast. Horses were never exported in quantity (Hrabak, 2008 (V): 173-187; Vinaver, 1960: 72). Finally, it should be noted that the middle of the nineteenth century saw the collapse of wool sales, competing with cotton fabrics imported either in bulk from Rumelia or as cloth from England (Zaplata, 1933: 80).

While products of beekeeping and animal husbandry (mainly sheep) fed the constant flow of exports, grain trade was more irregular. Quantities were often modest, but are obviously underestimated: depending on the period, Bosnia may have served as a granary for the coast. Until the seventeenth century, the main grain market was at the mouth of the Neretva River, from where cargoes were shipped to Ragusa, Venice, and Italy. It can be argued that the volume grew in the 1850s, representing more than 90% of the value of exports by the 1870s (Bogićević, 1949: 223; Hrabak, 2003 (I): 5-73; Palairet, 1997: 140-141; Fabijanec, 2011: 367). This relative share should not lead to the assumption that the absolute value was too great: Bosnian and Herzegovinian peasantry did not endure any impoverishment because of the stock market crash of 1873.

Fruit was not widely sent outside the country, except for prunes, which became an export item in the early nineteenth century. The Austro-Hungarian period (1879-1918) confirmed this trend, so much so that around 1900, prunes from Bosnia could be found all over Europe (Zurunić, 1895). Wine was exported to the coast from Herzegovina very late in the period (Paponja, 2008: 78; Beljo, 2014: 42-45; Mrgić, 2017).

Booming in the sixteenth century, forestry exports dried up a hundred years later, but resumed around 1800-1840. In the first phase, logging had taken place in Herzegovina due to the needs of Venetians and Ragusans for their shipyards and had radically transformed the landscape in the Neretva surroundings, whose woodland cover disappeared forever at that time, leaving the karst bare (for more complex reasons, however, than just logging: see Vilović, 2017). In the second phase, it was in northern and central Bosnia that logging was carried out, under the impetus of Austrian, but also French, and sometimes Serbian firms. While we do not know to what extent local peasants participated in the first wave of logging, we do know that they were rarely hired in the second (Begović, 1978).

All of these exports reached a considerable scale between 1600 and 1650, and again between 1740 and 1800. In the middle of the eighteenth century, it is estimated that in Dubrovnik – at a time when trade between this city and *eyalet* was in sharp decline, to the benefit of Split and Trieste – *eyalet* traders brought in an average of 120 tons of wax and tallow, 112,000 sheep and goat skins, 24,000 ox skins, and 940 iron bales each year, all worth 2 million pounds. Thus, it was thanks to trade with Bosnia and Herzegovina that Ragusa maintained its role in the Levant trade as a whole, competing with Ancona and overtaking Naples and Messina (Vinaver, 1960: 71-2). In Split, around 1800, no less than 20,000 oxen and 30,000 pigs arrived each year from Bosnia, as well as 2100 hl of wine, presumably exported from Herzegovina (Vinaver, 1970: 72, 259).

To put it another way, the products valued for export came directly or almost directly from peasant activity, particularly pastoral; urban crafts did not produce large quantities of goods, apart from iron. In return, of all the items from the coast on sale in Bosnian markets, only a few were likely to affect the peasant economy – first and foremost salt, so important that it was often used as a currency. Despite the Tuzla saltworks (northern Bosnia), salt was lacking in these mountainous regions and was necessary for the health of the livestock that was sold to the coastal inhabitants (Handžić, 1960-1961). Other items entering Bosnia and Herzegovina were consumed mainly in the urban centres: sugar, coffee, and cotton goods from the coast, then from Vienna or Trieste; and, arriving from the interior of the empire, tobacco, rice, okra, oil, and sometimes silk (on this point, see Jukić, 2017: 189).

II.3. Trade organization

On the whole, these products were transported to the borders by professional traders. The question of the Vlachs will be examined below. For the time being, it should be noted that the most powerful sponsors had long maintained a network of commercial agents in Bosnia and Herzegovina: colonies of Ragusans or Florentines had been established in Sarajevo and Novi Pazar since the Middle Ages, for example; the Republic of Ragusa also often sent emissaries to the authorities to request urgent aid. Until the end of the sixteenth century, local merchants were dominated by these foreign traders, but they gradually established themselves. In the seventeenth century, it was the Catholics who managed to hold their own against their Muslim and Orthodox counterparts; the twenty years of catastrophic warfare between 1680 and 1700 impoverished them or even compelled them to flee, and they almost disappeared from trading to the benefit of the latter in the eighteenth century (Vinaver, 1960: 66-7; Carter, 1970: 389-390; Skenderović, 2010).

The Muslims preferred to turn their attention to the port of Split. Their arrival on the markets was already evident at the end of the sixteenth century, and some sixty years later an autonomous Muslim trading network was formed, the members of which were overwhelmingly notables, clerics, or military leaders. This network was organized in dependence on Christian entrepreneurs, because they had no privileged access to Western markets, nor did they seek to obtain any (Filipović N., 1952; Hrabak, 2003 (I): 5-73; Popović, 1986).

As for the Jews, who had arrived in Sarajevo in dribs and drabs in the second half of the sixteenth century, where they were at first only the intermediaries of co-religionists established in Dubrovnik, they, too, took part in the exchanges with Split and held a prominent place there during the second half of the eighteenth century (Carter, 1970: 387; Husić, 2017; Ivić, 2019: 120-122). But soon the Edict of Toleration of 1782, by which Joseph II emancipated the Jewish community of the empire, allowed them to strengthen their ties with Trieste, where their co-religionists were powerful.

In Trieste, as in Vienna, the Orthodox were not passed over. If Constantinople's trade was in the hands of the Armenians, the Balkan trade routes were under the control of the Aromanian diaspora, which had come to Habsburg territory following the complete decline of Moscopolis (now Voskopojë, in Albania) in the 1780s (Sturdza, 1983; Djuvara, 1989; Elibol-Küçükkalay, 2011). There is no doubt that the Aromanians fostered the growth of an Orthodox network in the Ottoman Balkans, including Bosnia and Herzegovina, some of whose members in turn settled in the Military Frontier, in Austria, or even in autonomous Serbia.[2]

Thus, in the eighteenth century, a whole class of merchants consolidated in Bosnian towns; they came from the ranks of craftsmen, especially goldsmiths, tailors, and shoemakers, who bought their raw materials abroad, processed them locally, and then resold them at a margin (Teinović, 2018, provides a good overview of the literature on the subject; see also Slijepčević, 1969: 155; Vacalopoulos, 1979). Enrichment benefitted Jews and Orthodox as well as Muslims; religious differences did not, more often than not, prevent them from setting up joint business, and investment capital was sometimes loaned by Muslim pious foundations (*vakf*) (Sokolović, 1944; Handžić, 1983; Stefini, 2015: 162-168).

Not all Bosnian merchants had good practices. The creation of the Illyrian Provinces by Napoleon (1809-1813) gave rise to risky speculations that suddenly made some of them rich, and then caused them to suffer very heavy losses. Indeed, the continental blockade, combined with Serbian insurrection, made Bosnia a privileged corridor for cotton trade from Salonika to Kostajnica, a town in the Illyrian provinces on the border with Ottoman Bosnia. More generally, illegal practices and smuggling were

---

2 There is considerable literature on the subject. For a suggestive overview, see Stoianovich, 1960, and Davidova, 2012; for Vojvodina and Hungary, Gavrilović, 2007; 2008; for Croatia, Petrić, 2011.

common. Although regularly mentioned in the sources, illegal commercial movements are difficult to quantify; smuggling flourished at the time of export bans (*yasak*), which occurred during wars or diplomatic tensions and were quite numerous; we have scattered testimonies of it. But it does not seem to have been on a large scale, as many of Bosnia's neighbouring regions were in any case quite poor and their standard of living comparable to that of Bosnia; customs duties were low enough that no one found it worthwhile to smuggle. Thus, some traders under-declared their goods, lied about the tax rate, or bribed customs officers (Pelidija, 1997: 98-99) – but in what proportion?

III. Internal trade: organization of collection

Foreign trading is a tangible sign that the Bosnian *eyalet* peasant economy was at least indirectly integrated into a network larger than the village; in other words, we can assume that goods were collected throughout the province. But how was it done? And was it a province-wide market? Responses are not so simple. The sources are mainly concerned with agricultural production, as this was the main component of the Ottoman tax base, but they say almost nothing about its commercialization.

III.1. Trade infrastructure

In order to consider this second circle of the peasant economy, we will proceed in the same way as for the macro-economic level: first, the existence of structures and exchanges must be noted.

III.1.1. Roads and rivers

Bosnia is almost entirely surrounded by natural barriers and has difficulty communicating with its neighbours, whereas Herzegovina is a more open space. Trade routes, which emerged in the Middle Ages to transport ores to the Adriatic, supported the creation and development of marketplaces along their route in Herzegovina and present-day southern Serbia. From Ragusa, two routes went to the Herzegovinian hinterland and then to Serbia and Belgrade via the Drina or the Lim (*via Anagasti* and *via Drine*) and another reached Mostar (*via Narente*). Conversely, from Mostar most of the routes went to southern Herzegovina (Trebinje, Nikšić, Bileća) or to the Dalmatian coast (Imotski). Bosnia and Herzegovina did not communicate well with each other: from Mostar, the road to Sarajevo (*via Bosna*) was a very dangerous and inconvenient route even for horse-drawn caravans.

In fact, bypassed or neglected, Bosnia was barely connected to the Adriatic until the rise of Livno at the beginning of the seventeenth century. Until the 1590s, only the trade of Banja Luka, capital of the *eyalet* between 1533 and 1639, was directed towards the Adriatic market of Obrovac (Hrabak, 2003 (I): 377). This orientation was probably a consequence of the conquest effort, which came to a halt from that time onwards. Apart from this exception, Bosnia proper was for a long time oriented towards the Sava, the only river with a somewhat remarkable commercial dimension, as the Una and the Drina, navigable on part of their lower course, showed a very modest trade activity (Handžić, 1973; Uzunović, 2010: 252). But the Sava was never developed and towing remained poorly organized (Horbec-Vrbanus, 2015). And as its banks were the scene of many wars, it was only in the seventeenth century that Bosnia's trade increased in this direction; ports flourished there to some extent, conveying downstream (Belgrade and then the Black Sea via the Danube) as well as upstream (Sisak and further Trieste by land). Trade in the regions around the Sava and Slavonic Mesopotamia is not well studied, and no historian discusses the question of routes; we only know that Osijek was a powerful place at that time.

The main flows were by land. These, by all accounts, were impassable for cart transport until 1850; to connect the countryside to the towns, the towns to each other, and Bosnia to its neighbours, communications had to be done exclusively by horse. The roads were poorly maintained and presented paths strewn with obstacles; the many streams and rivers made them impassable during the bad season, and despite the forty or so stone bridges built by the Ottomans, the rivers remained an obstacle to transport. Even the peasants rarely possessed horse-drawn carts or wagons for their agricultural work (Ljiljak, 1975: 36-43; Tepić, 1981: 57; Kasumović, 2006).

In continuity from the Middle Ages, throughout the Ottoman period the roads were not safe for traders in Bosnia but especially, it seems, in Herzegovina. Convoying was an adventure that had to be prepared for, and the occupation of expediter (*kramar*), not to be confused with caravaneer, was a profession in its own right.

Only the locals were able to master these conditions, and they knew it well. For example, they refused to allow a road from Livno to the coast through the Prolog range, because they were afraid of competition from the Austrian-Dalmatians (Tepić, 1981: 68). So much so that even in the nineteenth century, goods from Trieste arrived in Split by boat, from there to Sinj by cart, and from Sinj to Sarajevo via Livno by horseback (Tepić, 1972-1973: 82). The situation improved slightly in the 1860s, and Bosnia owes to the Austro-Hungarians the creation of efficient communication routes.

III.1.2. Marketplaces

At the time of the conquest, the Ottomans kept the main medieval marketplaces, linked to mining centres – Fojnica or Srebrenica – or commercial nodes of the first order such as Foča. However, very quickly, markets were created *ex nihilo*, or almost (Novi Pazar), or developed strongly in the new administrative centres of *sancak* (Sarajevo, Banja Luka, Zvornik, Livno, Pljevlja) to the detriment of the Srebrenica region.

Northern Bosnia and Slavonia were long impacted by war operations (1460-1530); their markets, some of them flourishing in medieval times, would only resume their activity out of step with central Bosnia, which was better spared from devastation (Vasić, 1970-1971). In general, it was only between 1550 and 1620 that Bosnia experienced a commercial boom, i.e. around the time when this warlike march, a first-rate cog in the Porte's expansionist will, acquired the status of *eyalet* (1580) and stabilized. But on its fringes, sparsely populated areas emerged, where economic life was prevented by perpetual raids and skirmishes: thus the arid Dalmatian hinterland, the Banovina, and the Moslavina.

Accelerated from 1700 onwards, the slow shift of foreign trade northwards affected the internal economic balance of the *eyalet*, causing the gradual and inevitable decline of some of the most important marketplaces of the Middle Ages and the first centuries of the Ottoman era: Gabela/Neretva, Foča, Pljevlja, Novi Pazar, and, to a lesser extent, Banja Luka and Livno (Ljiljak, 1975: 38; Hrabak, 2003 (I): 280). Once again in the front line, northern Bosnia was slowly recovering from the wars of 1680-1740; exhausted, the old Sava ports, Kobaš and Dubočac, gave way to new trading places, but Brod and Brčko, also located on the river, represented a transit point between Sarajevo and the Habsburg Monarchy, in the north-south direction, and no longer a stage of the Danube trade.

It is not clear to what extent the large marketplaces drained trade flows from the many small market towns, many of which were large villages that had been granted *kasaba*, *varoş*, or *bazaar* status for strategic reasons. Some of these country markets visibly served as supply points for the larger centres, but others represented mere halts on major routes; sometimes one has the feeling that such a market exists only on paper and has only administrative or military value.[3] It is likely that the economic reality of the *eyalet* was quite similar to that of the neighbouring *sancak* of Smederevo, where village markets were absorbed by urban centres at the end of the fifteenth century (Miljković-Bojanić, 2004: 96). In other words, the export wholesale trade did not follow a pyramidal logic and was largely supplied

3 Handžić, 1974b; Spaho, 1984; Zlatar, 1988 (the article requires mitigation); Miljković-Bojanić 2007; Hodžić, 2020; Handžić, 1968-1969 gives very little information about Zvornik at this time.

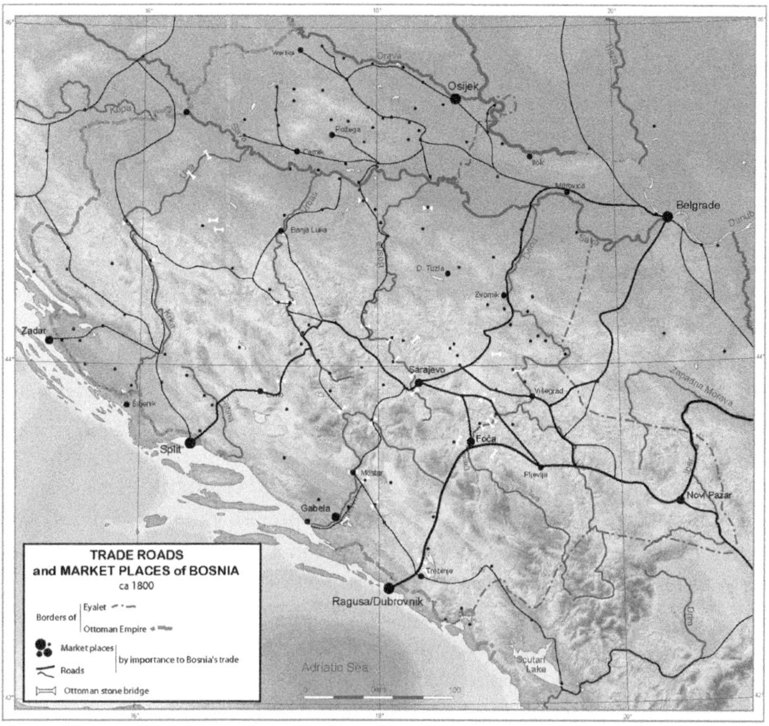

Map 7.2. Roads and markets 15th-17th c. Author: Ph. Gelez.
Sources: for marketplaces, i.e. all cities (*şeher*) and towns (*pazar*, *kasaba*, *varoş*) and excluding fairgrounds (too changeable), see Popis Zvornika 1519-1533; Popis Hercegvine 1585; Popis Bosne 1604; Handžić, 1974a; 1975; 1977; Spaho, 1989; Mažuran, 1998: 210-212; Moačanin, 2001; Popara, 2014: 53-54. In Slavonia, I have not been able to locate Sveti Vadislav, Karaš, and Sveta Katarina (and adapted Moačanin's map). In the Zvornik *sancak*, there are two unlocated markets: Poklica in 1519 and Turija in 1533 (Popis Zvornika 1519-1533: 38 n. 108, 86 n. 27 and 87 n. 31). On the map, Perin and Glasinac have been indicated, although they functioned as markets only for half a century. For roads, Dimitrijević, 1958; Zirojević, 1970; Bejtić, 1976; Čoralić, 1991; Moačanin, 2001; Slukan Altić, 2005; Šego-Dodig, 2019. I do not include Škrivanić, 1974, which is limited to the pre-Ottoman period. For bridges, Čelić-Mujezinović, 1969; Gojković, 1989.

by suppliers who were themselves located in larger places in the interior of Rumelia (Serbia, Priština, Plovdiv) or even outside the empire (Vienna, Leipzig, Venice, Italy) (Tepić, 1972-1973: 68, 72, 78, 87). Conversely, small traders in the towns were well supplied by the main centres and did not go through parallel networks.

III.2. Production and taxation

What was transported – with difficulty – to these markets? From the point of view of the peasant economy, which dominated almost all of Ottoman Bosnia and Herzegovina, it was a priori the agricultural surplus. However, it is not obvious that we can speak of surpluses in our case, and what follows will even lead us to reject this idea.

III.2.1. A largely natural economy

Part of the peasant economy of Ottoman Bosnia was at odds with that of medieval Bosnia. Indeed, if the export of livestock products to the West continued, the introduction of a new taxation system and the lasting position of the province as a war march (*serhat*), with all that this implies in terms of militarization and external contributions through booty and border robbery, profoundly disrupted commercial and economic exchanges.

Since it is virtually impossible to describe precisely the external inflows generated by booty, let us look at the Ottoman tax system. There were two ways of levying taxes on production: proportional tax (tithe) and flat tax (*filuri* or *maktu*), which affected different populations. As a matter of principle, peasants who were taxed proportionally paid their contribution in kind, while the others paid in cash. In addition, many villages and groups benefitted from exemptions, wartime requisitions temporarily caused a tax rebate (especially in the vicinity of the large towns where the army gathered at the beginning of the campaign: Banja Luka, Višegrad, Sarajevo and Mostar; Hrabak, 2003 (I): 358), and that the sultan could abolish and re-establish this or that mode of taxation. Therefore, the situation was particularly tangled in Ottoman Bosnia and Herzegovina, where populations and individuals with different tax statuses lived side by side and could switch from one taxation to another.

Taken as a whole, it could be argued that fiscal necessity pushed for a certain monetarization. Indeed, even if the tithe was levied in kind, other requirements induced the peasants to transform a part of their products into cash: the land tax and, for non-Muslims, the capitation. Finally, everyone still had to pay in cash the tax on sheep and goats, commercial taxes (market duties, tolls), taxation on alcohol, religious taxes, etc.[4]

However, the monetarization of trade met with three major obstacles. Firstly, a close examination of cash taxes shows that their payment did

4 Nenad Moačanin states that for peasants in Ottoman Croatia, payments in kind ranged from 40 to 60 per cent, with the remainder being paid in cash; he considers the share of drudgery (considered as payment in labour) to be negligible. To compensate for the almost non-existent payments in kind, the Vlachs were obliged to make a substantial payment in labour in the form of military service (Moačanin, 1999: 121).

not weigh too heavily on the peasant economy until around 1700. The non-Muslim inhabitants of the Bosnian *eyalet* benefitted until then from a flat-rate capitation tax per household; throughout the seventeenth century, moreover, the sheep tax was very advantageous for them. In addition, many people enjoyed notable exemptions: miners, townsmen, and janissaries always; various militias until the 1580s (*martoloz, derbentçi, çerahor, akıncı,* and *voynuk*) – a list to which some falconry villages and others have to be added. Even afterwards, other cash taxes were in practice not collected (Hadžibegić, 1958). Until the end of this century, therefore, there were hardly any peasant riots. Finally, the Ottoman financial crisis of 1584-1585 caused a liquidity shortage that the empire barely overcame within forty years, in the mid-1620s. A second liquidity crisis rocked the empire in 1690-1695.

The scarcity of money and payments made it easier to maintain a natural economy in the countryside and even encouraged it. Urban wage-earning groups (especially janissaries and garrisoners), tired of waiting for their pay, became artisans, farmers, small landowners, etc. (Jurin Starčević, 2006: 249). Sharecropping with fees in kind developed throughout the empire at this time, and to a particular extent in Bosnia. Peasants subject to the flat tax were gradually subjected to tithing (in kind) from 1700 and their fiscal category disappeared between 1835 and 1850. Even in the 1850s, an attempt to monetarize the tithe ended in failure (Aličić, 1980; Šljivo, 1990: 402-405; Kasumović, 2021: 109-110, 118, 127-129, 131).

Simultaneously, an opposite fiscal trend emerged: cash levies increased around 1700. Fighting and requisitions had exhausted a population diminished by numerous exoduses; the war effort had caused a growing demand for cash, exacerbated by the financial crisis. The authorities increased the number of cash taxes: perpetuation of extraordinary contributions, reassessment of capitation tax on an individual basis (albeit at the lowest rate for the whole *eyalet*), and tax for supporting provincial pasha, to which were added a host of other taxes, the total of which increased (Sućeska, 1960). A tangible sign of this monetarization of the economy is the numerous documents that testify to the convoying of large quantities of money from Bosnia (Vinaver, 1970: 59-61, 102).

These developments, which are very complex in detail, did not overly link the peasantry of the *eyalet* to the market economy. This can be seen from the fact that indebtedness of peasantry remains almost unnoticeable in the sources, except on the occasion of very bad harvests (Baltić, 1991: 95-96, 223, 234). Usurers, landlords, or lending institutions (*vakf*) lent to urban elites or rural notables – all religions included – but we barely see peasant indebtedness in the registers after the death of the powerful,[5] and

5 More often than not, published cadi protocols do not give any evidence about indebtedness (e.g. Čar-Drnda, 1989: 253-263), and when they do, we see that the debtors were wealthy

the practice of interest-bearing loans does not seem to be very ancient (Filipović M., 1949: 102).

Moreover, as everywhere in Europe, free labour was widespread: drudgery (*kuluk, zgon, angarija*) for public works, transport on horseback, and work on certain plots of land held directly by the lords, whether fields or forests. Mutual aid within the village at harvest time (*moba*) was a real institution. Only in exceptional cases did farms take in servants or farm boys to help with farm work, and rural wage employment remained marginal (4.25% of the working population in 1885, cf. Ortschafts- und Bevölkerungs-Statistik 1885[6]). Finally, the question of the division of communal land and its appropriation, which in the nineteenth century had been the subject of much debate in the European countryside and as far afield as Croatia, did not arise until the 1900s, so that no authority collected grazing rights. In other words, the possibility of monetary gain in the countryside was low.

III.2.2. Commercial consequences

The examination of a last fiscal development allows us to understand the way in which tithes entered the market: this is the leasing of tithes, or eventually of sharecropping fees. Before 1690, whatever one may read here or there, this omnipresent practice put large quantities of agricultural produce into the hands of wealthy individuals. It led to wholesale marketing of these products abroad, and if the foreign trade of the *eyalet* increased, it was not due to an improvement in yields, but to a better valuation of the tax payments.

In concrete terms, either the farmer delivered his share directly to the beneficiary of the tax or fee, or it went to a collector who was commissioned by the owner to sell it for export. In both cases, there was no monetary exchange. What circulated in trade came from the tithe and is not comparable to a surplus (Moačanin, 1999: 69). In order for such a collection network to be established, it was necessary for the politico-military cadres to be approached by the merchant class. The reality is even simpler: the cadres became merchants (Nagata, 1979; Filipović, 2020: 256-257; Kasumović, 2021: 116). Strictly speaking, they did not have correspondents

---

lords, military chiefs, or craftsmen (e.g. Buturović 1956-1957: 256; Popara, 2009; see also Berić, 1983: 134-135). I therefore do not accept the interpretation of Nihad Dostović, who identifies the inhabitants of the villages with peasants and therefore believes that many Christian as well as Muslim peasants were in debt to the vakf (Dostović, 2014: 229-230).

6 This figure was obtained by subtracting from the category of 'helpers, day labourers, domestic servants' those who lived in the city (see summary tables at the end of the publication), in relation to the working population and not to the total population. The total category in relation to the working population rises to 8.57 per cent, and in relation to the overall population to 2.56 per cent.

in the villages with fairs and markets to drain the surplus; rather, they relied on state agents in charge of collection in the villages.

The tithe was part of the gross income of the farm and its transfer to the agent or representative of the state was a heavy burden on the family budget. Indeed, grain yields – at least as deduced from Ottoman tax rolls – were barely sufficient to feed the households, and no surplus seems to have emerged (Miljković-Bojanić, 2004: 89-90).

This fiscal orientation turned the population away from agriculture. The peasants of the Bosnian *eyalet* never sought to improve their very rudimentary technical environment. The plough was only marginally used and in some places unknown until the First World War; the metal ploughshare was still a rarity at that time in all regions; and even in the predominantly agricultural regions, the horse-drawn cart was unknown. Horse-drawn ploughing appeared timidly in the 1880s; crop rotation (*ugar*) was not practised, with some exceptions. Finally, manuring was virtually non-existent (Landwirthschaft, 1899: 78-89; Filipović M., 1969: 13; Mrgić, 2008: 280-282).

Should this general picture be qualified? Should we distinguish, on the medieval model, between a complex economy in the vicinity of urban centres as well as in the agglomerations around international routes, on the one hand, and a food economy in the regions that were far from them, on the other? This seems obvious. The urban centres (Sarajevo, Novi Pazar, but also Srebrenica, Mostar, etc.), with a more or less large proportion of their population not engaged in agriculture, were centres of consumption, and the markets there were full of goods; travellers' accounts and, in the nineteenth century, other sources, testify to this. The markets were full of local products (cereals, fruit and vegetables, wax and honey, meat and livestock products, as well as metals, weapons, and urban handicrafts) in addition to products from the coast and the interior of the empire (salt, fish, olive oil, various fabrics, tools, cotton, silks, and jewellery). Were peasant handicrafts sold? Probably in small quantities, but unlike Serbia, village craftsmen in Ottoman Bosnia and Herzegovina did not become professional in the nineteenth century.[7]

As soon as we leave these cities, we assume more than we know. Statistics from the Austro-Hungarian period can help us to see a little more clearly. The administration strictly controlled the sales of cereals and drew up market prices lists, some of which have been preserved. We have a beautiful series for one year (July 1905-June 1906) for almost all the marketplaces in the province, with the quantities sold of wheat, rye, meslin (wheat + rye), barley, oats, and maize. Of course, the situation in that year

7 Aličić, 1985; Kreševljaković, 1949; Hrelja, 1961; Hauptman, 1967; Kovačević-Kojić, 1978: 197-199; Ćirković-Kovačević-Kojić, 1982-1983: 54-55; Tošić, 2001; Kovačević-Kojić, 2007: 339; Miljković-Katić, 2013.

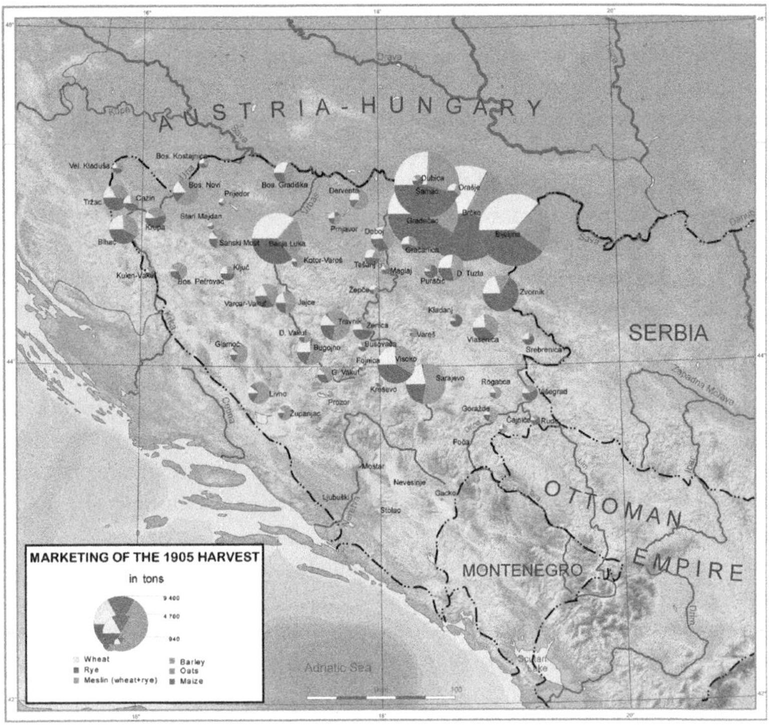

Map 7.3. Harvest marketing in 1905[8]
Author: Ph. Gelez.

cannot be generalized to the whole of the past centuries, but on this basis, a certain functioning can be deduced.

8 Sources: ABH ZVS opća 1906 27/16-7, 28/16-7 and 29/16-7; Landwirthschaft. The constitution of the series on the basis of the archives would lead to numerous remarks, for which we unfortunately do not have the space here. The series is almost complete; it has been corrected on the basis of estimates or other figures for Busovača, Jajce, Livno, Rogatica, Rudo, Sanski Most, Stari Majdan, Tešanj, and Zvornik (correction for one month), Bijeljina (correction for four months), Bihać and Prijedor (correction for five months). For Derventa, only the figures for July and August 1906 are available, which were used for an extrapolation for the previous year weighted from the province-wide monthly production percentages and assuming that the proportion put on the market was the same from one year to the next (although the 1906 harvest was overall very poor in the Derventa region except for oats, it seems that this market had a fairly large influence and that local quantities did not predominate in sales). For Gacko, the archives have only preserved a price list for the month of September 1906; I have estimated that it could be compared to the neighbouring market of Nevesinje. As for the Ulog market, nothing was sold there.

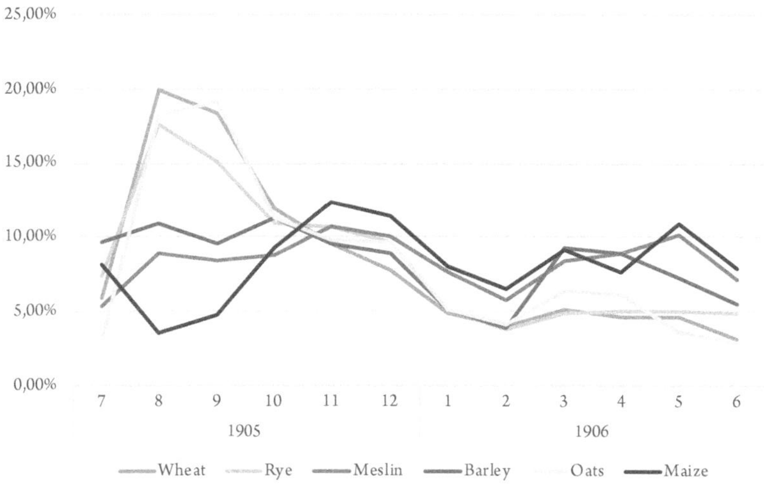

Graph 7.1. Monthly sales per 1905-1906 agricultural year (%). Author: Ph. Gelez. Sources: see Map 7.3, footnote 8.

The 1905 harvest had been slightly above average except for oats, where it had been quite poor. The Pannonian plain (Possavina) had the largest harvests and, as a result, the largest transaction volumes. Not surprisingly, Sarajevo and Banja Luka were relatively important places due to local consumption, which was a consequence of their tertiary activities. The Bihać region and Zvornik were home to numerous military garrisons. Visoko, Travnik, and Bugojno are located in fertile regions, in contrast to Herzegovina, where trade in agricultural products was almost non-existent.

In all likelihood, the grain sold represented mainly the tithe. This had been monetarized by the Austro-Hungarians since 1879, and even though other taxes had been reduced, the need to find money was greater than in previous centuries. The monthly rhythm of sales indicates a correlation with the tax calendar, since taxes were mainly due in the autumn (Graph 7.1).

Clearly it is wheat, rye, and oats which were used to pay the tithe just after the estimates of the decimators; wheat represents 29% of the annual valuation of these six products, and oats 32% (1% only for rye). As for maize (39% of the valuation), it was used in particular to feed the animals throughout the year and its sales are more constant, apart from the summer when the herds found abundant food in the mountain pastures.

To obtain cash, 19% of the wheat harvested in 1905 was sold on the markets between July 1905 and June 1906, 11% of the rye, 6% of the barley, 32% of the oats, and 9% of the maize. That is, a total of 13% of the volume of these cereals, which were valued at 7,547,458 Kr (kroner), i.e. 85% of the income from the 1905 tithe (Bericht, 1906), which was collected on many other products. In reality, the proportions must be smaller because some landowners owned many tenant farms and marketed the fees.

Unfortunately, these market prices lists, which were intended to provide comparative statistics for the whole of the Dual Monarchy, did not take into account the other products sold. We are left wanting for livestock and plums, for which we can nevertheless affirm that the considerable volumes exchanged created the real margin for the peasants – an observation that can be extrapolated without hesitation for the entire Ottoman period.

In the nineteenth century there was even a pastoralization of economic life in some regions, perhaps even accelerated in the Austro-Hungarian period (Landwirthschaft, 1899: 245-247). The primary cause was the abolition of the *timar* system (1826-1839) and the generalization in Bosnia (including the Sandjak) and Herzegovina (in its widest extension), but also in Macedonia and southern Serbia, of a regulated sharecropping (1843-1859) where the sharecropper's fees were quite significantly increased for all agricultural products. The many peasants under sharecropping contracts gave priority to livestock farming because livestock was not subject to fees. The loss of income for the landlords was significant and indirectly affected the state, which received the tithe on agricultural products from the landlords. In return, the Porte introduced a tax on small and large livestock, but its collection left much to be desired.

IV. IPE areas

From this examination, we conclude that at least since the mid-eighteenth century, a logic of agricultural specialization prevailed in the north-eastern quarter of Bosnia, while for probably much longer, Herzegovinian people had to resort to other activities apart from agriculture in order to survive. Before examining these two cases, however, we shall say a word about the monetarization of village exchanges, and in particular about rural handicrafts; although they were generally not very well developed and hardly part of a monetarized economy, they represented a small monetary source.

IV.1. A Picture of Exchanges in the Countryside

Generally speaking, according to the quantities exchanged on the small markets in 1905-1906, we can be sure that the sellers were indeed peasants who had come to collect a little money by selling cereals and, as we can see intermittently in the sources, some other commodity: hides, wood, etc. However, it remains very difficult to trace the monetary functioning of the countryside during the four Ottoman centuries (a very hypothetical attempt for the seventeenth to eighteenth centuries is found in Paponja, 2008: 99-104). Itinerant craftsmen often belonged to the Gypsy community, and in this case they seem to have been paid in money; specializing as tinsmiths, there is every reason to believe that they also traded to Slavonia (Slijepčević, 1969: 161; Vrbanus-Skenderović, 2016). In rare places, some women served as intermediary to order textiles from peasant women, which they then took back to their customers in town (Hadžibegović, 1980: 17). Unfortunately, what the ethnography of the early twentieth century says about rural handicrafts cannot be applied to the Ottoman period, as the peasant economy had already been disrupted by industrialization. In this context, it is important to note that the transport of goods was a significant source of monetary income (Filipović M., 1949: 28-30, 88-89; Filipović M., 1969: 29). Small entrepreneurs, usually from the families of village chiefs (*knez*), could organize the collection of goods (herds, timber) for direct sale for export (Karanović, 1930: 278; Slijepčević, 1969: 155; Hadžibegović, 1980: 19). A few rare villages were characterized by their secondary activity for example, in regions where the population was engaged in the mining industry, they nevertheless continued to be subject to the tithe in cereals (Handžić, 1982-1983: 334-337). And of course, there are peasants everywhere who offer their services on occasion.

All this remains unclear. If, in the big urban centres, exchanges were well monetized – this is obvious for Sarajevo in the nineteenth century – let us recall that on the markets of the Adriatic coast, Bosnians and Herzegovinians very often sold their goods in exchange for salt or other commodities. In the village, sales by exchange of goods (*trampa*) or services were still widespread in the 1920s and even the 1960s. Households covered their textile needs (linen was grown everywhere from the Middle Ages onwards) and the use of professionals or semi-professionals for certain tasks could be made in return for payment in kind, particularly for blacksmiths. In short, all this activity has never taken a protocapitalist form; the inertia was such that in the 1870s, attempts to launch a rural industry in textiles all failed, as did those to professionalize transport (Filipović, 1949: 110; Slijepčević, 1969: 161; Hadžibegović, 1980: 15).

The overall autarkic functioning existed at the village level rather than at the level of the family farm. The latter could not provide for all its needs, if only because, contrary to a widely spread view, households did not have many members. It is believed that the farms were all run by *zadruga*, i.e. multi-households, able to specialize in and diversify daily and seasonal tasks to cover all the needs of the farmers. However, quantitative sources show that households had no more than 7-8 members on average as early as the end of the seventeenth century, this proportion being most likely true as early as the fifteenth century (Mišić, 2015: 15-16;

Miljković-Bojanić, 2001: 110). This figure leaves little room for an entirely autarkic economy of large family farms.

IV.2. Possavina

For a long time the scene of destabilizing international conflicts, Possavina enjoyed a certain amount of prosperity for about sixty years in the first half of the nineteenth century. Its agricultural production increased considerably. However, in 1858, farmers saw their sharecropping fees increase significantly, in some cases tripling. In addition to renting themselves out as reapers, specialization and later, the economic crisis, seem to have been at least partially compensated for in some micro-regions by logging for potash production (Filipović, 1969: 29, 44, 128). In other places, such as Janja near Bijeljina, diversification was achieved through the cultivation of silkworms, probably in the wake of Croatia, where this activity was booming at the end of the eighteenth century. This undemanding female domestic craft produced a thread from which clothes were made for domestic use, thus compensating for the increasingly important share in domestic economy taken by agriculture (Sadiković, 1978; Buczynski, 2001; Režić Tolj, 2007).

IV.3. Karstic regions: Herzegovina and Western Bosnia

Finally, the karstic territories give rise to the most evident diversification of peasant activity. The agricultural dependence of the mountains of Herzegovina (especially in the south) or western Bosnia (Dinara massif), accentuated by deforestation (whatever is meant by *forest*, either woodland or scrub) and subsequent soil erosion in the sixteenth and seventeenth centuries, led their inhabitants to devote themselves to other activities in order to survive – which does not necessarily mean that they were monetized. In large households, a few members could work outside for one or two months, or even a whole season (*pečalba*) or several years (*gurbet*). This pluriactivity is well described: peasants from the south went to northern Herzegovina or Possavina to be reapers in the fields, to the coast to work the vineyards, to the whole of Herzegovina to offer their services as masons, to Serbia to offer commercial services, to Europe to sell small items on the street, but also to the big Adriatic ports to drive caravans of goods (Trifković, 1903: 628; Dedijer, 1991: 46-47).

It was also in Herzegovina that initiatives for agricultural diversification flourished in the nineteenth century, although it could not be called specialization. A local potentate, Ali Pacha Rizvanbegović, introduced sericulture (without much success) and tobacco (in the Brotnjo region); he expanded viticulture and olive-growing (Mostar, Stolac), and, in the Trebižat valley, had an irrigation system built that allowed the cultivation of rice, which was of rather poor quality but cheap and therefore easily exportable to Bosnia. Trials to plant sesame did not succeed. The volumes of wine and vinegar exported to Bosnia continued, maintaining an older tradition (Zaplata, 1933: 80; Alerić, 1993; Smoljan, 1996: 136).

Settled in the karstic regions as early as the eleventh and twelfth centuries, the inhabitants of the Dinaric Karst, most often referred to as 'Vlachs' although this label is rather labile, continued a tradition of transhumance that probably dates back to the Neolithic period in these mountains (Pijović, 2018). This system of animal husbandry reduces agricultural activities to a strict minimum and involves a great deal of trade; the transhumants are traders, they value wealth more than warlike prowess, and they participated amply in the commercial boom of Bosnia in the eighteenth century (Dedijer, 1916: 350; Filipović, 2020: 259-263). A mobile population, they roamed the territory of the *eyalet* by going up to the mountain pastures from May to September or October, also going down to winter in the Sava plain.

The pattern of transhumance (Map 5.4), coupled with that of the density of sheep in relation to the inhabitants of the districts (1895), tells us about this itinerant life which contributed to a lively circulation of the peasant economy in Ottoman Bosnia and Herzegovina. It was the Vlachs in particular who, from the Middle Ages until the twentieth century, transported their livestock and beekeeping products to Ragusa. In the first two Ottoman centuries, this trade was carried out by specialized Vlach traders who dealt directly with the peasants of their group for raw products but also for domestic crafts (coarse woollen cloth – *raša*). They transported their goods in caravans of 10-20 horses (Hrabak, 2003 (II): 351-371; Dinić-Knežević, 1983: 85). This manner contrasts with the larger convoys of the same goods arriving in Zadar or Split, led by traders from western Herzegovina.

V. Conclusion: IPE Model in the Bosnian Eyalet

From this overview of the market economy in rural Ottoman Bosnia and Herzegovina, we can see that livestock breeding represented the main margin of economic flexibility for the peasantry, as agriculture stagnated at a low level of development in most regions. Large quantities of livestock products were supplied by transit trade from the Ottoman Empire and Central Europe, but also by local production. In this context, two regions have specialized: in the nineteenth century, north-eastern Bosnia in cereal farming; since time immemorial, the karstic mountains of Dinara and Herzegovina in livestock farming. As a result of this specialization, both areas have developed a rather crude but fundamental IPE model for surviving. Although we are far from the 'capitalist integration' of the peasant

Map 7.4. Transhumance. Author: Ph. Gelez.
Sources: Trifunoski, 1963: 29; Marković, 1971; Glamuzina and Fuerst-Bjelić, 2015: 85; Kaser, 1992: 297, 369-370. The transhumance movements were described in the late nineteenth century, but they are most likely valid at least from the early eighteenth century onwards – the grey circled regions represent the main destinations of transhumance in the Middle Ages; only Romanija disappeared from later movements.

world under the leadership of 'agricultural professionals', as Henri Mendras highlighted in the French countryside in the twentieth century and as the Austro-Hungarians planned – unsuccessfully – in Bosnia-Herzegovina between 1878 and 1914, the fact remains that these two regions functioned as organs of a larger economic body than the *eyalet* alone. In this latter, there was no significant income integration by peasants – at least as read in the sources. Poverty does not seem to have distressed them. As with many ancient and traditional societies, many ethnologists and travellers have underlined that profit, accumulation, and the desire for comfort were foreign to them (belated testimony and all the more eloquent in Bogićević, 1949: 220-221).

Anyway, many historians and sociologists, with some nuances, hold the view that Ottoman Bosnia and Herzegovina functioned autarkically; the basic unit of this entirely self-sufficient society would have been the family organization in complex households (the *zadruga*). Without denying the fundamental tendency of any food-producing society towards self-subsistence, one should beware of this simplistic view, which leads to the opposition of a primitive collectivist and autarkic society to an evolved society based on individual property and dependent on the market. This interpretation is neither necessarily false, nor necessarily true; it is expressed in any case in evolutionary terms typically inherited from the nineteenth century, that the IPE model tries to reproblematize according to a more realistic framework, as this article tried to do.

Table 7.1: Integrated peasant economy checklist: the Bosnian Eyalet

Activity	Check
Primary sector	
Agricultural specialization	Sava area
Intensification of cultivation (no fallow, mixed-cropping, …)	None
Wage day-labour in agriculture and longer-term farmhands on larger farms	Almost none
Extension/intensification of animal husbandry	Extension because of favourable fiscality (Herzegovina, Dinara)
Intensification of forest exploitation (in primary sector, but also secondary and tertiary)	None by peasants, industry at AH time
Extension of cultivated land (reclamation of commons and woods)	None
Quarries	Herzegovina
Fishing	None
Secondary section	
Transformation of primary resources/products (e.g. wine, cheese, meat products; charcoal, lime)	Herzegovina
Rural crafts	Exceptionally
Domestic, putting-out system (proto-industry)	None
Work in 'centralized' industries and plants (manufactures, mining, etc.)	None
Migrant/mobile craftsmen (e.g. bricklayers)	Herzegovina
Wage labour in the industrial sector	None
Tertiary sector	
Services in the field of long and medium distance trade (draft animal lease, fodder, lodging and food – inns, etc.)	None
Transport of other people's products and goods over short to medium distances	Yes, above all in Herzegovina
Trade with own products and goods over short to medium distances	Yes, above all in Herzegovina
Peddling	None
Smuggling	Yes
Migrant/mobile workers (dock-workers, etc.)	Existing, but not to the same extent as in neighbouring Croatia at the end of the 19th c., or the tradition of mobile working in Macedonia
Works of trust (estimation of land value, testimonies, etc.)	None
Tourism	None

Bibliography

Archival sources

ABH ZVS opća – Arhiv Bosne i Hercegovine, Zemaljska vlada – 1906 27/16-7, 28/16-7 and 29/16-7.

Published sources

Die Landwirthschaft in Bosnien und der Hercegovina. Sarajevo, Landesregierung, 1899.

Ortschafts- und Bevolkerungs-Statistik von Bosnien und der Hercegovina nach dem Volkszahlungs-Ergebnisse vom 1. Mai 1885. Štatistika mjesta i žiteljstva Bosne i Hercegovine po popisu naroda od 1. maja 1885. Sarajevo, Landesdruckerei, 1886.

Aličić, A. S. (ed.) (1985), *Poimenični popis sandžaka vilajeta Hercegovina*, Sarajevo, Orijentlani institut.

——— (ed.) (2014), *Opširni katastarski popis za oblast Hercegovinu iz 1585. godine*, Sarajevo, Dobra knjiga.

Baltić, J. (1991), *Godišnjak od događaja crkvenih, svjetskih i promine vrimena u Bosni*, Sarajevo, Veselin Masleša.

Gavrilović, S. (2008), *Грађа о балканским трговцима у Угарској XVIII века*, Beograd, SANU.

Handžić, A. (eds) (2000), *Opširni popis Bosanskog sandžaka iz 1604. godine*, Sarajevo, Bošnjački Institut/Orijentalni Institut.

——— (ed.) (1986), *Dva prva popisa Zvorničkog sandžaka (iz 1519. i 1533. godine)*, Sarajevo, ANUBiH.

Jukić, I. F. (2017), 'Putovanje iz Sarajeva u Carigrad god. 1852. mjeseca svibnja', *Izabrana djela*, Sarajevo, Matica hrvatska, pp. 177-197.

Bibliography

Alerić, D. (1993), 'Neobično hercegovačko riječno ime *Mlade* ili *Mladi*', *Rasprave ZHJ*, 19, pp. 51-62.

Aličić, A. S. (1980), 'Desetina u Bosni polovinom XIX vijeka', *Prilozi*, 17, pp. 129-174.

Begović, B. (1978), *Razvojni put šumske privrede u Bosni i Hercegovini u periodu austrougarske uprave, (1878-1918), sa posebnim osvrtom na eksploataciju šuma i industrijsku preradu drveta*, Sarajevo, ANUBiH.

Bejtić, A. (1976), 'Stari trgovački putevi u donjem Polimlju', *Prilozi za orijentalnu filologiju*, 22-23, pp. 163-189.

Beljo, J. (2014), *Atlas vinogradarstva i vinarstva Bosne i Hercegovine / Atlas of Viticulture and Wine of Bosnia and Herzegovina*, Mostar, Sveučilište.

Berić, D. (1983), 'Diskusija i završna riječ', Filipović, N. (ed.), *Savjetovanje o istoriografiji Bosne i Hercegovine (1945-1982)*, Sarajevo, ANUBiH, pp. 131-135.
——— (1994), *Устанак у Херцеговини 1852-1862*, Beograd/Novi Sad, SANU.
Bičanić, R. (1936), *Kako živi narod. Život u pasivnim krajevima*, Zagreb, Gospodarska sloga.
Bogićević, V. (1949), 'Građa za proučavanje ekonomskih odnosa u Bosni i Hercegovini pred ustanak 1875 godine', *Godišnjak Istoriskog društva BiH*, 1, pp. 215-232.
Buczynski, A. (2001), 'The development of sericulture and the production of silk in Croatia', *Povijesni prilozi*, 21, pp. 171-180.
Buturović, D. (ed.), (1956-1957), 'Isprave spahiskih porodica iz nahije Neretve', *Prilozi za orijentalnu filologiju*, 6-7, pp. 193-258.
Čar-Drnda, H. (1989), 'Sindžil visočkog kadiluka (1755-1810) kao historijski izvor', *Prilozi za orijentalnu filologiju*, 38, pp. 253-263.
——— (2008), 'Integracija nekih Egipćana (Misirijun), u bosansko društvo', *Prilozi*, 37, pp. 31-43.
Carter, F. W. (1971), 'The commerce of the Dubrovnik Republic, 1500-1700', *The Economic History Review*, 24/3, pp. 370-394.
Čelić, Dž. and Mujezinović, M. (1969), *Stari mostovi u BiH*, Sarajevo, Veselin Masleša.
Ćirković, S. and Kovačević-Kojić, D. (1982-1983), 'L'économie naturelle et la production marchande aux XIIIe-XVe siècles dans les régions actuelles de la Yougoslavie', *Balcanica*, 13-14, pp. 45-56.
Coll. (1959), *Historija naroda Jugoslavije I-II*, Zagreb, Školska knjiga.
Čoralić, L. (1991), 'Izvori i literatura o povijesti cesta i puteva u srednjovjekovnim hrvatskim zemljama i Bosni', *Radovi Zavoda za hrv. povijest FFZ*, 24, pp. 23-40.
Davidova, E. (2012), *Balkan Transitions to Modernity and Nation-States: Through the Eyes of Three Generations of Merchants (1780s–1890s)*, Leiden/Boston, Brill.
Dedijer, J. (1990) [1909], *Херцеговина. Антропогеографске студије*, Sarajevo, Veselin Masleša.
——— (1916), 'La transhumance dans les pays dinariques', *Annales de géographie*, 137, pp. 347-365.
Dimitrijević, S. (1958), *Дубровачки каравани у јужној Србији у XVII веку*, Beograd, SAN.
Dinić-Knežević, D. (1983), 'Učešće Vlaha u preradi vune i prevozu sukna u XIV i XV veku', *Radovi ANUBiH*, 73, 22, pp. 85-92.
Djuvara, N. (1989), 'La diaspora aroumaine aux XVIIIe et XIXe siècles', *Les Aroumains*, Paris, Inalco, pp. 95-127.
Do Paço, D. (2019) [1998], 'Une collaboration économique et sociale: consuls et protecteurs des marchands ottomans à Vienne et à Trieste au XVIIIe siècle', *Cahiers de la Méditerranée*, 98, pp. 57-74.
Dostović, N. (2014), 'O gotovinskim vakufskim kreditima u tuzlanskom sidžilu 1644-1646', *Prilozi za orijentalnu filologiju*, 63, pp. 221-232.

Elibol, N. and Küçükkalay, A. M. (2011), 'Implementation of the Commercial Treaty of Passarowitz and the Austrian Merchants, 1720-1750', Ingrao, Ch., Samardžić, N. and J. Pešalj (eds), *The Peace of Passarowitz, 1718*, West Lafayette (Ind.), Purdue University Press, pp. 159-178.

Erceg, I. (1972), 'Trgovina između Habsburške monarhije i Turske preko sjevernojadranskih luka', *Jadranski zbornik*, 8, pp. 160-184.

——— (1986), 'Oživljavanje i razvitak trgovine između Habsburške monarhije i Turske u 18. stoljeću', *Acta historico-oeconomica Iugoslaviae*, 13, 1986, pp. 115-140.

Fabijanec, S. (2007), 'Trgovački promet Kvarnera na Jadranu krajem srednjeg vijeka', *Zbornik Odsjeka povijesnih znanosti ZPDZ HAZU*, 25, pp. 103-152.

——— (2011), *Le développement commercial de Split et Zadar aux XVe-XVIe siècles. Un commerce transitaire entre l'Europe Centrale et la Méditerranée*, Saarbrücken, Editions universitaires européennes.

Filipović, M. (1949), *Живот и обичаји народни у Височкој нахији*, Beograd, SAN.

——— (1969), *Prilozi etnološkom poznavanju severoistočne Bosne*, Sarajevo, ANUBiH.

Filipović, N. (1952), 'Nekoliko dokumenata o trgovini za vrijeme turske vladavine u našim krajevima', *Prilozi za orijentalnu filologiju*, 2, pp. 57-81.

——— (2020), 'Ibrahım-alemdar Pinjo, Jeftan Kovačević i sarajevska izvozna trgovina preko Dubrovnika (*c.* 1824-1825)', *Tragovi*, 3, 2, pp. 225-298.

Gavrilović, S. (2007), 'Извори и литература за историју балканских трговаца на подручју данашње Војводине', *Istraživanja*, 18, pp. 89-97.

Glamuzina, N. and Fuerst-Bjelić, B. (2015), *Historijska geografija Hrvatske*, Split, Sveučilište, 2015.

Gojković, M. (1989), *Stari kameni mostovi. Anatomija, patologija, zaštita, sanacija, konzervacija*, Beograd, Naučna knjiga.

Hadžibegić, H. (1958), 'Porez na sitnu stoku i korišćenje ispaša', *Prilozi za orijentalnu filologiju*, 8-9, pp. 63-109.

Hadžibegović, I. (1980), *Postanak radničke klase u Bosni i Hercegovini i njen razvoj do 1914. godine*, Sarajevo, Svjetlost.

Handžić, A. (1960-1961), 'Uvoz soli u Bosnu u XVI vijeku', *Prilozi za orijentalnu filologiju*, 10-11, pp. 113-148.

——— (1968-1969), 'Zvornik u drugoj polovini XV i u XVI vijeku', *Godišnjak Društva istoričara BiH*, 18, pp. 141-196.

——— (1973), 'Izgradnja lađa kod Novog na Savi u XVI vijeku', *Prilozi za orijentalnu filologiju*, 22-23, pp. 83-132.

——— (1963), 'Postanak i razvitak Bijeljine u XVI vijeku', *Prilozi za orijentalnu filologiju*, 12-13, pp. 45-74.

——— (1974a), 'Najraniji turski izvori o rudnicima i trgovima u Bosni', *Prilozi*, 10/2, pp. 155-162.

——— (1974b), 'Postanak i razvitak Dervente u XVI stoljeću', *Prilozi*, 10/2, pp. 111-133.
——— (1975), 'O formiranju nekih gradskih naselja u Bosni u XVI stoljeću (uloga države i vakufa)', *Prilozi za orijentalnu filologiju*, 25, pp. 133-169.
——— (1977), 'O značaju putova za razvitak gradskih naselja u Bosni u XVI i XVII stoljeću', *Prilozi*, 13, pp. 73-78.
——— (1982-1983), 'Rudarstvo u Bosni. XV do XVII stoljeće', *Istanbul Üniversitesi, Iktisat Fakültesi Mecmuası*, 41, pp. 321-360.
——— (1983), 'Vakuf kao nosilac određenih državnih i društvenih funkcija u osmanskom carstvu', *Anali Gazi Husrev-begove biblioteke*, 9-10, pp. 113-120.
Hauptman, F. (1967), 'Pregled tržišnih cijena nekih artikala u Bosni 1852-1862', Glasnik arhiva *i* Društva arhivskih *radnika BiH*, 7, pp. 163-189.
Hodžić, M. (2020), 'Pazar Ustikolina i sedmični pazarni dan u 16. stoljeću', Prilozi za orijentalnu filologiju, 69, pp. 287-305.
Horbec, I. and Vrbanus, M. (2015), 'Sava – poticaj i prepreka trgovini u 18. stoljeću', Ostajmer, B. (ed.), *Rijeka Sava u povijesti*. Slavonski Brod, HIP, pp. 281-312.
Houssaye Michienzi, I. (2015), 'Les milieux d'affaires florentins, le commerce des draps et les marchés ottomans à la fin du XVe et au début du XVIe siècle', Mélanges de l'École française de Rome – Moyen Âge, 127, 2, DOI: https://doi.org/10.4000/mefrm.2753
Hrabak, B. (2003-2010), *Из старије прошлости Босне и Херцеговине I-VII*, Beograd, Hrabak/Arhivar.
Hrelja, K. (1961), *Industrija Bosne i Hercegovine do kraja Prvog svjetskog rata*, Beograd, Ekonomska biblioteka.
Husić, A. (2017), 'Razvitak jevrejske zajednice u Sarajevu do kraja 17. stoljeća', *Anali Gazi Husrev-Begove Biblioteke*, 24, 38, pp. 105-132.
Ivić, A. (2019), 'Prometna i trgovisnka povezanost Splita i Bosne u prošlosti', *Zbornik radova Pravnog fakulteta u Tuzli*, 5, 2, pp. 109-131.
Jurin Starčević, K. (2006), 'Krajiške elite i izvori prihoda: primjer jadranskog zaleđa', *Prilozi za orijentalnu filologiju*, 55, pp. 243-266.
Karanović, M. (1930), Саничка жупа у Босанској Крајини, Beograd, SKA.
Kaser, K. (1992), *Hirten, Kämpfer, Stammeshelden*, Wien, Böhlau.
Kasumović, F. (2006), 'Prilog proučavanju saobraćaja u dolini rijeke Bosne. Skele u blizini sela Bičer i Desetnik u XVIII st.', *Anali Gazi Husrev-begove biblioteke*, 25-26, pp. 297-308.
——— (2021), 'Rekonceptualizacija transformacijskih procesa na periferiji Osmanskog carstva: filurija i prijelaz na režim naturalne desetine u agrarnoj ekonomiji osmanske Bosne, *c.* 1699-1852', *Historijska traganja*, 19, pp. 95-149.
Katić, S. and Popović, B. (2013), 'Смедеревска варош од 1459. године до краја 16. века', *Istorijski časopis*, 62, pp. 79-115.
Kovačević-Kojić, D. (1978), *Градска насеља средњовјековне босанске државе*, Sarajevo, Veselin Masleša.

——— (2007), Градски живот у Србији и Босни (XIV–XV вијек), Beograd, Istorijski institut.

——— (1987), 'Privredni razvoj srednjovjekovne bosanske države', Čović, B., Kovačević-Kojić, D. and Redžić, E. (eds), *Prilozi za istoriju Bosne i Hercegovine I.* Sarajevo, ANUBiH, pp. 85-190.

Kreševljaković, H. (1949), 'Gradska privreda i esnafi u Bosni i Hercegovini (od 1463 do 1851)', *Godišnjak društva istoričara BiH*, 1, pp. 168-209.

Krkić, S. (2000), *Ekonomija Bosne u turskom periodu – polovi rasta*, Mostar, Univerzitetska knjiga.

Ljiljak, M. (1975), Pošta, telegraf i telefon u Bosni i Hercegovini. I. Razvoj i razmještaj mreže poštanskog i telegrafskog saobraćaja za vrijeme osmanlijske vlade, Sarajevo, Preduzeće PTT Saobraćaja.

Marković, M. (1971), 'Stočarska kretanja na dinarskim planinama (antropogeografska promatranja)', *Zbornik za narodni život i običaje*, 45, pp. 523-549.

Mayhew, T. (2008), *Dalmatia between Ottoman and Venetian Rule.* Contado di Zara *1645-1718*, Roma, Viella.

Mažuran, I. (1998), *Hrvati i Osmansko carstvo*, Zagreb, Golden Marketing.

Miljković-Bojanić, E. (2007), 'Караван сарај у Пљевљима, трговачка станица на дубровачком друму', *Glasnik zavičajnog muzeja*, 6, pp. 15-21.

——— (2001), 'Породица у пљеваљском крају у првом веку османске владавине', *Glasnik Zavičajnog muzeja*, 2, pp. 103-116.

——— (2004), *Смедеревски санџак 1476-1560. Земља – насеља – становништво*, Beograd, Istorijski institut/Službeni glasnik.

Miljković-Katić, B. (2013), 'Сеоско професионално занатство Кнежевине Србије (1834-1866)', *Istorijski časopis*, 62, pp. 309-329.

Mirković, M. (1958), *Ekonomska historija Jugoslavije*, Zagreb, Ekonomski pregled.

Mišić, S. (2015), 'Инокосне породице и задруге у средњовековној Србији', *Glasnik Zavičajnog muzeja*, 14, pp. 9-28.

Moačanin, N. (1999), *Turska Hrvatska. Hrvati pod vlašću Osmanskoga carstva do 1791. Preispitivanja*, Zagreb, Matica Hrvatska.

——— (2001), *Slavonija i Srijem u razdoblju osmanske vladavine*, Slavonski Brod, HIP.

Moroni, M. (2011), *L'impero di San Biagio. Ragusa e i commerci balkanici dopo la conquista turca (1521-1620)*, Bologna, Il Mulino.

Mrgić, J. (2008), *Северна Босна 13-16. век*, Beograd, Istorijski institut.

Nagata, Y. (1979), *Materials on the Bosnian Notables*, Tokyo, Institute for the study of Languages and Cultures of Asia and Africa.

Nikašinović, B. (1901), *Bosnien und die Herzegovina unter der Verwaltung der österreichisch-ungarischen Monarchie u. die österr.-ungar. Balkanpolitik*, Berlin, Thormann et Goetsch.

Palairet, M. (1997), *The Balkan Economies c. 1800-1914. Evolution Without Development*, New York, CUP.

Panzac, D. (1986), *Quarantaines et lazarets. L'Europe et la peste d'Orient, XVIIe-XXe siècles*, Aix-en-Provence, Édisud.

Paponja, A. (2008), 'Gospodarske prilike u ljubuškom kraju pod turskom vlašću do početka 17. stoljeća', *Hercegovina*, 22, pp. 71-108.

Pelidija, E. (1997), 'O privredi Sarajeva u 18. stoljeću', Juzbašić, Dž. (ed.), *Prilozi historiji Sarajeva*. Sarajevo, Institut za istoriju/Orijentalni institut, pp. 93-105.

Petrić, H. (2011), 'The Navigation and Trade Agreement of 1718 and Ottoman Orthodox Merchants in Croatia and the Military Border', Ingrao, Ch., Samardžić, N. and Pešalj, J. (eds), *The Peace of Passarovitz, 1718*, West Lafayette, Purdue University Press, pp. 179-189.

Pijović, M. (2018), *Vlasi u dubrovačkim spomenicama do 14. stoljeća*, PhD thesis, University of Zagreb.

Popara, H. (2009), 'Tri neobjavljena dokumenta o banjalučkom mutesellimu i muhafizu Ali-begu Grošiću – prilog historiji Banje Luke 1738-1740', *Anali Gazi Husrev-begove biblioteke*, 29-30, pp. 5-40.

——— (2014), 'Tragom popisa ostavine jedne pašinice iz 1727. godine', *Anali Gazi Husrev-begove biblioteke*, 35, pp. 51-92.

Popović, T. (1986), 'Трговци Муслимани у балканској спољној трговини у ХВИ веку', Istorijski časopis 33, p. 57-82.

Radojčić, D. (2004), 'Санитарни кордон', *Glasnik etnografskog instituta SANU*, 52, pp. 301-310.

Režić Tolj, Z. (2007), 'Svilarstvo u Konavlima. Oživljavanje jedne tradicije', *Etnološka tribina*, 30, pp. 95-116.

Sadiković, A. A. (1978), 'Gajenje svilene bube u Janji', *Članci i građa za kulturnu istoriju istočne Bosne*, 12, pp. 73-78.

Salihović, A. (2014), *Trgovačke prilike u Bosanskom ejaletu (1793-1831)*, Tuzla, Arhiv Tuzlanskog Kantona.

Scandola, M. (2020), 'Une hypothèse sur la bibliothèque de travail d'Armand-Louis-Maurice Séguier, consul français à Trieste (1810-1813)', *Acta Histriae*, 28, 3, pp. 379-396.

Šego, D. and Dodig, T. (2019), 'Razvoj građenja cesta u Republici Hrvatskoj kroz povijest', *Zbornik radova Veleučilišta u Šibeniku*, 1-2, pp. 121-132.

Skenderović, R. (2010), 'Zapisi o doseljenim sarajevskim katolicima u najstarijoj brodskoj matici (1701.-1735)', *Scrinia Slavonica*, 10, pp. 143-160.

——— (2015), 'Sanitarni kordon na Savi i začetci javnog zdravstva u Slavoniji', Ostajmer, B. (ed.), *Rijeka Sava u povijesti*, Slavonski Brod, HIP, pp. 315-327.

Škrivanić, G. (1974), *Путеви у средњовековној Србији*, Beograd, Turistička štampa.

Slijepčević, M. Đ. (1969), *Samobor, selo u Gornjoj Hercegovini*, Sarajevo, ANUBiH.

Šljivo, G. (1990), *Bosna i Hercegovina 1849-1853*, Banja Luka, Institut za istoriju.

Slukan Altić, M. (2005), 'Kartografski izvori za rekonstrukciju i praćenje razvoja prometnih komunikacija', *Ekonomska i ekohistorija*, 1, pp. 85-101.

——— (2006), 'Povijest sanitarnih korodona i njihova uloga u razvoju dalmatinskih gradova', *Ekonomska i ekohistorija*, 2, pp. 55-64.

Smoljan, V. (1996), Poglavlja iz ekonomske *historije Hercegovine*, Mostar, Gospodarska komora Herceg-Bosne.

——— (2006), *O nekim uzrocima siromaštva Hercegovine u prošlosti*, Mostar, Matica Hrvatska.

Sokolović, O. A. (1944), *O kreditima u Bosni za turske uprave (1463.-1878), (naročito obzirom na vakufske i pupilarne gotovine)*, Sarajevo, Bosanska pošta.

Spaho, F. Dž. (1984), 'Livno u ranim turskim izvorima', *Prilozi za orijentalnu filologiju*, 32-33, pp. 147-162.

——— Dž. (1989), 'Neke karakteristike varoških naselja u kliškom sandžaku u XVI i XVII stoljeću', *Prilozi za orijentalnu filologiju*, 38, pp. 241-252.

Stefini, T. (2015), 'Ottoman Merchants in Dispute with the Republic of Venice at the End of the 16th Century. Some Glances on the Contested Regime of the Capitulations', *Turcica*, 46, pp. 153-176.

Sturdza, M. D. (1983), *Dictionnaire historique et généalogique des grandes familles de Grèce, d'Albanie et de Constantinople*, Paris, M. D. Sturdza.

Stoianovich, T. (1960), 'The Conquering Balkan Orthodox Merchant', *The Journal of Economic History*, 20, 2, pp. 234-313.

Sućeska, A. (1960), 'Promjene u sistemu izvanrednog oporezivanja u Turskoj u XVII vijeku i pojava nameta tekalif-i sakka', *Prilozi za orijentalnu filologiju*, 10-11, pp. 75-112.

——— (1984), 'Прилике у Босни прије и послије освајања Сарајева од стране принца Еугена Савојског (према домаћим и османско-турским изворима)', *Prilozi*, 19, pp. 143-149.

Taslidža, F. (2011), 'Trgovina Hercegovačkog sandžaka u prvim decenijama XVII vijeka', *Prilozi*, 40, pp. 55-76.

Teinović, B. (2018), 'Босански ејалет у првим годинама Првог српског устанка (1804-1806)', *Зборник Матице српске за историју*, 97, pp. 83-105.

Tepić, I. (1972-1973), 'Trgovina Despića u prvoj polovini XIX vijeka (Prilog proučavanju nastanka buržoazije u Bosni i Hercegovini)', *Godišnjak Društva istoričara BiH*, 20, pp. 65-100.

——— (1981), 'Изградња сапбраћајница у Босни и Херцеговини од средине 19. вијека до аустроугарске окупације', *Prilozi*, 18, pp. 45-71.

Tomasevich, J. (1955), *Peasants, Politics, and Economic Change in Yugoslavia*, Stanford/London, SUP/OUP.

Tošić, Đ. (2001), 'Земљорадња пљеваљског краја у првим годинама турске владавине', *Glasnik Zavičajnog muzeja*, 2, pp. 91-102.

Traljić, S. (1965), 'Izvoz bosanske robe preko splitske luke u XVIII stoljeću', *Pomorski zbornik*, 3, pp. 809-827.

——— (1971), 'Rapporti commerciali della Bosnia con le Marche nei secoli XVII e XVIII', *Quaderni storici*, 6, 16-1, pp. 246-253.

Trifković, S. (1903), 'Вишеградски Стари Влах', *Srpski etnografski zbornik*, 5, 2, pp. 611-668.

Trifunoski, J. (1963), 'Geografske karakteristike srednjovekovnih katuna', Filipović, M. S. (ed.), *Simpozijum o srednjovjekovnom katunu*, Sarajevo, Naučno Društvo SR BiH, pp. 19-43.

Uzunović, A. (2010), *Zvornik. Historijska monografija*, Tuzla, BMG.

Vacalopoulos, C. Ap. (1979), 'Tendances caractéristiques du commerce de la Bosnie et le rôle économique des commerçants Grecs au début du XIXe siècle', *Balkan Studies*, 20, 1, pp. 91-112.

Vasić, M. (1970-1971), 'Uticaj ratova na naselja i privredu osmanskog graničnog područja u Srbiji i Bosni (1480-1536)', *Radovi Filozofskog faulteta u Sarajevu*, 6, pp. 461-471.

Vilović, I. (2017), *Deforestacija u mletačkoj Dalmaciji (16.-18. st.), Ekohistorija*, MA Thesis, University of Zagreb.

Vinaver, V. (1960), *Дубровник и Турска у XVIII веку*, Beograd, SAN/Naučno delo.

——— (1970), *Преглед историје новца у југословенским земљама (XVI-XVIII век)*, Beograd, Istorijski institut.

Vrbanus, M. and Skenderović, R. (2016), 'Trgovački promet na tridesetnici Brod od 19. studenoga 1719. do kraja lipnja 1721', *Scrinia Slavonica*, 16, pp. 91-146.

Zaplata, R. (1935), 'Carinska tarifa u Bosni i Hercegovini polovicom XIX. vijeka (Dokumenti iz arhiva austrijskog generalnog konzulata u Sarajevu, 1850-1878)', lost ref.

——— (1933), 'Privredne prilike Bosne i Hercegovine polovinom XIX vijeka. (Iz povjerljive arhive austrijskog generalnog konzula u Sarajevu)', *Glasnik Zemaljskog muzeja*, 45, 2, pp. 77-90.

Zirojević, O. (1970), 'Цариградски друм од Београда до Софије (1459-1683)', Zbornik Istorijskog muzeja Srbije, 7, pp. 3-196.

Živković, P. (1986), *Ekonomsko-socijalne promjene u bosanskom društvu u XIV i XV stoljeću*, Tuzla, Univerzal.

Zlatar, B. (1986), 'Sarajevo kao trgovački centar bosanskog sandžaka u XVI vijeku', *Prilozi za orijentalnu filologiju*, 38, pp. 225-240.

Zurunić, P. (1895), *Die bosnische Pflaume*, Wien, Verl. der Bosnisch-Hercegovinischen Landesreg.

VOLODYMYR KULIKOV

8. Peasant Agency and Off-Farm Incomes in the Ukrainian Provinces of the Late Russian Empire

I. Introduction

This chapter scrutinizes one of the pillars of the Integrated Peasant Economy concept (hereinafter IPE), that is, 'giving economic agency' to the peasants. According to Aleksander Panjek, 'Integrated Peasant Economy emphasizes a bottom-up process, where peasants had agency and took decisions about their own economy and how to expand it outside agriculture' (Panjek, 2017: 8). But *how much* agency did peasants have in making decisions about earnings beyond their own farm? This chapter answers the question by analyzing three samples of household budgets collected in the Ukrainian provinces of the late Russian Empire, supplemented by narrative sources. After introducing the problem and describing previous approaches to solve it, the chapter provides some general context about off-farm earnings, followed by the analysis of off-farm earnings based on household budgets and their interpretation. The last part explores the applicability of the IPE to the peasant economy in the Ukrainian provinces.

Geographically, this study focuses on that part of the Russian Empire which today is within the borders of Ukraine. At that time, it was nine provinces: Volhynia, Kyiv, Podolia, Kharkiv, Poltava, Chernihiv, Kherson, Katerynoslav, and Taurida. In the Russian Empire, a province *(guberniya)* was subdivided into several districts *(uyezd)*. Chronologically, the study covers the period from the 1880s until 1914. 'Agency' in this chapter refers to the ability to choose an action from several alternative possibilities limited by certain constraints. Agency is bounded by structures, such as social class, gender, and customs, determining or limiting an agent and their decisions.

The results of the analysis show that most peasants made ill-informed decisions about off-farm labour allocation. However, wealthy households were in a better position than their poorer peers. The former had resources to travel closer to better-paid jobs and were better equipped

Integrated Peasant Economy in Central and Eastern Europe, ed. by Aleksander Panjek, Rural History in Europe, 18 (Turnhout: Brepols, 2024), pp. 203–230
BREPOLS PUBLISHERS 10.1484/M.RURHE-EB.5.142469

with working tools. Another conclusion is that the researcher should consider intra-household relations instead of treating peasant households as a single decision-making unit. This approach also reveals reasons behind behavioural patterns that have been labelled as economically irrational.

II. The Problem: Why did peasants in the Russian Empire have so many idle days?

Until the 1860s, the peasants of the Russian Empire were deprived of political power, enabling other social groups to exploit them economically. The series of emancipation reforms in the 1860s and 1870s granted personal freedom to the peasants. However, they remained economically subordinated to 'external forces', driven mainly by capitalism. One of the main reasons was a shortage of production resources, primarily arable land. Therefore, the peasants had to either purchase or lease land or sell their workforce to meet the consumption demand.

Many peasants experienced a shortage of arable land already by the 1860s. In the following decades, due to the rapid natural increase in population, the average size of arable land per peasant household decreased rapidly. This caused a phenomenon that their contemporaries called 'agrarian overpopulation'. The term refers to a situation when, due to the low level of peasant agriculture (compared to Western Europe), the peasant household could not fully utilize all the labour force and accumulated a significant share of 'redundant' workers (Kaufman, 1908). The disparity between the labour force of a household and the maximum productive capacity of its farm caused a labour surplus.

Peasant households with a shortage of arable land and a labour surplus had three main options to increase their income: 1) increase the production capacity by purchasing or renting land; 2) increase the productivity of the farm by intensifying labour; and 3) embrace off-farm earnings such as crafts, trade, and wage labour. They used all these options, but often not to their full capacity.

Recent studies demonstrated that in the last hundred years of the Russian Empire, the well-being of the peasantry steadily improved (Mironov, 2015: 329-330). Nevertheless, a large share of the peasant population lived in extreme poverty and experienced malnutrition (Klepikov, 1920; Simms, 1982). At the same time, most adult peasants worked only from 100 to 120 days per year. Some households increased that amount up to a dozen percentage points more, but the overwhelming majority of peasants did not work all workdays (Chelintsev, 1919: 7). Aleksandr Chaianov calculated that peasants in the Kharkiv province annually dedicated 27% of their time to work on their farms, 4% was spent on off-farm income, 27% were holidays, and 42% was occupied by housework, illnesses, and leisure time.

Chaianov compared these numbers with Moscow and Vologda provinces and found similar results, with a slightly higher percentage of workdays on their own farm (28% and 25%) and off-farm income (8% and 18%) (Chaianov, 1915: 91).

If the shortage of production capacity determined so many idle days, it would be logical to expect peasants to utilise the labour surplus in the job market outside their farms. However, sources about the history of industrial work show that it was not that straightforward. Many industrialists complained about the deficit of workers, especially in the summer months (Kulikov, 2019: 115-120). Then why did peasants with insufficient assets refrain from grasping every opportunity for wage jobs? How did they make decisions about their level of self-employment?

Several microeconomic theories explain decision making in peasant households (Ellis, 1993: 167, 278-283). The most detailed one, developed on peasant household statistics collected in the Russian Empire, is the neopopulist theory of resource allocation. Aleksandr Chaianov and Aleksandr Chelintsev, the two most influential contributors to the theory, say that the goal of a peasant household is simple reproduction rather than profit maximisation. According to them, the level of consumer demand in the family and the working capacity of the family (the consumer-worker ratio) determines the intensity of a household's economic activity. A household works to satisfy consumer demand rather than to employ all available family labour. Chaianov and Chelintsev claimed that peasant work motivation follows, in part, social concepts about the minimum acceptable level of material income and work ethic (Chelintsev, 1919: 8; Chaianov, 1989: 70-71). Diana Hunt eloquently summarized the idea as follows: 'Each household works to the point where the household's subjective evaluation of the marginal disutility of work equals its estimate of the marginal utility of the output gained' (Hunt, 1979: 248).

In approaching the issue from the Marxist perspective, Mark Harrison criticized Chaianov's assertion that 1) 'peasant society was stable or homogeneous' and 2) 'idle labour is voluntarily unemployed'. Harrison argued that underemployment could be involuntary, especially in the case of poor peasants who lacked access to resources and when 'the marginal productivity of labour is declining sharply, and when they cannot save or accumulate because they are already very poor' (Harrison, 1975: 408, 11). He thus distinguished between the involuntary unemployment of the poor and the voluntary idleness of rich peasants. Harrison rejected the idea that all peasants 'ate and worked as much as they wanted' because it was 'an ideological mask for famine, disease, and scarcity' (Harrison, 1975: 412).

Both approaches discuss how peasants make decisions about how much to work but present peasant agency as highly limited by structures. Chaianov and Chelintsev refer to the demographic characteristics (ratio of workers to consumers), which strongly impacted the peasants' decisions.

For Marxist scholars, it was capitalism and the invisible hand of the market that determined the economic choices of the peasants. The book 'The Socio-Economic Structure of Peasant Agriculture in European Russia During the Era of Capitalism' by Soviet scholars (Koval'chenko-Moiseenko-Selunskaia, 1988) is a striking example of such super-determinism. The authors found a positive correlation between the main components of peasant households, which they interpreted as the 'deep involvement of Russian peasants in the market-oriented capitalist system' (Koval'chenko-Moiseenko-Selunskaia, 1988: 127). They concluded that the market 'rigidly determined the economy of poor and wealthy peasants' and 'market relations penetrated all spheres of production and other activities of the peasants'. In their opinion, all economic activities of all layers of peasants were subordinated to the 'objective requirements dictated by the market laws'. The researchers emphasised that even the most impoverished households with a scanty land plot, i.e., the 'rural proletarians', obeyed market laws. The authors also argued that even poor households 'could organise production at a level' that it could be part of the market: 'the laws of the market knew no exceptions' (Koval'chenko-Moiseenko-Selunskaia, 1988: 93).

Still, the positive correlation between the main components of peasant households does not explain the paradox of the coexistence of agrarian overpopulation and the high number of idle days. Some scholars assume that the economic factor, in principle, cannot provide a satisfactory explanation for the labour-related behaviour of the peasants. Boris Mironov argues that most Russian peasants were bearers of a 'minimalist' work ethic (Mironov, 1999). According to Mironov, reasonable restriction in consumption and modesty in work was an ethical ideal for the peasants. Russian peasants rejected the attitude that strove to maximize profit but also despised idleness in poverty as extremes (Mironov, 1999). Instead, they chose moderation in work and a reasonable restriction of needs that acted as a normative concept of economic behaviour, 'a lifestyle with its advantages and disadvantages'. From the perspective of the market economy, such an approach seems to be 'economically irrational', but Mironov says that peasants' choices were rational within the mindset of the 'moral economy'.

All microeconomic theories on the peasant household acknowledge the relevance of the context, especially factors such as consumption and demand, labour capacity, agricultural productivity, the off-farm labour market, and work ethics. So, it is important to understand the economic environment in which peasants were supposed to decide how to utilize their workforce.

III. Context: Off-Farm Earnings for the Peasant Households

The peasant household was a family unit, which made its living from agriculture. It was based primarily on family labour and served the consumption needs of the family. This economic unit was partly engaged in input and output markets, including the labour market. Utilizing its workforce on its own farm was an ideal model. However, many peasants lacked enough arable land to sustain their living needs. The size of arable land per household shrank quickly due to the rapid growth of the population. Besides that, land assets were distributed unequally among the peasants.

Considering the scarcity of land, many households had to resort to off-farm earnings to cover the budget deficit. Contemporaries used two terms related to off-farm earnings: *promysly* and *otkhod*. *Promysly* refers to all earnings beyond the peasants' own farm, sometimes used in a narrower sense and applied to non-agricultural activities. *Otkhod* is a similar term that denoted various occupations in agriculture, industry, and the service sector, but geographically outside of the peasant's village (Häfner, 2019: 552-553). So, *promysly* is a broader category including migratory (*otkhod*) and local (*mestnie*) off-farm earnings.

Off-farm incomes earned through wage labour, crafts, and trade contributed significantly to the budgets of peasant households all over Europe in the nineteenth and early twentieth centuries. The Russian Empire was no exception. According to the observations from the local self-governments (*Zemskie podvornie perepisi*), around 50% of households in the Ukrainian provinces practised off-farm earnings (Table 8.1). The level of engagement in off-farm activities varied both among the provinces and within them (Tverdova-Svavitskaia-Svavitskii, 1926: 234-235). Several factors impacted the involvement of the peasants in off-farm earnings, such as proximity to large labour markers, arable land scarcity, and local traditions (Chelintsev, 1919: 8).

For most off-farm workers, it was a part-time job. In Katerynoslav province in 1898-1902, 88% did not break away from the farm, having off-farm earnings occasionally or seasonally, and only 11% cut off all connections with the farm. In Kharkiv province in 1913, the share of those who separated from their farm was higher, 23%, while 36% had an occasional income not far from the farm and 40% practised seasonal wage labour (Tverdova-Svavitskaia-Svavitskii, 1926: 234-235). Most off-farm activities were determined by the shortage of production assets in the peasant farms. In Poltava province in the 1890s, around 25% of households with migratory off-farm earners had no arable land, while such households constituted only 2.8% of all households in the entire province (Tverdova-Svavitskaia-Svavitskii, 1926: 298).

Table 8.1. Off-farm work (*promysly*) in selected Ukrainian provinces from 1883 to 1913 (Tverdova-Svavitskaia-Svavitskii, 1926)

Province and year of survey	Households engaged in off-farm work	The ratio of off-farm workers to adult members of the household	Households having commercial or artisan enterprises
Katerynoslav, 1883-1886	51%	n/a	n/a
Katerynoslav, 1898-1902	66%	18%	6%
Poltava, 1910	40%	n/a	9%
Taurida, 1885-1887	21%	n/a	n/a
Taurida, 1900, 1904	49%	33%	n/a
Kharkiv (Starobel'sk district), 1905	52%	30%	7%
Kharkiv, 1913	60%	46%	n/a
Kherson, 1883-1887	26%	n/a	n/a
Chernihiv, 1881-1883	58%	25%	n/a

According to some estimations made by *zemstvos* (organs of rural self-government in the Russian Empire) in the mid-1890s, the occupational structure of migrant peasants in Poltava, Katerynoslav, Chernihiv, and Kherson provinces was as follows: 57% agricultural labourers, 22% artisans, 2% industrial workers, and 20 miscellaneous (Häfner, 2019: 554). Another survey conducted by the state commission in 1900 showed that 84% of off-farm earners in the Ukrainian provinces found opportunities in their village or nearby and 16% in distant settlements (Table 8.2). Local off-farm earnings in agriculture contribute 54% of all off-farm earnings, while the industrial sector's contribution was 25% and 14% came from artisanship (Dep. oklad. sborov, 1903: 216-219). Table 8.2 demonstrates a significant difference in income between local and migratory off-farm earnings as well as earnings in different sectors (e.g., quadruple difference between industry and artisanship), which mean that peasants had to make difficult economic decisions.

Aleksandr Rybnikov aggregated materials from surveys conducted by *zemstvos* in the period from 1910 to 1913, and his calculations show that in the Ukrainian provinces, the majority of artisans were in the textile (37%), wood processing (27%), and leather processing (14%) sectors (Rybnikov, 1922: 108-118). Among the most popular artisanship activities

Table 8.2. Off-farm earnings in the 9 Ukrainian provinces and the 50 provinces of European Russia (Dep. oklad. sborov, 1903: 216-219)

Off-farm earning	Structure in the Ukrainian provinces	Structure in the 50 provinces of Eur. Russia	Annual income per earner in the Ukrainian provinces	Annual income per earner in the 50 provinces of Eur. Russia
Local	**84%**	**73%**	**114**	**85**
In industry	13%	14%	172	167
In agriculture	41%	27%	141	92
Artisanship	30%	33%	44	44
Migratory	**16%**	**27%**	**45**	**54**
Total	100%	100%	105	77

were weaving, woodworking, shoemaking, leatherworking, blacksmithing, and pottery.

The industrial sector offered a higher average wage than agriculture and profits from artisanship (Table 8.2 and Table 8.3). However, higher wage rates did not necessarily mean a higher monthly net income. A few hundred kilometres to the South of Kharkiv, in the Donets basin industrial region, an unskilled worker could earn up to 120 kopeks (that is 1.2 roubles) per day for work in a mine (Kulikov, 2019: 199), twice as much as what they could get in the agricultural sector. In practice, the net monthly salary of a coal miner varied between 10 and 30 roubles per month (Cheremukhin, 1910: 4). Since many mines practised a piece-work system, the real income depended on how hard a miner worked. A miner, Klimov, wrote about his first day as a toboggan in his memoirs. 'Full of energy, just out of the village', he made four times the norm and earned 4.8 roubles from one shift. But he made it through extreme overstrain. Klimov mentioned that he 'worked in just underpants' and was 'tottering due to extreme tiredness' (Zaks, 1955: 86). The wage rates of miners were significantly higher than those of manufacturing and agricultural workers. However, due to more intense production fluctuations, miners worked fewer days per year, so their real income was comparable with that of factory workers.

Peasants willing to sell their labour faced fragmented and distorted labour markets. While there was a workforce surplus in some regions, in others, labourers were lacking. Besides the unequal spatial distribution of work and workers, job seekers had to make ill-informed decisions on when and where to go. Market information was patchy and erratic.

Table 8.3. Daily wages in kopeks in Kharkiv province in 1910 (Opatskii, 1912: 59)

Type of work	Male	Female
Agricultural worker	57	41
An unskilled temporary worker in Kharkiv	82	52
A worker in a sugar beet plant	60	32
House servant in Kharkiv	41	27

Job seekers relied on their experience, followed rumours about available jobs, and made guesses about good crops and the need for working hands. Some tried to find more reliable information about the job market in the newspapers. It was tricky, however, because some landowners deliberately disseminated false information about exceptionally high crops to attract many labourers and force down wages. Contemporaries describe how every year, 'millions of people roamed haphazardly in search of a job' and often failed in their endeavours (Iaroshko, 1894: 38; Brave, 1899: 17). A contemporary, Aleksandr Iaroshko, illustrates the chaotic process of contracting labour, typical for the 1890s, with the example of the Kakhovka market, one of the main localities where labourers could find a contractor in Southeastern Ukraine: 'Crowds of people roam with sore eyes. They try to figure out the established rates for work and information about the expected harvest. These bazaar rumours are driving the demand for working hands' (Iaroshko, 1894: 39; Brave, 1899: 18).

Many jobseekers endured a relatively long period of unemployment or even returned home with no income. Nevertheless, the next year they would try again. Iaroshko cites an interview with an experienced worker, whose words reveal the logic behind this: 'Assume that we know that only one out of three job seekers will get income, but it does not decrease the influx of people. Everyone expects that it will be them who will get the job, while the others fail. So, they go and try their luck' (Iaroshko, 1894: 38). The practice of job seekers in such conditions can be characterised as a probabilistic labour search with considerable uncertainty due to information asymmetry.

In addition to the high level of market uncertainty, wage labour had other drawbacks. High transportation costs, passport requirements, and residual institutional rigidities were among the main constraints (Nafziger, 2010: 390). The process of seeking a job was unpleasant and stressful. Journalist Luigi Villary shares his observation from around 1905: 'Crowds of peasants wrapped up in rough sheepskin coats fill the third-class railway carriages or are seen trudging along the muddy roads towards the great towns in search of work. The same man may be attending to cotton spindles one year, to silk looms the next, and be employed in a sugar refinery the third, with intervals of agricultural labour in between' (Villari, 1905: 223). This and similar evidence show that searching for a job was harsh and stressful. Young female migratory peasants were exposed to sexual harassment. Many job seekers left behind families and unfinished work on their farms, which added to the anxiety and stress.

Both employees and employers suffered from fragmented and distorted labour markets. Job seekers risked getting low wages or finding no employment at all. Another risk was to accept an offer with poor working conditions. Employers tried to squeeze out all the working capacity from their employees, threatening immediate dismissal if a worker underperformed (Brave, 1899: 9). At the same time, employers would face problems if they failed to hire enough workers in the harvest season or for an industrial enterprise. The industrialists' complaints about the deficit of workers in the summer months was a recurrent topic until the end of the imperial epoch. High volatility of wages, sometimes fluctuating hundreds of percentage points within a day, contributed to uncertainty and increased risks for both workers and their employers (Brave, 1899: 16).

Distorted and poorly regulated markets caused unethical behaviour because all actors tried to take advantage of the opportunities. Emelian Kolodub, a mining engineer, mentions a vivid example of the opportunistic behaviour of the workers in the Grushevsk mines, the Donbas, in the early twentieth century. According to Kolodub, in the years of good crops, all diligent workers used to come back to their villages to work on the farms. However, many chronic drunkards stayed in the coal towns. Despite the high wages offered by agricultural enterprises and the mines, they did not want to work and preferred hanging around in the local bazaars. They willingly accepted offers from employers, required alcohol and food, but kept postponing the starting date of work, using a wide range of tricks to fool the employers. Eventually, an employer would lose his patience and confront the worker. Then, the worker pretended to be offended and went back to the market, waiting for other employers whom he would trick the same way. The enterprises needed workers, so they 'had to tolerate such behaviour' (Kolodub, 1905: 41-43). Kolodub notes that both the employees and employers suffered from labour opportunism, the former from a precarious job market, the latter from a 'half-drunk, incompetent and non-reliable worker' (Kolodub, 1905: 44).

Another example of labour opportunism in the agricultural sector was described by Iakov Brave. In 1893, south-eastern Ukraine had exceptionally good crops, and seasonal workers were in high demand. On the Kakhovka market, a place in Kherson province where workers and potential contractors could meet, the workers behaved as follows: 'When potential employers asked about the price for their service, a worker did not respond but stretched out a leg, with a piece of paper indicating the numbers, glued to the sole of his shoe' (Brave, 1899: 96). Brave noted that in other years with regular crops, such rude behaviour would have been unthinkable.

To eliminate the risks of opportunistic behaviour among workers, employers contracted workers in winter or spring, when the peasants were running out of resources and were ready to accept payments in advance, which were half of those in the summertime (Lipskii, 1902: 140-141). Then they signed a contract, which included a fine to be paid by the peasant if he failed to fulfil his obligations (Morachevskii, 1903: 204; Brave, 1899: 58-59). Nevertheless, peasants found ways to outmanoeuvre the system. When it was time to do the job in seedtime or the harvest, workers deliberately performed so badly that the employer had to end the contract, and the workers were free to find another job with higher wages (Brave, 1899: 59; Iaroshko, 1894: 98). There was no efficient way to eliminate risks in the context of poor work ethic, weak labour regulations, and institutional voids. That is why agricultural and industrial enterprises were unable to find a solution for workers leaving before their contracts expired (Morachevskii, 1903: 204).

Some employers, having to deal with an insufficient workforce, tried to rely on a network of agents who travelled to regions with a surplus of workers. The agents provided information on working conditions, contracted peasants, and sometimes offered them a prepayment and covered their travel expenses. However, this did not prevent waged workers from using slowdowns and other forms of obstruction. In such cases, the employers tried to motivate workers by providing adequate treatment (e.g., better food and housing, higher wages) or asking a government representative to intervene and punish obstructionists (Brave, 1899: 58-59). Still, both economic incentives and administrative coercion had their limitations.

Governments attempted to regulate the labour market on different levels from the 1870s onwards. These were projects with various levels of *zemstvo* or state engagement (Brave, 1899: 58-59; Iaroshko, 1894: 82-83, 86, 92-93). The simplest attempts targeted refuting false rumours and disseminating adequate information about job offers and wages. The most ambitious undertakings aimed at establishing special agencies that would act as intermediaries between employers and hired labour (Iaroshko, 1894: 81-93). However, none of these projects lasted long enough to significantly improve the situation and make markets more secure and balanced. The initiatives failed because they had insufficient human and financial capacity, and job seekers obstructed them. As Lutz Häfner pointed out, 'migrant labourers were afraid of tax increases or even believed that the surveys served to trace migrants without domestic passports' (Häfner, 2019: 551). As a result, labour markets failed to achieve equilibrium until the end of the imperial era.

Table 8.4. Aggregated information from three samples. *For Poltava province, data is available only on migratory off-farm income ** A dessiatin is approximately equivalent to 1.09 hectares.

	Kherson	Poltava*	Kharkiv
Year of observation	1897/98	1902/03	1910
Households in the sample	124	100	101
Arable lands per household, dessiatines**	17.0	10.4	9.6
Households having off-farm income	85%	16%*	86%

IV. Data: Household Budgets

This section presents the results of the analysis of budget censuses conducted by *zemstvos*; this is a particularly rich source of statistics on peasant households. Three surveys from the late nineteenth and early twentieth century provide detailed data on off-farm earnings (Table 8.4). One budget census is from Kherson district, Kherson province, undertaken in 1897/98 (Arnol'd, 1902), one from Poltava province in 1902/03 (PoltZemstvo, 1907), and one from Starobel'sk district, Kharkiv province in 1910 (Chaianov, 1915).

The *zemstvos* surveyed the peasant budgets for fiscal purposes and informed policies for rural development. Most information about the budgets was collected on the spot by professional statisticians who interviewed the peasants and filled in the survey forms. The published results provide hundreds of indicators about different aspects of the peasant households, including labour resources, farming assets, annual revenues and expenses, and the amount of time the peasants dedicated to various activities. The source allows the analysis of the economic behaviour of peasant households on a micro-level, which makes this dataset invaluable for researchers of the peasant economy (see the details in: Chaianov, 1929; Korenevskaia, 1954).

The limitation of budget censuses is that the number of households involved was usually low (a few hundred per observation), making the conclusions insufficient to be applied to the entire region. They are also rarely directly comparable across sources. Nevertheless, scholars have developed efficient methods of using peasant budgets to measure inequality among the peasants (Field, 1989) to estimate the level of development of capitalism (Koval'chenko-Moiseenko-Selunskaia, 1988) and explain patterns regarding work intensity and consumption (Chaianov, 1989). Projects like 'The Historical Household Budgets' (A'Hearn-Amendola-Vecchi, 2016) and 'Integrated Peasant Economy in a Comparative Perspective' (Panjek,

2017) offer new, promising research tools and approaches to unifying scattered budget censuses and combining them into a single database.

In the **Kherson sample** (Table 8.5), 85% of households had off-farm income, but only 14% received more revenue from such activities than from their farm (Table 8.6). On average (median), off-farm income contributes 16% of all gross income (minus taxes). Off-farm earnings were much more important for poor peasant households than their wealthier peers (Table 8.6). A third of households with a small amount of arable land per capita sold their labour, while only one out of ten with an above-average amount of land did so. Wealthy peasants chose to increase their income by renting land and occasionally hiring their poorer fellows to perform some tasks during the growing season.

The structure of off-farm income varied depending on wealth. The poor households mostly relied on wage labour, while wealthy peasants generated off-farm income by using their assets, such as working animals, mills, and fishery equipment. Households from the upper quartile used their mills, grinders, and mowing machines to generate income. Among the wealthiest ones, only two households (3%) had income from wage labour. In contrast, 71% of households in the lowest quartile were selling their workforce.

There was also a difference between rich and poor peasants in terms of off-farm income category. For instance, while five households from the upper quartile earned income from fishing and only one from collecting reeds, the poorest households only collected reeds and had no access to fishing. While the wealthiest households mostly relied on machine-based activities, the poorest ones focused on trade services and manual artisanship, such as carpentry (Arnol'd, 1902: 182-190).

The off-farm incomes show no correlation with any of the other important indices, such as means of production, movable and immovable property, incomes and spendings. The correlation analysis did not reveal high correlation coefficients ($r \geq 0.5$) for any of the 84 variables selected for the analysis. Artisanship and earnings outside their own farm were opportunities rather than an entrepreneurial strategy for most households in the sample. A possible explanation is that the population density in the Kherson province was lower than the average in European Russia; therefore, agricultural overpopulation was less evident compared to the northern regions.

However, when one takes into consideration only those households in which off-farming activities contribute with at least 40% of the gross income (minus taxes), off-farm income positively correlates with the cost of draught animals ($r=0.44$) and tools and machines ($r=0.32$). This means that the availability (or scarcity) of working tools was a factor in part determining the involvement of peasants in off-farm earnings.

Table 8.5. The Kherson sample ranged by arable land per capita and divided into four groups (Arnol'd, 1902)

	Upper	Upper middle	Lower middle	Lower	All
N	31	31	31	31	124
Arable land per capita, dessiatines	5.7	2.6	1.6	0.8	2.7
Income per capita, roubles	85.3	31.9	17.6	10.2	36.1
Spending on food and vodka per household, roubles	106.3	59.5	39.7	42.0	61.9
Rented land per household, dessiatines	12.9	3.8	3.0	2.5	5.5
Income from farm per household, roubles	500.5	186.7	98.5	52.1	231.3
Household buying workforce	32%	6%	0%	0%	1.0%
Balance of buying/selling workforce, people	1.2	0.2	-0.1	-0.6	0.6
Percent of households selling labour	3%	19%	35%	32%	23%

Table 8.6. The structure of off-farm income and renting out assets in the Kherson sample ranged by arable land per capita and divided into four groups (Arnol'd, 1902)

	Upper	Upper middle	Lower middle	Lower	All
Arable land per capita, dessiatines	5.7	2.6	1.6	0.8	2.7
Share of households having off-farm income					
Commodity transportation	29%	58%	52%	35%	44%
Mills, forges, trade, shoemaking	26%	6%	10%	16%	15%
Wildcrafting and fishery	23%	13%	6%	10%	13%
Renting out buildings, tools, land	3%	6%	6%	6%	6%
Wage income	3%	32%	55%	71%	40%
Total	74%	81%	90%	94%	85%
Off-farm income from:					
Commodity transportation	35%	50%	41%	24%	37%
Mills, forges, trade, shoemaking	29%	7%	5%	11%	13%
Wildcrafting and fishery	29%	9%	1%	2%	9%
Renting out buildings, tools, land	2%	7%	3%	4%	4%
Wage income	4%	27%	50%	59%	37%
Total amount	100%	100%	100%	100%	100%

Table 8.7. The Poltava sample split into quartiles after ranging according to arable land per capita (PoltZemstvo, 1907).

	Upper	Upper middle	Lower middle	Lower	All
N	25	25	25	25	100
Arable land per capita, dessiatines	2.8	1.5	0.9	0.5	1.5
People of working age per household	2.7	3.4	3.1	3.0	3.1
Consumers to workers	1.5	1.4	1.6	2.2	1.7
Absent members of the household	0.0	0.0	0.1	0.4	0.1
Household with absent	0	0	8	8	16
Households with non-family consumers	21	8	5	3	37
Balance of workforce, workers	1.1	0.1	0.0	-0.3	0.2
Livestock, units	9.0	6.3	5.0	3.4	5.9
Gross production of grain per capita in poods (16.38 kg)	48	30	20	11	28

The Poltava sample includes data on 100 households observed in 1902/03. This survey focused on the dynamics of household income and consumption of agricultural products and concentrated on the balance of consumers instead of the off-farm earnings. Nevertheless, it provides some information about migratory off-farm earners. Out of 100 households, 16 had migratory workers, all in the lower-middle and the lowest category. Wealthier households, in contrast, hired rather than sold workforce. Consequently, the balance of the workforce was positive (1.1) in the wealthy and negative (-0.3) in the poor group (Table 8.7).

The number of migratory workers shows no correlation with the other important factors. Within sixteen households with migratory workers, their ratio correlated with the number of workers in the household (r=0.54) and the size of arable land per household (r=0.53). The lack of arable land stimulated peasant households to leave their village and sell their workforce. However, there is no significant correlation with the ratio of consumers/workers in the household (Chaianov's assumption). Alas, these data are non-representative: they show only missing members in the households who could be away for reasons other than off-farm work. Moreover, it does not count local off-farm income, which was more important in the Ukrainian provinces than migratory work.

In the **Kharkiv sample**, most households (86%) had off-farm earnings. They allotted from one to seven members (average 2.1) for such activities. Surprisingly, not only peasants with little or no arable land were involved in off-farm earnings, but so were the wealthy households.

The nature of these earnings was different for wealthy and poor households (Table 8.8). In the upper category, less than one-third of the adult workers' workforce was dedicated to off-farm earnings. In the lower category, it exceeded 100% of the adult workforce, meaning poor households had to mobilize children and retired family members to make ends meet.

Net income from off-farm earnings per worker in the upper group was twice as much as in the lower category. It explains how the wealthiest peasants, using fewer human resources, made almost the same amount per household as the poorest. The two middle groups had an even smaller net income per worker from off-farm earnings than those on the extremes. Since they were not forced to sell their labour by necessity like the poor, and had no surplus of production capital, either, as opposed to the wealthy group, off-farm earnings had marginal relevance to the middle peasant class.

Not only the quantity but also the structure of off-farm work depended on the level of peasant wealth. The diversity of sources for additional income was similar in all groups, but the poor households tended to be involved more in off-farm earnings in industry (Table 8.9). Work in industrial enterprises was monotonous, hard, and fraught with the danger of injuries, so wealthy peasants, probably, tried to abstain from it, even if high nominal wage rates were offered. Poor households had more wage labourers and fewer self-employed workers than wealthy ones.

Table 8.8. The Kharkiv sample ranged by arable land per capita and divided into four groups (Chaianov, 1915)

	Upper	Upper middle	Lower middle	Lower	All
N	25	25	25	26	101
Arable land per capita, dessiatines	3.1	1.7	1.2	0.4	1.6
Households with off-farm earnings	72%	76%	96%	100%	86%
People of working age per household	4.0	3.7	3.4	2.6	3.4
Off-farm earners per household	1.4	1.7	2.2	2.9	2.1
Off-farm earners to people of working age	43%	44%	74%	119%	71%
Net income from off-farm earnings per household, roubles	91.9	42.4	77.5	109.6	80.7
Net income from off-farm earnings per worker, roubles	86.5	26.3	37.9	40.1	46.1
Net to gross income from off-farm earnings	94%	90%	94%	78%	88%
Arable land, dessiatines	34.9	24.5	16.0	5.1	20.0
Agricultural machines and tools per household, roubles	212.2	113.1	81.3	29.9	108.3
Gross income, roubles	857.1	501.6	372.1	243.1	491.0

Table 8.9. The structure of off-farm income in the Kharkiv sample, grouped according to the size of arable land per household, in dessiatines (Chaianov, 1915: 90)

	>15 D.	>7.5 AND ≤15 D.	>3 AND ≤7.5 D.	>0 TO ≤3 D.	0 D.	ALL
N	22	25	26	17	11	101
Days spent on work on own farm	35%	24%	12%	12%	5%	24%
Days spent on off-farm work outside own village	0%	2%	4%	6%	26%	4%
Women among off-farm earners	18%	30%	19%	41%	42%	29%
Literate among household members	45%	38%	37%	31%	13%	38%
Off-farm earning in economic sectors						
In industry	3%	2%	10%	0%	12%	5%
In agriculture	18%	34%	29%	36%	21%	28%
Artisanship and crafts	26%	12%	19%	13%	9%	16%
Trade, service, and other economic activities	54%	52%	42%	51%	58%	51%
Type of off-farm income						
Wage labour	57%	70%	67%	69%	72%	67%
Self-employed	43%	22%	26%	14%	16%	24%
Wage labour and self-employed	0%	8%	8%	17%	13%	9%

The poorer the household, the more days its members spent outside their village, and the more they had to involve women and children in generating off-farm earnings. The involvement of children and teenagers in off-farm work in poor households distracted them from receiving education: the level of literacy in wealthy households was double compared with the poor ones.

V. Discussion: Summary of the analysis

The narrative sources interpret the idea of selling labour power as something unnatural for peasants, caused by poverty and the scarcity of land. Qualitative evidence confirms that land was the most valued resource for the peasants. They rented plots from the landlords, the state, or their peers who, for various reasons, could not or did not want to work there. However, the means of production, labour resources, and opportunities for supplemental earnings were distributed unequally geographically and among the peasant households. Therefore, off-farm earnings were an important means of balancing family needs, production resources, and labor surplus.

Work on one's farm produced more economic value than off-farm earnings. Aleksandr Chelintsev calculated that in 1915, peasants made 54% from off-farm earnings compared to what they would make on their own farm in the same working time (Chelintsev, 1919: 71). The amount of earnings outside of their own farm was inversely proportional to the peasants' wealth. Nevertheless, many wealthy households also tapped off-farm income opportunities when they had spare time and labour surplus.

Off-farm earnings constituted an important but supplementary source of income for the peasants in Ukraine. In principle, peasants had several options to generate revenue from outside their farm, through self-employment and wage labour. In practice, their ability to make their own free choices depended on their wealth. For wealthy peasants, off-farm earnings were a 'nice to have' option. They were not compelled to take the first opportunity they got; instead, they could wait for a fair option and earn good money for their work. In contrast, necessity pushed poor households to take any job, and, in this respect, they had little agency; the existing structures determined their economic actions.

It is not only the level of wealth that determines peasant agency. Many external factors, such as proximity to large urban settlements or industrial clusters, also contributed to their decisions. Peasants from the villages located close to cities had more opportunities for temporary work without leaving the farm than did their peers in the remote rural areas.

Working tools and machines, draught animals, and other means of production significantly increased peasant agency in terms of off-farm incomes. Besides providing more options, they impacted the productivity and profitability of work. Data on wage prices in Kharkiv province in the period from 1906 to 1910 shows that a waged worker with a horse received double, and with a pair of oxen, triple remuneration compared to a worker without draught animals (Khar'k. gub. zem. uprava, 1913: 66-69, 82-85).

Agricultural machines helped to save time during hectic harvest periods and provided the possibility of converting this time into an additional income. Viktor Vasilenko, who conducted an expeditionary survey of the weaving industry in Poltava province in 1898, noticed that wealthy peasants were weaving for sale. It surprised Vasilenko because, traditionally, rich peasants limited production only to family needs. He explained the new phenomenon by the proliferation of agricultural machines. The machines significantly increased the productivity and speed of agricultural work, so the well-equipped peasants could spare time and spend it to get extra income by undertaking some side income (Vasilenko, 1900: 44).

Access to the means of production created opportunities for the wealthy, while the lack of it severely limited the agency of poor peasants. The same survey by Viktor Vasilenko demonstrated that weaving, one of the most popular forms of side income in the area, was 'inextricably linked with agriculture and animal husbandry, processing their products into fibre and wool'. Poor farms with little land and livestock 'could not fully use their capacity for work'. They lacked productive capital, so they either had to buy raw materials from their wealthier neighbours or sell their labour (Vasilenko, 1900: 102).

Finally, the economic standing of a household could add to their wage bargaining power. The Kherson and Kharkiv samples show that clothing expenditure in the upper quartile of peasant households was three times more than in the lower quartile. The wealthiest peasants were twice as educated as their poor counterparts. Better clothing, more advanced hygiene practices, and better education increased the human capital of the wealthy peasants, which they could convert into economic value. Wealthy households had more advanced networks and influence on the members of the local community. Finally, they had more means to apply informal practices to seek better side income opportunities, such as bribing managers at industrial enterprises to get better jobs (Kulikov, 2018).

Off-farm earnings impacted farm production differently for wealthy and poor peasants. For poor households, side earnings competed with their own farm and hindered its development. For wealthy households, off-farm earnings were a useful addition to utilize excessive labour resources more organically. In households with enough arable land, the peasants decided whether to intensify labour in their household or embrace off-farm income-generating activities. For them, it was not a big dilemma. For poor households, it was a trade-off. Poverty-stricken workers often had to accept a job during the harvest season when there was a lot of work on their farms and redirected labour to off-farm activities (Efimenko, 1884: 555), thus decreasing the productivity of their own farms (Chelintsev, 1919: 73). For wealthy peasants, off-farm earnings were the source of additional resources that could improve both the farm and the household members' well-being. In the case of poor peasants, off-farm earnings hampered the development of the household and decreased the quality of life of its members.

The peasants were only partly engaged in the markets, which is why their economic rationale was only partly determined by profit maximization (Ellis, 1993: 278). Such half-hearted involvement in the markets led to inconsistent economic behaviour. Along with economic structures, many non-economic reasons shaped the working practices of the peasants. Family conflicts, curiosity, interest in new experiences and adventures, and tiredness of the monotony of farm life were among the reasons to seek migratory off-farm work.

Besides that, to better understand peasant agency, it is worth zooming in to look at the actions of individual peasants within a household. Frank Ellis reasonably pointed out that scholars often treat a peasant household as a single decision-making unit and ignore the impact of intra-household relations on economic behaviour (Ellis, 1993: 282). However, peasants were not a homogeneous group with the same standings and pursuits; rather, household members could have different, even conflicting, interests and inter-house relationships that varied from cooperation to conflict.

This also applies to off-farm earnings. Traditionally, income from one's own farm was considered a household asset, and the male head of household (the patriarch) disposed of it. But only part of the money earned outside of the household went to the common pot, while the rest accumulated in the earners' pockets. That is why young, unmarried family members preferred off-farm earnings to work in their household, even if the former was less profitable and riskier (Efimenko, 1884: 551). A contemporary, Aleksandr Iaroshko, noted that a peasant girl who stays at home has 'nothing except for linen spun during winter months'. In contrast, a girl who chose wage labour 'in three years has an excellent dowry'. 'No wonder' – says Iaroshko – 'that as soon as a girl grows up, wage labour opportunity magnetises her' (Iaroshko, 1894: 39).

Quantitative data shows that the share of female off-farm workers significantly increased during the late nineteenth and early twentieth century. In 1885, in Poltava province, 9234 female peasants had migratory off-farm earnings. This number increased to 23,399 by 1910 (153% increase). Compared to that, the increase of male earners – from 50,500 to 58,276 (15% increase) – looks very modest (Tverdova-Svavitskaia-Svavitskii, 1926: 298-304). A contemporary statistician, Viktor Vasilenko, found that from 1877 to 1896, the number of female migratory earners among the Poltava peasants increased threefold. Commenting on this trend, Vasilenko compared it to 'a rapidly increasing snowball rolling down a steep hill' (Vasilenko, 1900: 104).

The growing involvement of young family members increased their economic independence and led to social and cultural structural changes within peasant communities. Income earned by young migrant workers considerably contributed to undermining the authority of the head of the household (Häfner, 2019: 556). This inevitably caused conflicting situations within families. Statistician Stepan Bleklov recalls that when he surveyed peasants in Poltava province, many household heads complained that their children did not bring home enough money, excusing themselves with high living costs (Bleklov, 1894: 53). Bleklov acknowledges that heads of the household had insufficient power to force their junior family members to 'reveal the real financial situation' (Bleklov, 1894: 53). The modernization process introduced new models that undermined patriarchal dynamics within households. One such model was "voice," which refers to the right and ability of household members to participate in decision-making. Another was "exit," which involves the socially and economically viable alternatives available to household members if cooperative solutions cannot be reached (Katz, 1997: 25).

The examples mentioned by Vasilenko and Bleklov present a typical agency problem: what was desirable for the household was not a priority for the workers. Since increasing the productivity of individuals was a common interest of the household and the employers, they tried to cooperate. Iakov Brave mentions that some heads of peasant households used to sign contracts with the agents of potential employers. The agents offered the household heads lower wages for the junior family members than the job seekers could get on the spot. Instead, the agents guaranteed to keep the co-opted earners 'from vacillation, idleness, drunkenness, and unnecessary expenses', in which, apparently, many of them were involved (Brave, 1899: 58-59). In practice, the agents had a limited arsenal of methods to keep the hired peasants at the workplace for a long time and make them work hard.

The analysis of budget samples shows that the economic decisions of peasants in the Ukrainian provinces were less determined by the markets than was suggested by the Soviet scholars (Koval'chenko-Moiseenko-Selunskaia, 1988), and peasants were more economically rational than hypothesized in Chaianov's model. Mark Harrison provides the most accurate model that describes peasant economic decisions from the region explored in this study. The evidence presented in this chapter aligns with his suggestion to distinguish between the involuntary unemployment of the poor and the voluntary idleness of rich peasants (Harrison, 1975: 411).

VI. Peasants in the Ukrainian Provinces and the Integrated Peasant Economy Concept

This section applies the results of the analysis to the IPE framework. It starts with the table of activities identified by Aleksander Panjek (Panjek, 2017: 21), which will allow a comparison of the peasant economy in the Ukrainian provinces with that in other European countries.

Table 8.10 shows that most of the activities identified for the Western European and southern Alpine, as well as for the western Slovenian area, apply to the case of the Ukrainian provinces. Just as in the western Slovenian lands, the presence of such activities in Ukraine varied 'in time, at the local level as well as in the whole area, not least as a response to the wider economic conjuncture or change' (Panjek, 2017: 22).The factual material presented in this chapter shows that the peasant economy in the Ukrainian provinces of the Russian Empire met most of the criteria characterizing the integrated peasant economy (Panjek, 2017: 25).

Peasants in the Ukrainian provinces combined agriculture and market-oriented activities to make a living and raise their living standards (**Criteria 1**). Off-farm income was generated by most peasant households (**Criteria 2**). It was a crucial income source for poor peasants and a supplementary option for middle-class and wealthy peasants. The peasants had to make a choice between farm work, off-farm income activities, and leisure, where farm work was considered toilsome, and off-farm work was even less desirable (but there were exceptions when peasants decided otherwise, for personal reasons). Peasants relied on income sources from primary, secondary, and tertiary economic sectors (**Criteria 3**). The combination of these sectors depended on the local opportunities and traditions.

Off-farm peasant earning practices were dynamic. They adapted to changes in the availability of income sources (**Criteria 4**). However, most off-farm income opportunities were related to fragmented and distorted labour markets. Peasants made ill-informed decisions about off-farm labour allocation. Wealthy households were in a better position compared to their poorer peers. The former had resources to travel closer to better-paid jobs and were better equipped with working tools.

By the 1870s, peasants in the Ukrainian provinces had already failed to have enough arable land to absorb all the potential workforce. The following decades brought a rapid increase in the population, and the shortage of land became a pressing problem. More and more peasants had to look for off-farm income in the agricultural sector, industry, and service. Industrialization and urbanization presented a wide range of opportunities to job seekers from villages (**Criteria 5**). Income sources related to the use of commons (**Criteria 6**) played a marginal role, but community forests, ponds, and pastures provided crucial resources for crafts.

The peasants were only partly engaged in the markets, which is why their economic rationale was only partly determined by profit maximization (**Criteria 7**). Such partial involvement in the markets led to a diversity of economic behaviour of the peasants.

When discussing peasant economic agency, it is necessary to consider intra-household relations instead of treating peasant households as a single decision-making unit. Besides economic reasons, there were other factors behind the decisions peasants made, which led to patterns of behaviour that have historically been labelled as irrational. Even so, one can better understand such underlying motivations by considering the variety of individual interests within a peasant household.

Acknowledgements

I thank the editors and Kyra Lyublyanovics for their comments and guidance through the review process.

Funding

This study was accomplished during a visiting scholarship at Matej Bel University, supported by the National Scholarship Programme of the Slovak Republic.

Table 8.10. Economic activities providing income to peasants: Ukrainian provinces of the Russian Empire in the Late Nineteenth and Early Twentieth Century

Activity	Check
Primary sector	
Agricultural specialization	Only in some regions. The majority focused on grain production
Intensification of cultivation	Only a minority of the wealthy households. The agricultural system is backward compared to Western peers
Wage day-labour in agriculture and longer-term farmhands on larger farms	Yes, very popular
Extension/intensification of animal husbandry	Only in some advanced, wealthy households or in those that received support from the agronomists
Intensification of forest exploitation	No evidence
Extension of cultivated land (reclamation of commons and woods)	Yes, where it was possible
Quarries	Yes, where it was possible
Fishing	Yes, where it was possible
Secondary sector	
Transformation of primary resources/products	Yes
Rural crafts	Yes
Domestic, putting-out system (proto-industry)	Yes
Work in 'centralized' industries and plants	Yes, mostly poor households
Migrant/mobile craftsmen	Yes, often in the form of an artel, a working cooperative association
Wage labour in the industrial sector	Yes
Tertiary sector	
Services in the field of long and medium distance trade	Yes
Transport of other people's products and goods over short to medium distances	Yes
Trade in own products and goods over short to medium distances	Yes
Peddling	Probably, but no evidence
Smuggling	Probably, but no evidence
Migrant/mobile workers	Yes
Works of trust	No evidence
Tourism	No evidence

Bibliography

A'Hearn, B., Amendola, N. and Vecchi, G. (2016), 'On historical household budgets', *Rivista di storia economica*, 32, pp. 137-176.

Arnol'd, V. F. (1902), Obshchie cherty agronomicheskoi tekhniki i sel'skokhoziaistvennoi ekonomii krest'ianskikh khoziaistv Khersonskogo uezda, Kharkiv, Khersonskoe uezdnoe zemstvo.

Bleklov, S. M. (1894), Za faktami i tsiframi: Zapiski zem. statistika, Moscow, tip. D. I. Inozemtseva.

Brave, I. F. (1899), Naemnye sel'skokhoziaistvennye rabochie v zhizni i v zakonodatel'stve: Obshchestv.-iurid. ocherki, Moscow, Knizhnoe delo.

Chaianov, A. V. (1915), Biudzhety krest'ian Starobel'skogo uezda Khar'kovskoi gubernii, Kharkiv, Khar'kovskoi gubernskoi zemskoi upravy.

——— (1929), Biudzhetnye obsledovaniia: Istoriia i metody, Moscow, Novyi agronom.

——— (1989), Krest'ianskoe khoziaistvo. Izbrannye trudy, Moscow, Ekonomika.

Chelintsev, A. N. (1919), Teoreticheskie osnovaniia organizatsii krest'ianskogo khoziaistva, Kharkiv, Agronomiia.

Cheremukhin, N. M. (1910), 'Kak zhivut i kak pitaiutsia rabochie Rykovskikh kopei v pos. Iuzovke', Vrachebno-sanitarnaia khronika Ekaterinoslavskoi gubernii, pp. 1-21.

Dep. oklad. sborov (1903), Materialy vysochaishe uchrezhdennoi 16 noiabria 1901 g. Komissii po issledovaniiu voprosa o dvizhenii s 1861 g. po 1900 g. blagosostoianiia sel'skogo naseleniia srednezemledel'cheskikh gubernii, sravnitel'no s drugimi mestnostiami Evropeiskoi Rossii. Chast' 1, St. Petersburg, tip. P.P. Soikina.

Efimenko, P. S. (1884), 'Otkhod krest'ian iz Khar'kovskoi gubernii.', Khar'kovskii kalendar' i pamiatnaia knizhka na 1885 god, Kharkiv, tip. Gubernskogo pravleniia.

Ellis, F. (1993), Farm households and agrarian development, Cambridge, Cambridge University Press.

Field, D. (1989), 'The Polarization of Peasant Households in Prerevolutionary Russia: Zemstvo Censuses and Problem of Measurement', *Research in Economic History*, 5, p. 477-505.

Häfner, L. K. (2019), 'Engines of Social Change? Peasant Migration and the Transgression of Spatial, Legal and Cultural Divides in Late Imperial Russia', *Journal of Borderlands Studies*, 34, pp. 547-570.

Harrison, M. (1975), 'Chayanov and the Economics of the Russian Peasantry', *The Journal of Peasant Studies*, 2, pp. 389-417.

Hunt, D. (1979), 'Chayanov's model of peasant household resource allocation', *The Journal of Peasant Studies*, 6, pp. 247-285.

Iaroshko, A. A. (1894), Rabochii vopros na Iuge. Ego proshedshee, nastoiashchee i budushchee, Moscow, Tipo-lit. T-va Kushnerev i Ko.

Katz, Elizabeth. (1997) 'The intra-household economics of voice and exit', *Feminist economics*, 3, no. 3, pp. 25-46.

Kaufman, A. A. (1908), Agrarnyi vopros v Rossii: Lektsii, chit. v Mosk. nar. un-te v 1907 g. 1-2, Moscow, Tip. t-va I.D. Sytina.

Khar'k. gub. zem. uprava (1913), Svodnye dannye za 5-letie 1906-1910 g. o podennykh i srokovykh platakh, ob urozhae khlebov i o bazarnykh tsenakh na produkty polevodstva, Kharkiv, Khar'k. gub. zem. uprava. Otd. tekushchei statistiki.

Klepikov, S. A. (1920), Pitanie russkogo krest'ianstva. Ch. 1. Normy potrebleniia glavneishikh pishchevykh produktov, Moscow, Tip. III Internatsional.

Kolodub, E. K. (1905), Trud i zhizn' gornorabochikh na Grushevskikh antratsitnykh rudnikakh, Moscow, Tip I. Ia. Poliakova.

Korenevskaia, N. N. (1954), Biudzhetnye obsledovaniia krest'ianskikh khoziaistv v dorevoliutsionnoi Rossii, Moscow, Gos. statisticheskoe izd-vo.

Koval'chenko, I. D., Moiseenko, T. L. and Selunskaia, N. B. (1988), Sotsial'no-ekonomicheskii stroi krest'ianskogo khoziaistva evropeiskoi Rossii v epokhu kapitalizma, Moscow, MSU.

Kulikov, V. O. (2018), 'Neformal'ni trudovi vidnosyny na promyslovyh pidpryjemstvah Rosijs'koi' imperii' v ostannij tretyni XIX – na poch. XX st', Misto: istorija, kul'tura, suspil'stvo. E-zhurnal urbanistychnyh studij.

——— (2019), Pidpryjemstva j suspil'stvo v zavods'kyh i shahtars'kyh poselennjah Donbasu ta Prydniprov'ja v 1870-1917 rr., Kharkiv, Vyd-vo HNU imeni V. N. Karazina.

Lipskii, (1902), Tseny na rabochie ruki pri zablagovremennom naime na sel'skokhoziaistvennye raboty, St. Petersburg, izd. A. Novikova.

Mironov, B. N. (1999), '"Vsiakaia dusha prazdniku rada": Trud i otdykh v russkoi derevne vtoroi poloviny XIX – nachala XX veka', Problemy sotsial'no-ekonomicheskoi i politicheskoi istorii Rossii XIX – XX vekov, St. Petersburg, Aleteiia.

——— (2015), Rossiiskaia imperiia: ot traditsii k modernu. V 3 tomakh. Tom 3, St. Petersburg Dmitrii Bulanin.

Morachevskii, V. V. (1903), 'Promysly i zaniatiia naseleniia [Malorossii]', Semenov, V. P. (ed.), Rossiia: polnoe geograficheskoe opisanie nashego otechestva. Nastol'naia i dorozhnaia kniga dlia russkikh liudei. Tom 7: Malorossiia, St. Petersburg, Izd-vo A. F. Devriena.

Nafziger, S. (2010), 'Peasant communes and factor markets in late nineteenth-century Russia', *Explorations in Economic History*, 47, pp. 381-402.

Opatskii, A. N. (1912), Fabrichno-zavodskaia promyshlennost' Khar'kovskoi gubernii i polozhenie rabochikh, Kharkiv, Tip. firmy 'Adol'f Darre'.

Panjek, A. (2017), 'The Integrated Peasant Economy as a Concept in Progress', Panjek, A., Larsson, J. and Mocarelli, L. (eds), Integrated Peasant Economy in a Comparative Perspective. Alps, Scandinavia, and Beyond, Koper, University of Primorska Press.

PoltZemstvo, 1907. Statisticheskii ezhegodnik Poltavskogo gubernskogo zemstva na 1907 god, Poltava, Statisticheskoe biuro Potavskogo gubernskogo zemstva.
Rybnikov, A. A. (1922), Melkaia promyshlennost' i ee rol' v vosstanovlenii russkogo narodnogo khoziaistva, Moscow, Koop. izd-vo.
Simms, J. Y. (1982), 'The Crop Failure of 1891: Soil Exhaustion, Technological Backwardness, and Russia's "Agrarian Crisis"', *Slavic Review*, 41, pp. 236-250.
Tverdova-Svavitskaia, Z. M. and Svavitskii, N. A. (1926), Zemskie podvornye perepisi 1880-1913: Pouezdnye itogi, Moscow, TsSU SSSR.
Vasilenko, V. I. (1900), Ocherki kustarnykh promyslov Poltavskoi gubernii: Vyp. 1: Priadenie i tkachestvo v Zen'kovskom i Mirgorodskom uezdakh, Poltava, Tipo-litografiia I. A. Dokhmana.
Villari, L. (1905), Russia Under the Great Shadow, London, London T.F. Unwin.
Zaks, A. B. (1955), 'Trud i byt rabochikh Donbassa', Pankratova, A. M. (ed.), Istoriko-bytovye ekspeditsii. 1951-1953: Materialy po istorii proletariata i krest'ianstva Rossii kontsa XIX – nachala XX veka. 1951-1953, Moscow, Gosizdat.

LEV CENTRIH AND POLONA SITAR

9. 'Those who had paid jobs and worked on farms were living the best lives'

Integrated peasant economy in socialist Slovenia

I. Introduction

The aim of the following article is to check the presence of and elucidate the integrated peasant economy in socialist Slovenia between the 1960s and 1980s. The period was marked by a steady decline of the peasant population and an extensive deployment of agricultural machinery to the private farming sector. Modernization was in full swing but not without contradictions. Social scientists claimed that at the beginning of this period a new urban-rural type of family emerged (Klemenčič, 1965: 610). The share of peasants in official statistics for Slovenia in 1981 was only 9.1% – however, as much as 58% of the population still lived in the countryside (Barbič, 1990: 296).

The development in question was shaped by two factors: a) changes in agricultural policy and attitude regarding the peasantry by the socialist state; and b) rapid industrialization immediately after 1945 but relatively slow urbanization until the 1960s.

The Yugoslav socialist revolution, with certain restrictions, maintained the right of private property over land. Until 1953, peasant households could own as much as 30 ha of land, from then on (until 1988) the maximum was lowered to 10 ha. The constitution of 1974, however, left open the option of unlimited private lease of arable land (Veselinov, 1987: 33). The agrarian reform of 1945 in Slovenia confiscated (with no compensation) large estates, mostly owned by foreigners with a feudal background, land owned by enterprises or banks, and church estates above 10 ha. Arable land over the amount of 30 ha owned by famers, and small rural businessmen, who could retain up to 5 ha of land, had been expropriated, but their former owners were entitled to financial compensation. Land had been confiscated from all adversaries of the national liberation movement and later also from other prosecuted individuals. Nonetheless, the total share of the confiscated or expropriated land was not very large. When the agrarian reform was completed in 1949, the share of private property

Integrated Peasant Economy in Central and Eastern Europe, ed. by Aleksander Panjek, Rural History in Europe, 18 (Turnhout: Brepols, 2024), pp. 231–264
BREPOLS PUBLISHERS 10.1484/M.RURHE-EB.5.142470

over arable land, compared to state-owned, in Slovenia was still between 82 and 93%. The state took over forests, confiscated mostly from the Catholic Church, while the confiscated or expropriated arable land was either transformed into state agricultural enterprises, or assigned to other institutions and enterprises sponsored by the state. No one was allotted a substantial share, and only a small part was actually transferred to small and landless peasants as their private property or to the peasants' cooperatives, amounting to about 13% of all confiscated land. On a Yugoslav scale, the state retained half of the confiscated and expropriated land (Čepič, 1995: 111-129, 244-245).

How to integrate small landowners into the national economy in order to boost agricultural surpluses for the industrialization had been a challenge for the communist authorities ever since the agrarian reform. Until the early 1950s, the policy was very tough: peasants were obliged to sell their surpluses to the state and there had even been an unsuccessful attempt at collectivization. These measures were accompanied with political campaigns but also with coercion (Čoh Kladnik, 2012). In the late 1950s, the regime adopted a more favourable policy ('cooperation') regarding the peasantry, which included much better terms of trade between farmers and the state through cooperatives. The authorities hoped to integrate small land producers through the renting of agricultural machinery. However, due to the lack of interest and economic effects, the regime gave up and from 1967, private farmers finally became eligible to receive credits to buy their own machinery (Čepič, 1999; Veselinov, 1987: 62). Shortly thereafter, in the 1970s, the number of privately owned tractors skyrocketed.

After the war, industrialization pumped the labour force from the countryside to the towns and cities. In Slovenia/Yugoslavia in the late 1940s, at the time of the first five-year plan, quitting farm work for industry was not always voluntary or an individual choice. For example, it was estimated that in 1949 no less than 26,000 new workers in Slovenia were required to meet plan targets in industry, construction, forestry, and mining. According to the data considered by the bureau of the Central Committee of the Communist Party of Slovenia (CC CPS), only 10,000 individuals were expected to apply, while the rest were supposed to be 'mobilized' (Drnovšek, 2000, Zapisnik seje biroja CK KPS, April 20th 1949: 150). This mobilization took several forms: some individuals were administratively assigned to factory jobs after they were dismissed from military service (Čepič 1991: 87), and there were also cases when participants in voluntary Sunday work (labour brigades) were bullied in order to be employed as a regular labour force (AS 1589, Dnevne informacije, March 11th 1950: 7). The Party also anticipated that some peasants would quit farming due to high taxation, and increasing quotas of mandatory sale of products to the state (Čepič, 1991: 89; Drnovšek, 2000: 150). This policy changed in the early 1950s and searching for employment in industry became again a matter of individual choice. At that time a significant number of workers still lived in the countryside. In 1953, as much as 70% of construction workers, more than 60% of miners, and 55% of industrial workers lived in rural areas (Levstik, 1964b: 14). The state saved substantial resources for housing as a consequence. In the late 1960s, a polycentric development model had been introduced in Slovenia. More and more industrial enterprises were opened in the countryside: between 1951 and 1984, townships with industry more than doubled in number (Klemenčič, 1991: 27; Čepič, 2005: 1133).

In the post-war period, labels such as 'semi-proletarians', 'part-time farmers', 'workers-peasants', or just 'peasants' were coined to comprehend the reality of the significant part of the labour force who were migrating from their small family farms to industrial centres on a daily basis (Levstik, 1964a: I). As in socialist Slovenia also in Hungary after the forced collectivization commuting from the villages to industrial towns was easy and widespread. According to Varga (2013: 212) after the third wave of collectivization that occurred in the winter of 1958-1959 farming families in Hungary rediscovered their interest in satisfying subsistence needs outside the cooperatives and, if the industrial sector offered possibility of employment, men were quick to avail of it while women or elder members of the family joined the cooperative in his place. It was typical for members to work in the cooperative only on the understanding that this granted them the right to have household plots. Day-labour opportunities were thus exploited, as were those that involved working illegally in construction or on nearby state farms where labour could expect to be paid. From this example we can see that also the cooperative households were able to integrate different income sources. Although in the beginning this represented a temporary survival strategy, later these families became financially the most successful ones in the village, as they had two active earners and also an income from the household plot.

From the 1960s, Slovenian scholarship adopted the terminology and typologies developed in western agrarian economics, rural sociology, and international institutions such as OECD and FAO: 'full-time households', 'part-time households' (sometimes subdivided in two categories according to the number of the household members employed outside the holding), 'residential farm households', etc. (Kovačič, 1983: 25-40). Social scientists like Stane Krašovec, Jože Levstik, Vladimir Klemenčič, Ana Barbič, and Matija Kovačič focused on rural households rather than individuals. Rural households by no means combined their incomes exclusively from agriculture and off-farm work. For that reason, Ana Barbič paid attention to complementary activities, performed on the farms but only indirectly related to agriculture, such as lumbering, beekeeping, transportation services, crafts, tourism, etc. (Barbič, 1990: 137-142; Barbič, 2000).

In the following article, the concept of the integrated peasant economy (IPE) is used in order to comprehend this complex historical reality. The concept in question has proved to be very useful in order to explain economic strategies conducted by peasant households in the Alpine region, Scandinavia, and partly also in Japan through the modern era up to the twentieth century. Numerous case studies elucidated economies in which peasant households combined several different economic activities to make their living. Primary, secondary, and tertiary sector activities were recognized as equivalent components of the whole, which formed the peasant economy in a certain time and place (Panjek-Larsson-Mocarelli, 2017). According to the IPE concept, self-consumption agriculture may thus not necessarily be the primary economic activity of the peasant's household. Market-oriented activities may represent an equally important income source for the peasant's families (Panjek, 2017: 24-24). With the IPE concept it is also possible to comprehend the resilience of small peasant holdings in the period of development of capitalism which introduced large scale and, above all, market-oriented farming and global market competition. The family farm economy through the modern age proved to be flexible; it adapted not only to internal (family structure and its needs) and external (market, politics) changes but also to the limits posed by the environment. According to Panjek, the integrated peasant economy 'enabled rural societies to overcome natural and technical limits, and to significantly raise the carrying-capacity of the environment they lived in, since it allowed sustaining a population beyond the level that would have been possible based solely on agricultural land and the self-consumption of its produce' (2017: 25). IPE's applicability to rural Slovenia has already been proven not only for the preindustrial period (Beguš, 2017), for which it was originally developed, but for the industrialization and interwar period as well (Lazarević, 2018a).

The case of peasant holdings and households in socialist Slovenia, dealt with here, is challenging for the IPE holistic approach. In the modern age up to the twentieth century, a capitalist market economy significantly shaped the environment of the peasants. The socialist revolution in Slovenia/Yugoslavia, however, introduced an attempt to replace the market economy with a planned economy. Initially, this attempt considerably shrank traditional market opportunities for the peasant households but it eventually introduced others – especially the peasants' sale of their labour in quickly developing industry at unprecedented levels. The relevance of the IPE concept for socialist Slovenia has already been proven fruitful to comprehend certain phenomena of the period and environment in question: the peasant's response to reform of agricultural policy in Slovenia/Yugoslavia in the late 1950s which halted collectivization of the Soviet type (Centrih, 2020) and the case of Slovenian peasant-workers and their leisure opportunities (Sitar, 2020).

In the following article the realities of IPE strategies in socialist Slovenia through the 1960s–80s will be closely elaborated. Two basic questions will be addressed: 1) what were the main economic activities combined by the peasant households between the 1960s and 1980s and what were their motives; and b) how did these activities influence the gender division of labour within the individual peasant household?

In the second part we discuss the sources and methodology; the third part explores the economy of Slovenian peasant households, and their combination of different income sources in the broadest perspective according to the official statistical data and research conducted on large samples; the fourth part presents a case study on individual peasant households, which is based on interviews. The last part is dedicated to concluding remarks.

II. On sources and methodology

Literature that studies the history of economic life in the socialist countryside as a past process is relatively rare in Slovenia. Scholarship has been focused on the period between 1945-1965, including well elaborated topics, such as the agrarian reform of 1945 (Čepič, 1995), coercions in the late 1940s (Mikola, 2006; Čoh Kladnik, 2012), the relaxation of private initiative in agriculture in the 1950s and 1960s (Novak, 1996; Čepič, 1999; 2005; Lazarević, 2018b), migrations from rural to urban areas (Čepič, 1991), and the public image of peasantry and part-time farmers since the late 1960s in Slovenia (Visković Razpotnik-Serućnik, 2013).

Since the period from the late 1960s until the 1980s has been relatively neglected by the current historiography, we relied on scientific elaborations conducted in the corresponding socialist period. We made great use of the pioneering research on the semi-proletariat in Slovenia conducted by a group of scholars, (agrarian) economists, and their students in the early 1960s, led by Jože Levstik (1964). Besides the elaborations of official statistical data, which already took into account the phenomenon of part-time farming households, their research included detailed surveys of one hundred semi-proletarian households from different parts of Slovenia, largely selected according to the residence of the students who conducted them (Levstik, 1964b: 26-27). Dragan Veselinov's book *Sumrak seljaštva* [Twilight of the Peasantry] (1987) is the most in-depth study on the history of agrarian policies in socialist Yugoslavia up to date. Veselinov's book is rich with statistical data and references on sources. According to his thesis, part-time farm households had been the most typical feature of 'deagrarization' in Yugoslavia that was in full speed through 1957-1974, meaning the transition of the population from agriculture to industry. The developmental tendency of agricultural households appeared to be the following: the income originating outside of agriculture obtained by a household member, typically employed in industry, is initially considered as supplementary. According to Veselinov, the process ends when agriculture itself becomes a supplementary or even a recreational activity for the household. In Yugoslavia in 1965, the farming households' income share from non-agricultural activities was 35.7%, while in 1975 the share had already risen to 50.8% (Veselinov, 1987: 118-120). It is also worth noting the important monograph of the Croatian economist Branko Horvat entitled *The Postwar Evolution of the Yugoslav Agricultural Organization*. The study is especially useful for the scientific community not eloquent in Serbian, Croatian or Slovene. It is true, however, that Horvat's analysis takes into account only data up to 1970, while Veselinov's findings are also relevant for the middle 1980s. Like Veselinov, Horvat is interested in the agricultural policies of the Yugoslav authorities, especially when it comes to finding reasons for the successes and failures of connecting private farmers with the social/state economic sector. It should be added, however, that Horvat pays slightly less attention to the phenomenon of workers – peasants or mixed households. Nevertheless, he noted that in 1960s Yugoslavia, the size of a holding (land ownership) no longer played a role in the economic differentiation in the village. A certain differentiation then existed between purely agricultural farms and mixed farms. Designating income per household member in 1967 on the average as 100 (Yugoslav average), then on agricultural farms amounted to 91 and on mixed farms 111, due to the greater income outside agriculture at the latter (Horvat – M. Kramer, 1974: 15).

Rural sociologist Ana Barbič contributed numerous researches on part-time peasant households in 1980s Slovenia. Her work is best summarized in the book *Kmetov vsakdan* [Everyday life of a farmer] (1990). The core of the book is research on the economic life of 2052 agricultural holdings in different parts of Slovenia, conducted in 1982-1983. The study explores the market orientation of the households, the strategies of combining incomes from several activities, education levels of household members, their aspirations and motivations, political affiliations, and access to health-care, pensions, and other social provisions, but also how their leisure time was been spent (Barbič, 1990). Statistical data analysis, interpretations, and typologies of Slovenian peasants' households had been provided by geographer Vladimir Klemenčič and agrarian economist Matija Kovačič (Klemenčič, 1968; 1991; Kovačič, 1983).

The primary sources for our research are divided into two types: a) the Statistical yearbook published by the Statistical Office of the Socialist Republic of Slovenia in 1990 that includes interesting data regarding part-time peasant households' sources of income from 1955 until 1988 (Statistični letopis RS, 1990); selected results from the 1991 Slovenian census of the population, households, housing, and agricultural holdings and their equipment with agricultural machinery (Ilić et al. 1994); and b) in-depth semi-structured interviews.

In the period between 2019 and 2020, we conducted interviews on the basis of common themes and questions. Through our own social network, we established contact with people from rural areas of Slovenia and conducted semi-structured interviews with them.[1] Interviews enable us to identify certain phenomena that are embedded in the broader social context to show the dynamics between the individual and the social. The selection of interlocutors was carried out using the principle of ethnographic research in the form of a snowball sampling. After we got closer to the main interlocutor in the village and conducted a semi-structured interview with him/her we asked him/her to introduce us to his/her network of people. We conducted interviews with thirty-five interlocutors throughout Slovenia born before the second World War, and with the generation of their children, born in the 1950s and 1960s. What they all had in common is that they were engaged in farming, and most of them were also involved in non-agricultural activities. The inclusion of both generations enables the understanding of the period of socialism in the Slovenian countryside through a generational perspective, which illuminates possible generational discontinuities and also common understandings.

In the study we used an oral-history-based approach, which is based on the collection of spoken and written memories of everyday life that record past events of historical significance and the attitudes of individuals towards them. Oral history narratives are written from a personal (subjective) rather than a real (objective) point of view (Ritchie, 1995; Thompson, 2000; Thomson, 2005). Oral histories have the potential to tell us 'not just what people did, but what they wanted to do, what they believed they were doing, and what they now think they did' (Portelli, 1981: 99-100). The method of oral history enabled us to gain access to the peasants' microworld. It gave us an insight into the main economic activities in the individual peasant households and their management in the daily work cycle. We were able to learn about the types of non-agricultural activities on the farm, peasants' motives, and the gender division of labour within the individual peasant household.

1 We will not name interlocutors by their real name and surname. Instead, we will use fictitious names to ensure their anonymity. However, information about gender, age, profession, year, and place of birth is real.

III. The economic activities of peasant households in socialist Slovenia in figures

The Yugoslav agriculture was an exception within the socialist agriculture in eastern European countries where communist parties in 1950s and the early 1960s followed Soviet-style collectivization policies. Just like Poland, the collectivization of agricultural land had never been completed in Yugoslavia, which abandoned collectivization altogether after 1953. This is the reason why the individual farming based on privately owned land could survive during the whole state socialist period. As pointed out by Bokovoy (2014: 197) from 1945 to 1953 the Communist Party of Yugoslavia's collectivization program was met with varying degrees of resistance and compliance among national and regional mid-level officials, their advisors, state and local party bureaucrats, and peasants. Party leaders in Yugoslavia abandoned collectivization in the face of peasant resistance, which was not the case for all other communist regimes. As observed by Swain (2014) collectivization in Eastern Europe was a complex process, and the conditions within which it was implemented varied considerably. He emphasized that the relationship between ideal type and practice was a complex one in each country. The political leaders of Eastern Europe had a common project, which was to establish rural structures that conformed to the Model Charter. However, they could not avoid entanglements with their pasts, the Soviet Union or their fellow Eastern Bloc members (Swain 2014: 498).

After the failed attempt at collectivization in Slovenia and the whole of Yugoslavia in the 1949-1951 period, it eventually became clear that it was impossible to exercise total state control over rural life in general and over agriculture in particular. At about the same time, the centrally planned economy also lost its steam on the level of industrial enterprises with the gradual introduction of workers' self-management, which initially meant more independence for companies. With the economic reform of 1965 bringing commercial credit through banks rather than state funds, the gradual deregulation of prices as well as the decentralization processes moved the system closer to the western type of a market economy (Prinčič, 1999: 215-276). Even though the 1970s brought a halt in that direction, there was no real return to the Soviet style of economy.

To be sure, the leading political force in Slovenia and Yugoslavia, The League of Communists of Slovenia (Yugoslavia), as late as the 1970s preferred a strong integration of private farming households with social agricultural enterprises and cooperatives. Preferably, a peasant would hand over his land to the social agricultural enterprise and become its employee. In return he would receive a wage, all social benefits (including pension, social, and health insurance) and a rent revenue for his formerly private land, now incorporated into the socialist agricultural enterprise. By 1982, less than 3% of all Yugoslav agricultural holdings (around 30,000 peasants) had chosen this option (Veselinov, 1987: 231-232). In fact, many other much more attractive choices were at hand for the peasant households. Combining farming and full-time jobs in industrial enterprises proved to be one of the favourites.

In general, it can be argued that at least since the mid-1950s, private peasants in Slovenia have operated within the framework of a specific Yugoslav version of socialism, which was characterized by a fragile balance between the market and the plan, accompanied with severe economic/political crisis followed by reforms. If, for the purposes of the present paper, we ignore the bitter 20th century controversies about the similarities and differences between a market and planned economy, and rely on the explanation of economist Branko Horvat, then we can say that the market and planning were not incompatible but rather complementary in the Yugoslav socialist project (2016: 328-338). If we summarize and somewhat simplify Horvat's arguments, the self – managed (market-plan) socialism should ideally work when three preconditions are met: 1) sovereignty of consumers; 2) autonomy of producers in self-managed enterprises; 3) non-market means of coordination in various nationwide agreements, consultation and arbitration. 'Planning means the perfection of market choices in order to increase the economic welfare of the community' (Horvat, 2016: 332). It might be argued that in the Slovenian/Yugoslav reality, after the abolition of ration cards/consumer coupons in the early 1950s, but especially since the 1960s, sovereignty of consumers increased enormously and so did social differentiation, autonomy of enterprises (above all the autonomy of managements and considerably less the working collectives) also grew steadily since the late 1950s until the early 1970s but became considerably limited afterwards, until the late 1980s. Through 1970s enterprises were artificially divided into smaller units, officially autonomous in decision making but in fact limited by many legal regulations. Social agreements between companies and communities were in practise frequently enforced or curtailed by the political authorities (republic League of Communist leaderships), especially due to the chaos which erupted after divisions of enterprises and later due to the debt crisis (Horvat, 1989: 31-37). For that reason, social planning never actually evolved as a democratic tool, a mere coordination between companies and local communities/republics of Yugoslavia, to perfect socialist market. It was a regulatory mechanism imposed from above. It might be argued that private peasants in Slovenia/Yugoslavia at least since the late 1950s enjoyed far more autonomy in making their economic decisions than working collectives in enterprises under social ownership. Since their plots of land were on average relatively small, it is appropriate to mention the old remark by Karl Kautsky who said that 'the commodity which the small farmer produces "in abundance" is [...] *labour power*' (1988: 166). More often than not, buyers of peasants' labour power were in Yugoslav socialism industrial enterprises and sometimes also large socially owned farms, equivalents of capitalist large farms that Kautsky had in mind. When the administrative employment system was abolished in the 1950s, employment finally became more than less a matter of a personal choice, this also enlarged the autonomy of private peasants in making their economic decisions, including an option to combine income from different sources. A major obstacle was further removed in the late 1960s, when the so called system of 'cooperation' either collapsed or was reformed, largely in favour of the peasants. In late 1950s, during the 'cooperation' policy period, peasants were not forced to join collective farms, at least not by extra-economical means (intimidation, violence), but cooperatives had monopolies on crop purchases and on supplying villages with agricultural machinery, fertilizers etc. The economic reform of 1965 abolished most of monopolies enjoyed by cooperatives. To cover losses, cooperatives increased prices for their services, but since 1967 private peasants became eligible for credits to get their own machinery which expanded their economic autonomy. To be sure, cooperatives maintained certain extra income by collecting certain fees, for example if peasants bought machinery via cooperative, but a certain number of them eventually integrated or connected with processing industry and larger trade enterprises. 'These cooperatives then began to bind more lastingly to themselves those producers who could produce for the market' (Horvat, 1974: 82-83).

If we now turn back to the phenomenon of the semi-proletarians or part-time farmers, it might be argued that it became widespread in Yugoslavia in general and in Slovenia in particular. Veselinov called part-time farming the basic form of Yugoslav deagrarization-modernization (1987: 118). Levstik and his associates, in the research project on the semi-proletariat in Slovenia in the early 1960s, carefully criticized the old (orthodox) Marxist presumption that semi-proletarians necessarily belong to the strata of poor (if not the poorest) peasantry, who are unable to survive on their holdings and are forced to sell their labour to more prosperous farmers or need to find jobs in industry. According to Levstik and others, the situation significantly changed after the Second World War. Thanks to the improvement in wages and social legislation, semi-proletarians in western, but also in socialist countries, earned better wages and invested in their holdings (land and machinery) in return. In his view, the semi-proletarian came to a relatively better standard of living because his off-farm income enabled him to invest in land and agricultural machinery. The material position of a farmer-worker was often better than the position of a farmer who had a large estate and therefore could not earn additional income outside of agriculture (Levstik, 1964a: II-III).

Indeed, the war and the post-war developments significantly changed the fortunes of the rural poor in Slovenia and Yugoslavia. According to the popular census of 1931, in the Drava Banovina (today's Slovenia without the Littoral) there were as many as 81,550 farmhands, housemaids and day labourers on the farms out of the 1.1 million population (Levstik, 1964b: 6). In the post-war period, these rural proletarians were considered lost for agriculture. A report of the local communist party branch in the Ljubljana area in 1949 claimed, for example, that some farmers faced difficulties because of the lack of labour force, since farmhands and housemaids found jobs in industry. Research on the semi-proletariat later confirmed this fact. The move of the labour force from the countryside, which was not replaced by agricultural mechanization, and unfavourable agricultural policies by the young revolutionary regime encouraged even some of the remaining farmers who could make a living from farming alone, to look for revenues outside their family holdings (Levstik, 1964b: 8; Čoh Kladnik, 2012: 163). Due to these processes, between 1931 and 1948, the Slovenian peasant population decreased by 110,533 persons. By 1949, up to 250,000 individuals had quit farming as their principal occupation (Čepič, 1991: 86, 94). The situation was made even more difficult by the fact that the war had taken an extremely heavy toll among the Slovenian population – no less than 6.7% perished (Čepič et al. 2017: 426). Later, the agrarian maximum, introduced in Slovenia/Yugoslavia in 1953, which limited private property of land at 10 ha hardly motivated ambitious farmers to focus on commercial agriculture (Čepič, 1991: 91). In the following decades new motives emerged, which are discussed in the third part of this article.

The economist Stane Krašovec assumed that peasants earning their living both from industrial jobs and agriculture, as a typical phenomenon of modernization, would continue to exist for some time in the future. Yet he still considered the strata of part-time farmers ('peasant-workers') something essentially transitional (Levstik, 1964a: 3). In the following decade, the Slovenian economist Marijan Klemenčič refuted the thesis on part-time farming as a transitional phenomenon to be withered away by industrial society. As the ultimate proof, he outlined the fact that part-time farming was also widespread in the most advanced industrial societies. He observed, for example, that Italian part-time farms with 10 ha of land were better equipped with machinery than full-time farms (Klemenčič, 1974: 65).

The statistical data and our interviews support Klemenčič's argument. In fact, according to the 1991 population census, 13% (114,612) of the working population in Slovenia was employed in agriculture and fishing, but at the same time, out of a total of 640,198 households, as many as 156,531 (24%) possessed an agricultural holding. In the official statistics the latter were defined as households which used a) at least 10 Ares of arable land; or b) less than 10 Ares of land but owned at least one cow and a calf, or five full-grown sheep, or 50 heads of full-grown poultry, etc. (Ilić et al., 1994: 38, 44, 127, 259). The census further provided data on the

Table 9.1. The share of agricultural holdings by source of income in the Republic of Slovenia in the 1969, 1981, and 1991 censuses

Source of income (%)	1969	1981	1991
Purely agricultural	44.5	11.3	11.9
Mixed	44.4	27.1	36.9
Non-agricultural	8.2	60.7	50.6
Without any labour force	2.9	0.9	0.6

Source: Ilić et al. 1994: 73.

Table 9.2. Dimension, workforce, and mechanization of holdings by their source of income (1991 census)

Source of income	Average per agricultural holding			
	Total land (ha)	Annual work units	Livestock units	Power of double axle tractors (kW)
Pure-farming	7.40	1.2	3.5	17.6
Mixed	8.36	1.4	4.4	23.5
Non-farming	3.75	0.2	1.2	9.7
Without labour force	2.07	0.1	0.3	6.7

Source: Ilić et al. 1994: 376.

distinction of agricultural holdings by the source of income. Results from earlier surveys were included (Table 9.1).

Holdings with purely agricultural income (full-time farming) were considered those whose household members' activities were limited to their own agricultural holding; mixed income (part-time farming) applied to those households whose members were employed inside and outside their holdings; non-agricultural sources of income (residential farm households) were assigned to the households with all members employed outside their holdings (Ilić et al., 1994: 39). The data clearly show how full-time farming steadily declined between the late 1960s and the early 1980s, with the situation later stabilizing, but in favour of a renewed growth in the share of mixed-income holdings. The most interesting phenomenon, however, might be the strong emergence of residential farmers, that is, peasant households with officially no income from agriculture (Table 9.1). Evidence reveals that in the 1980s, part-time holdings were clearly better off in regard to the possession of land, livestock, farming machinery, and labour power (Table 9.2).

In the part-time households, among the active members of the household, males accounted for as much as 61% of all who were economically active outside their holding, while at the residential farm households this share was slightly lower, around 58% (Illić et al., 1994: 354).

Slovenian peasant households by no means combined their incomes exclusively from farming and regular jobs. Annual statistical surveys conducted by the Statistical Office of the (Socialist) Republic of Slovenia offer more detailed data on different economic activities and on the structure of peasant households' incomes. The numbers varied: in 1987, for example, 13 full-time farming households and 236 part-time households were surveyed, while in 1988 they were 10 and 238 respectively (Statistični letopis RS, 1990: 476).

Since the number of households in the survey is quite low, the data in Table 9.3 have a limited analytical value. Nonetheless, considering the data from Table 9.1, we can assume that these figures correctly indicate a declining share of income from the peasant holdings in favour of external sources. A further data comparison between Tables 9.1 and 9.3 suggests that a notable disruption took place in Slovenian peasant economies in the 1980s. From 1955 to 1975, the share of income from the peasant holdings was in steady decline, but for the later period, data in Table 9.3 suggest ups and downs in the development. In a similar way, Table 9.1 records a slight increase in the number of full-farming households through 1981-1991, and a substantial increase of part-time farming along with a remarkable decline of residential farming. Even more telling is the sudden increase of income deriving from agriculture between 1985 and 1988 which is close to the mid-1950s figures. A notable disruption, between 1985-1988, apparently also took place in supplementary activities such as transport services and handicrafts. Major disruptions took place in the sale of real estate and machinery, and in obtaining loans, dowries, etc. Between 1980 and 1985 these types of income considerably increased but then, between 1985 and 1988, decreased by half. The causes of this disruption in this period can be attributed to the severe economic and political crisis in Slovenia and Yugoslavia.[2] In 1981, Yugoslavia's foreign debt reached 20 billion USD, while the foreign trade deficit jumped from 1.7 billion in 1973 to 7.9 billion USD in 1979. Yugoslavia was unable to service its debts and was forced into austerity measures. Between 1986 and 1988, the pressures of

2 This interpretation was proposed by dr. Žarko Lazarević during the discussion of the draft version of this paper.

foreign creditors were intensified and the Yugoslav government was forced to deregulate prices, press on wages, and reduce expenditures for the public sector (Lorenčič, 2012: 46-47).

How did Slovenian peasant households manage in this period of social and political disturbances? Some insights are provided in the research by Ana Barbič carried out in 1982-1983 on 2052 agricultural holdings from different parts of Slovenia, which provides more details than public census survey results. Babič's survey divided these households into three basic groups according to occupation activities of core family members (male householder – husband, female householder – wife; male/female heir): 1) full-time farming households – all core family members worked in agriculture: 28.1%; 2) part-time farming households 1 – at least 1 core member worked at the farm, at least 1 was employed outside: this group was the largest, 59% of all cases under survey; and 3) part-time farming households 2 – all core members were farming but were also employed outside their holding: 12.9% (1990: 74).

These data are not directly comparable with data from Slovenian public censuses (Table 9.1) because different methodologies were applied. Table 9.1 reveals a high number of peasant households with non-agricultural income (no family members whose working occupation was farmer, as much as 60.7% in 1981 but dropping to 50.6% by 1991). Comparable data from Babič's survey suggests only a 12.9% share of such households (part-time farming households 2) for 1982/83. Such enormous difference between these data might be explained only by the fact that Babič's survey took into account only peasant households with possession of at least 1 ha of arable land (1990: 55), while public census surveys in Slovenia/Yugoslavia included also households with possessions as little as 10 Ares of arable land or the required number of farm animals. Available data for 1991 from the public census survey suggests that a considerable share (42%) of the Slovenian peasant households with non-agricultural income possessed less than 1.01 ha of arable land; but only 24% of those who had between 1.01-3.00 ha of land. In 1981, 32.5% of all agricultural holdings in Slovenia comprised less than 1.01 ha of land used for agricultural activities; in 1991, this share dropped to 28.4% (Ilić et al., 1994: 71-72). Apart from the different methodologies, both public census surveys and results from Babič's research suggest that pure agriculture in Slovenian peasant households was far from dominant in the 1980s. To be sure, Babič's number regarding full-time farming households is considerably higher as suggested by Table 9.1, and yet its share still makes less than one third of all households under survey.

Table 9.3. The share of income of peasant households in Slovenia by income source on average per surveyed household (1955-1988)*

Year	On-farm					Off-farm					Total %
	Agriculture %	Fruit, viticulture %	Livestock%	Other %	On-farm total %	Employment, social benefit %	Transport, handicrafts %	Other employ. related income %	Other** %	Off-farm total %	
1955	14.69	7.99	36.53	7.66	**66.87**	17.77	3.59	8.07	3.70	**33.13**	**100.00**
1960	5.16	6.84	42.94	3.28	**58.22**	19.95	4.43	10.75	6.65	**41.78**	**100.00**
1965	4.95	3.57	29.29	2.04	**39.85**	42.64	2.95	8.32	6.24	**60.15**	**100.00**
1970	1.55	3.59	25.01	1.28	**31.43**	48.39	1.55	12.31	6.32	**68.57**	**100.00**
1975	4.82	0.92	19.67	2.21	**27.62**	57.59	3.86	3.34	7.60	**72.59**	**100.00**
1980	3.88	3.79	22.31	2.51	**32.49**	53.55	3.20	7.17	3.59	**67.51**	**100.00**
1985	5.58	1.84	21.09	0.70	**29.21**	48.30	4.10	0.79	17.60	**70.79**	**100.00**
1988	12.87	1.19	18.22	1.28	**33.56**	56.78	0.41	0.92	8.33	**66.44**	**100.00**

Source: Statistični letopis RS, 1990: 488).

*In the original survey, the distinct sources of income are represented in the monetary form (dinars). Due to the hyperinflation of the 1980s, the data on revenues are comparable only in the form of shares (%) that reflect the income ratio.

**These incomes include: real estate sale (land, buildings), machinery sale, gifts, dowry, repaid and borrowed loans.

Table 9.4. The share of peasant households (n=2052) engaged in on-farm supplementary activities by type of holding and economic sector (1982-1983)

On-farm supplementary activities	Full–time farming households (all core members work at the farm)	Part–time farming households 1 (at least 1 core member works at the farm; at least 1 is employed outside)	Part – time farming households 2 (all core members are farming but also employed outside their holding)	Total (%)	
n=576	n=1211	n=265	n=2052		
Primary sector					
Forestry	25.0	15.7	14.0	**18.1**	
Work with own agricultural machine on other farm	0.5	0.2	0.4	**0.3**	**20.4**
Herb & mushroom picking & drying	0.3	1.4	1.5	**1.1**	
Beekeeping	0.5	1.1	1.1	**0.9**	
Secondary sector					
Wood processing	0.9	1.0	1.1	**1.0**	
Crafts	1.2	1.2	1.1	**1.2**	**2.8**
Construction	0.3	0.5	0.6	**0.5**	

On-farm supplementary activities	Full–time farming households (all core members work at the farm)	Part–time farming households 1 (at least 1 core member works at the farm; at least 1 is employed outside)	Part – time farming households 2 (all core members are farming but also employed outside their holding)	Total (%)	
Sewing, tailoring	0.2	-	-	**0.1**	
Blacksmithing, barrel production	-	0.2	-	**0.1**	
Tertiary sector					
Tourism	0.2	-	-	**0.1**	
Transport	0.3	1.2	0.8	**0.9**	
Agricultural machines repair	0.3	0.3	0.4	**0.3**	
Household machines repair	0.2	0.2	1.1	**0.3**	**2.2**
Automobile repair	0.2	0.1	-	**0.1**	
Inn-keeping	0.2	0.3	1.9	**0.5**	
Maximum share* (%)	**30.3**	**23.4**	**24.0**	**25.4**	

Source: elaboration of data from Barbič, 1990: 138.

*Values calculated as if each farm was active in only one activity, while in reality the same farm may have been active in more than one. This is why the values shown represent the upper possible limit; real figures would be lower.

Babič's survey also suggests that core family members were employed in the secondary sector. Few of them were fully employed in their own private enterprise. Since only 4.2% of male householders, 3.5% of female householders and 16.3% of heirs finished high school or a higher education level, it is safe to assume that most of them found jobs in industry, construction, transport, and mining (Barbič, 1990: 72-73.) The marketing of agricultural products was present in 1810 households (out of 2052) and almost 2/3 were reportedly selling up to three commodities. Peasant households were selling a minor share of their actual production. Regarding all cases under survey (2052): 85.6% of farms produced milk and 62.2% were selling it on the market, while as many as 96.5% of farms were growing vegetables, but only 8.5% also sold them on the market (Barbič, 1990: 83). Barbič believed that Slovenian peasant households could improve their well-being by expanding their on-farm supplementary activities. These activities were poorly developed (Table 9.4). It appears that the largest share was occupied by forestry – 18.1% on average, while most of the other activities were completely marginal or almost non-existent. Also, the share of certain on-farm supplementary economic activities considerably varied among Slovenian regions. In the Ljubljana municipality of Bežigrad not a single household was engaged with forestry, while in the municipality of Velenje (Styria region, eastern part of Slovenia), forestry made up as much as 99 percent of income of all on-farm supplementary activities. Transportation services, for example in two Ljubljana municipalities (Bežigrad and Moste–Polje), had as much as a 72.9 and 82.2% share of income among supplementary activities (Barbič, 1990: 137-138). Considering all reservations regarding different methodologies, these data complement well the data presented in Table 9.3 where the share of income from transport and handicraft, as compared with income from employment outside the holding, also appears very low.

IV. An oral history study on income integration in Slovenian peasant households

The oral history method offers an insight into events, their perception, and values in individual households on the topic presented in the previous section through quantitative indicators and broader social and economic processes and trends. In general, our thirty-five interviews show that most peasant households did not rely only on agriculture for their survival but often integrated agriculture with non-agrarian activities. Peasants were highly motivated to be involved in non-agrarian activities and their main motive was making money. Also, they were motivated to achieve a better standard of living and consequently improve their social status. The main motivation for off-farm activities was the realization that a peasant 'works all day and has nothing', although he still had to pay taxes and other living costs. Interlocutors often said they were not able to make a living from the farm only, since 'there was no money from the farm', usually because it was too small. Indeed, out of the twenty-two peasant family households we interviewed one family had less than 1 ha of the land, nine had between 1 and 2 ha, five between 3 and 5 ha, two between 5 and 10 ha, and five between 10 and 20 ha of land.

The majority of the interlocutors we interviewed pointed out that they sold the surplus of their agricultural products, such as vegetables, fruit, eggs, milk, and forest fruits to agricultural cooperatives, hospitals, taverns, and corporate canteens. Only two families were selling it on the nearest market. Another important source of income deriving from their farms was the intensification of forest exploitation by selling firewood, wooden boards, beams, logs, or even buying wood and reselling it. Animal husbandry was also a very common income source with approximately half of the interviewed households selling livestock, most often to the agricultural cooperative.

The agricultural cooperatives had a large impact on agricultural and non-agricultural peasant activities during socialism. They coordinated the direction of the activities on the farm and, if necessary, redirected them. This was implemented by sending out the cooperative's field promoters, who introduced peasants to new types of seeds on the market, taught them how to better manage the barn, etc. Cooperatives also provided farmers with favourable credit for buying agricultural machinery. Most importantly, they organized fruit, vegetable, milk, and livestock sales and purchased all the surplus crops from peasants. As remembered by Jože, born in 1932 in Dobrna, manager of an agricultural cooperative, this was organized also on the federal Yugoslav level:

> I bought all the fruit from the surrounding peasants in Dobrna for a little money and sold it well. I was buying and selling all over Yugoslavia because I was certified. In Split and Zadar, I had many customers for buying fruit. I also bought wood, charcoal, and lime from peasants. I picked up the goods, paid the peasants, and shipped them to the wagons.

All the interviewed members of peasant households grew their food at home and were motivated to be completely self-sufficient. In the case of lacking a particular foodstuff, peasants could acquire it by exchanging foodstuff with their neighbours. Free mutual work assistance was extremely important and favours were common among relatives, friends, and neighbours, especially for chores where a larger workforce was needed, such as building a house, mowing grass by hand, or doing fieldwork. During the expansion of agricultural mechanization, favours that involved the use of agricultural machinery came to the fore, as in the case of owning a tractor:

> In most cases it was a mutual favour. I had to pay for tractor fuel and I charged for that, but minimally. It was an atmosphere of comradeship. Some of the farmers nearby borrowed the tractor attachments from me or I went to their farm to load the hay with a loading trailer. I bought a tractor in 1968, two years before everyone else did. (Ludvik, a farmer, born in 1948 in Gornji grad near Upper Savinjska Valley)

The least common non-agrarian activity on the farm was rural tourism and owning a tavern or a shop. Only two peasant families working in this sector are present among our interviewees.

More common were migrant workers, who went to work abroad for several months, for example in Germany, Switzerland, Australia, Sweden, Argentina, Canada, or Libya. Such a case is represented by six families in our study. In this way, these migrant workers earned a larger sum of money in a relatively short period of time, which helped them to build a house or buy a tractor and other agricultural machinery. As remembered by Janez, a farmer, born in 1946 in Celje, who went to work in Libya in 1966 and returned home in 1969:

> I worked there day and night for three years in an iron works. I found Slovenians there and I also got a private job with them so I worked also on weekends. Iron works had contracts because they needed people who knew how to roll in iron works. There were several Yugoslav companies in Libya. I went to work to earn more. If you worked there for half a year, you earned enough money for the house. Various directors from here also went to work down there. At first, wages were good, in U.S. dollars, but eventually they were getting smaller.

The most common off-farm activity in socialist Slovenia according to our research was wage labour in the industrial sector and we will therefore explore this phenomenon in greater detail. Among approximately three quarters of the interviewees, at least one member of the family worked in a factory. As already pointed out by the examples in the previous section, the semi-proletariat in socialist Slovenia was a wage labour-force, often working in factories, which also retained access to the land, cultivating the land by themselves or via members of their family, and was not wholly dependent on the wage work for economic subsistence. This section offers an insight into those examples.

The interlocutors pointed out that many decided to find employment outside the farm because they realized that working at home on a farm did not provide them with regular monthly earnings. Monetary income was only occasional, often too small and seasonal in nature. Miha, born in Rakovec in 1948, who worked as an ironworker in Štore iron plant, remembered: 'I made money at work, there was no money at home. If we sold a cow or a calf, that money went for taxes or to repair something'. If no one in the peasant family was employed outside the farm, the interlocutors described this way of life as much more modest.

By being employed, peasants had a regular monthly salary, which gave them a feeling of financial security:

> By the 1980s the salaries were good. My sister's son worked in *Gorenje factory* and received a salary of 170,000 dinars. A peasant got 40,000 dinars per month for selling milk. Who was in a better position? Some workers also wanted to farm at home to be able to earn twice. Those who had paid jobs and worked on farms were living the best lives. They were protected, I was not. (Albin, born in 1936 in Zaloška Gorica near Petrovče, peasant)

Also, by being employed, peasants were entitled to a pension and health insurance. In fact, until the early 1960s, farmers were excluded from the health insurance system and had to pay for all medical expenses, while after that date the ones who were involved in the co-operative system were covered by health, pension, and disability insurances. If not, they had the opportunity to contract with state institutions and pay for their own insurance. In socialist Slovenia, general social insurance for all farmers was introduced in 1972 (at the national, Yugoslav, level only in 1979) (Centrih, 2020: 163; Lazarević, 2018b: 414).

For peasants, being employed and also working at home on the farm meant a better standard of living due to the additional income. Some people would refer to them as 'sophisticated peasants', because they could buy better clothes or a car and build better-looking houses:

> They went to work because they had no income on the farm. They earned money there and they were able to manage at home better. Let's say a farmer had three cows and he wanted one more. He could buy it now, but before no. Also, they could repair their houses. (Fanika, born in 1928 in Prožinska vas, financial clerk)

With the money from their salary, they would pay for taxes and electricity costs on the farm and maintain farm buildings, but a relevant additional motivation was the possibility of getting a loan at the workplace. Even more important seems to be the fact that additional money could be invested in their farms – buying fertilizers or new and better seeds, which meant a bigger harvest. Some peasants would invest in buying a cow or other livestock, but especially in buying agricultural machinery. Prior to the use of agricultural machinery, farmers produced less with a much greater physical burden, and its introduction into the agricultural economy enabled the expansion of production and less manual labour.

Janez, born in 1936 in Idrsko near Kobarid, a farmer and postman, recalled:

> Wealthier farmers made a living easier, they bought clothes and things like that easier. They had more money. In our village there were 80% of poor farmers and 20% of those who lived better lives. This was soon after the war and also in the 1960s, but after that those suffered. A large farmer couldn't get a job in a factory because he had to work at home.

Janez points out an interesting turn of events that occurred when smaller farmers became employed, namely that they were in a better position than larger farmers, as non-agricultural income from employment in addition to afternoon work on the farm allowed them a better standard of living compared to large farmers as their estate was too large to enable them to look for additional income outside of agriculture, since they had no spare time for an extra job.

The organization of peasant work reflects the spatial and gender division, both inside and outside the household. In the case of peasant households in which their members also had a wage, mostly men were employed, while women remained working on the farm. This feature was interpreted as a phenomenon of the feminization of Yugoslav agriculture (Vadnal, 1979: 35). As a confirmation, among our interviewees, only four families had a situation in which the husband was farming at home and his wife went to work. According to Barbič (1990: 252), peasant women were employed in smaller numbers compared to men because they had poorer employment opportunities and because someone had to stay on the farm to cultivate it. Another reason was the common belief that their place was at home with their family.

When the peasant came home from work in the factory in the nearest town, he continued working on the farm, which interlocutors described as 'working two shifts'. Alenka, born in Šempeter in the Savinja Valley in 1946, who farmed on an 8 ha farm while her husband was employed in the company *Strojna industrija SIP*, recalled:

> My husband and I worked together in the afternoon. By the time he came home from work, I had to have prepared hay in the form of a line for gathering. He drove the tractor; I threw the hay in the blowpipe. I went to the barn to feed the animals in the morning. I did also drive the tractor and I worked in the forest.

With the increasing orientation of peasants towards acquiring income from non-agricultural activities, the working role of a woman on the farm became more emphasized. The active role of women within the families as performers and also assistants in performing agricultural work with modern agricultural machinery is evident. Marina, a cook, born in 1942 in Slatina, remembered that her husband stayed at home working on the farm while she was employed as a cook at a health resort in Rogaška. Although by earning her own money at work she was able to invest the money in the purchase of a new tractor, which she bought by taking a loan at the workplace, it was her husband who was more involved in the technological investments on the farm: 'I was not for this. He managed the household economy and I went to work, cleaned, and cooked'. One may see them in the role of active managers and investors on the farm, too, although most often it was the male head of the farm who decided about vital issues, especially economic and developmental ones.

'Female work activities' would consist of the household chores, milking the cows, growing a vegetable garden, making butter, and selling dairy products, eggs and poultry on the market. 'Male work activities' were mostly connected with highly physical tasks, such as working in the woods and the usage of agricultural machinery, but also feeding livestock, except pigs and chickens, because this task belonged to women. The participation of men in the 'female work activities' as named in the literature, which entailed household chores, remained relatively small (for example, babysitting, very occasional cooking or cleaning the dishes, helping with rural tourism), while the opposite, that is, the participation of women in 'male work activities' on the farm, was much more common.[3] Vlado, born in 1953 in Široko village near Tolmin, described his involvement in 'female work activities' as following: 'There was no time. When I came home from work, I had to perform hard work on the farm'.

Oral history narratives point out some exceptions to the rule of a strict gender division of labour. Characteristics of the division of labour by gender based on male superiority and male power were not always maintained, since women also worked in agriculture and forestry, were trading, blacksmithing, doing field ploughing, driving tractors, and doing specific housework chores that required extraordinary physical strength and were demanding and dangerous. As stated by Ramšak (2003: 161), for each task that was considered exclusively male or female, many opposite examples can be found. Similar findings were pointed out by Makarovič (2002: 65), who stated that the notions of 'women's work' as value constructs are components of historical mentalities and include the types of work that women are supposed to be capable of and/or which they perform according to the traditional division of labour. The content of the concept of 'women's work' did not overlap with the work that women actually performed, as they have almost always also performed 'men's work'. However, 'men's tasks' on the farm were performed by all members, sometimes also by children, and 'female tasks' were mainly performed only by women (compare with Destovnik, 2002).

3 Our interlocutors would not refer to them in this way, but would use the expression 'women's work' or 'male work'.

When one or more members of the farm household became regularly employed outside agriculture, most of the work on the farm had to be done by other family members. Consequently, a new division of labour in the family emerged. The role of 'master' was usually taken over by a non-employed member; most often these were peasant women who, besides the role of mother and housewife, also took on the role of female master of the holding, regardless of the formal ownership of the land. Interlocutor Elizabeta worked on a farm and sold field crops on the market, while her husband was employed. Since her husband was not used to working with agricultural mechanization, she had to be resourceful and would drive the tractor, plough the fields, and use rotary tillers, while her husband would milk the cows and work in the field. The changes in the ways of working in farming techniques and its mechanization in the middle of the twentieth century, which shortened technological procedures, had a remarkable influence on the working identity and the peasant working mentality as well. In the process of mechanization on the farm, more and more women began to operate machinery. As Ludvik, a farmer, born in 1948 in Gornji grad near Upper Savinjska Valley, remembered:

> In large peasant families, there was a lot of work outside the house done by women. They were real heroines. They also worked with chainsaws. More than half of peasant housewives also operated machines – tractors and attachments. The hay was turned and dried by women driving a tractor with a tedder attached. I said to a colleague: 'She is better than us'.

As we can tell from this narrative, being able to operate machines brought women respect from their fellow male farmers. Iza, born in 1964 in Orehovo near Sevnica, a peasant, proudly recalled how she used a tractor while farming: 'I was working with a tractor mower and also I was mowing the grass by hand. When we got the tractor, I turned everything, put it together, picked it up and threw it on the drying rack. When my husband came home from work, I had already brought two loading trailers home and scattered everything'. At first Iza was extremely afraid of the tractor and did not want to drive it. Her husband Franci, a farmer and a doorman, born in Poklek nad Blanco in 1952, recalled: 'She was forced to. When we got married, I told her: "You have to learn to drive the tractor", and she replied: "I won't". I said: "Then you're going to carry a basket"'.

In the interviews, female interlocutors tried to express equality with men at work. In doing so, they proudly listed tasks that were considered stereotypically male to highlight how they were equal to the physically stronger gender. They expressed that they work 'as men', that is, more and harder. As Brandth (2002: 188) states, the cultural constructions of masculinity are expressed by the notion of masculine power and symbolized by agricultural mechanization. The division of labour emphasizes the predominant value of productive, hard work with heavy machines and the tractor functions as an important indicator of male gender identity. Mechanization is part of performing masculinity, and the tractor lets others know that a person possesses the qualities of a 'real man'. The tractor acts as a marker between male and female work on the farm and as such symbolizes and maintains the gender division of labour in farming (Brandth, 2006: 20-21).

Women who operated agricultural machinery on a daily basis, thus performing tasks that fell within the domain of men, broke with the traditional position of female peasants. The new peasant woman, who used mechanization on the farm, to a certain extent transformed the Slovenian rural collective imagination and social identity and created new expectations regarding the role of women. As stated by Brandth (2002: 194-195), in addition to the inclusion of peasant women in the labour market and generating the earning of female peasants outside the farm, changes in technological and work processes also helped men and women in peasant households to reposition themselves and for men to at least partially lose their position as absolute leaders of the patriarchally organized peasant family.

Although we can observe the active role of women within peasant families as being not only assistants in farm work, but also active managers on the farm, the peasant woman mostly remained 'invisible' to other family members and a wider society. Despite agricultural mechanization there was a lot of statistically invisible work on women's shoulders, which was usually unpaid and regarded as unimportant. According to Barbič (2000: 99), her roles as mother and housewife are not only taken for granted, but are seen as inseparable components of the female farmer's role as a work force on the farm. As stated by Brandth (2002: 184), peasant women do not have independent status; their occupational identity is weak and barely recognized. Accordingly, peasant women in farming are often unable to describe their work on the farm as a profession at all.

As observed by Brandth and Haugen (2010), peasant women were perceived as occupying the private sphere of the peasant household and according to many qualitative studies, agricultural statistics under-report women's work on the farm. As pointed out by Barbič, a female farmer who works only on the farm while other members are employed outside agriculture is often – even in statistical censuses – registered as a housewife (this is also the case in our statistic data), that is, as a dependent member, and she attributes the role of the master on the farm to her husband and not to herself. Thus, her work on the farm is merely 'informal', not only because she is not recognized as having a suitable role in agricultural production, but also because it does not guarantee her the rights deriving from paid work (Barbič, 1990: 130).

Although the position of peasant women in socialist Slovenia was characterized by the patriarchal character of gendered positions, the narratives of oral history presented here show that we must perceive peasant women as active agents who shaped the future of Slovenian family farming as there was always room for manoeuvre within the frame of the family farm. This situation seems to be aligned with the one pointed out by O'Hara (1998: 38), in which women's involvement in the work process on the family farm is not only a result of material and patriarchal power relations, but must be seen as a complex negotiation process that involved women in various relationships within the farm. Indeed, many of our female interlocutors have resisted their subordinate position in various ways, including by operating agricultural machinery. It implied that women were able to perform all farm work, which gave them a greater sense of autonomy and increased their self-reliance and confidence in their own abilities. They also felt empowered while talking about possessing qualities and statuses traditionally reserved for men and thus formulated new practices and discourses on gender division of labour.

V. Conclusions

The results of our study on peasant income integration in socialist Slovenia, carried out by combining written and oral sources as well as a quantitative and a qualitative approach, suggest that interlocutors' narratives strongly coincide with the general trend of Slovenian peasant economy in two important aspects. Firstly, in approximately three quarters of the interviews, at least one member of the family appears as working in a factory, while the results from Babič's survey, conducted on a much larger sample, indicate that in the early 1980s, in 59% of all cases, at least one core family member worked on the farm and at least one was employed outside. Data from public census surveys (Tables 9.1 and 9.3) also clearly indicate that incomes of peasant households since 1965 originated predominately from sources other than agriculture. Secondly, an interlocutor's narrative stating that since the 1960s, small farmers with off-farm employment enjoyed a better position than larger farmers, can be confirmed by evidence. His argument was that non-agricultural income from employment in addition to the work on the farm enabled small farmers to possess a better standard of living compared to farmers with larger estates, which were more time consuming and therefore prevented them from gaining additional income from off-farm employment. Indeed, Levstik's research group on the Slovenian semi-proletariat in the 1960s reached a similar conclusion (1964a: II – III). The same has been suggested also by Horvat on the Yugoslav level as a whole (Horvat – M. Kramer, 1974: 15). Moreover, as indicated by Table 9.2, at the end of socialist period (in 1991), part-time farmers were better equipped with tractors and livestock units than full-time farmers. It should be noted, however, that by 1991, part-time farmers (on average) also possessed more land (8.36 ha) than full-time farmers (7.40 ha).

If we take a look at all integrated peasant economy activities in socialist Slovenia according to sectors (primary, secondary, and tertiary), and if we compare the results from official statistical data research with narratives from interlocutors, we get the following picture.

In the primary sector, intensification of cultivation was present with the growing of hops, potatoes, wheat, buckwheat, maize, carrots, salad, beans, strawberries, and raspberries. Also, work in the form of wage day-labour in agriculture and longer-term farmhands at larger farms was performed on socially-owned farms with employed workers. Intensification of animal husbandry was also present with the breeding of cattle, pigs, horses, chickens, sheep, goats, rabbits, and donkeys. For comparison, Table 9.3 suggests that livestock breeding was a very profitable activity in Slovenia. Until 1960, livestock income accounted for the largest single share of all earnings. Afterwards, livestock accounted for the largest share of all on-farm earnings. The majority of interlocutors pointed out that they sold the surplus of their agricultural products to agricultural cooperatives, hospitals, taverns, and corporate canteens. Babič's research results similarly show that two-thirds of respondents were selling up to three agricultural products, but while as much as 96.5% were growing vegetables only 8.5% of all respondents were selling them.

In the secondary sector, the transformation of primary resources and products was performed by producing wine, apple juice, cheese, cream, butter, meat products (for example Upper-Savinja stomach), charcoal, lime, wood cutting, pork fat, yeast, and honey. Also, different rural crafts were performed, such as: carpentry, shoemaking, blacksmithing, weaving wooden baskets, making wooden sticks for picks and hoes, making carved artefacts from wood, making wooden spoons, producing wooden wheels for wooden carriages, bobbin lacemaking, producing roof tiles, etc. It needs to be pointed out that according to interlocutors' narratives, the presence of handicrafts was quite modest, which can also be observed in official public census surveys and Babič's research (see the results in Tables 9.3 and 9.4). An example of work in centred industries and plants was the profession of coal miner. Migrant and mobile craftsmen were also represented by bricklayers and their assistants, by painters, and also by farmers who went to other farms to saw planks with a handsaw.

As already emphasized, the most common off-farm activity in socialist Slovenia was wage labour in the industrial sector in the form of working in the factory in the nearest town (as a fork-lift driver, textile worker, etc.). In approximately three quarters of the interviews, at least one member of the family appears as working in a factory, which corresponds with data regarding off-farm employment from Tables 9.1 and 9.3, and Barbič's research as well. As concerns the land size of the farm estate, seventeen families in our sample had an estate smaller than 10 ha and five families larger than 10 ha. Oral history narratives reveal that some farmers with larger estates (more than 10, even 20 ha) also worked as wage labour in the industrial sector, not only those with smaller estates. However, we need to take into account that most of the land on large farm estates was covered by forest, which did not require as much work as farming in the field.

In part-time peasant households, in which their members were also receiving non-agricultural income in the form of wage labour, mostly men were employed. The fact that peasant women were employed in smaller numbers was reflected in the oral history narratives, as in our sample only four families included an employed peasant woman. Moreover, according to the data from the public census survey for the year 1991, in the part-time households, among the active members of the household, males accounted for as much as 61% of all who were economically active outside their holding, while at the residential farm households, this share was around 58% (Illić et al. 1994: 354), which shows a slightly higher proportion of women working on the farm only. With the increasing orientation of peasants towards acquiring income in the industrial sector, the working role of women as non-employed members on the farm became more emphasized and the gender division of labour within the individual peasant household changed. Because their husbands were working outside the farm and because the process of mechanization of farms intensified in the early 1970s, more women began to operate agricultural machinery. Consequently, they broke with the traditional position of female peasants and thus formulated new practices and discourses on gender division of labour while performing tasks that fell within the domain of men.

In the tertiary sector, under services in the field of long and medium distance trade we can place taverns, shops, butcher's shops, gas station workers, and road menders. Transport of other people's products and goods over short to medium distances was performed in the form of buying wood and reselling it to the Forest Administration (Slovenian *Gozdna uprava*) or buying fruit, charcoal, or lime from peasants and reselling it to the south of Yugoslavia. Also, buying olive oil in Primorska [Littoral] and reselling it, or buying and reselling cigarettes in Italy occurred. We can also place horse and cart drivers and truck drivers here. Trafficking with one's own products and goods over short to medium distances was performed by selling charcoal and baked lime at people's homes, selling wood, wooden beams, buying and reselling livestock, and selling vegetables, fruit, eggs, milk, and forest fruits on the nearest market or to the agricultural cooperative, hospitals, and corporate canteens. Smuggling also occurred in the buying of nylon socks, jeans, coffee, hair sprays, perfume, and tracksuits in Italy and smuggling them back to Slovenia. Migrant and mobile workers were also present in the form of migrational workers who went to work in Switzerland, Germany, Canada, America, Argentina, Australia, Libya, Sweden, or Italy. Also, Slovenian women living in Primorska were performing paid housework in Italy. Under the works of trust, we can list a postman. In the sector of tourism, we find rural tourism and also taverns as examples of integrated peasant economy activities in socialist Slovenia. But these activities were rare, only two families reported them. Similarly, Barbič's research data (Table 9.4) suggest that inn-keeping was marginal and tourism almost non-existent.

To discuss the functioning of the IPE system from the point of view of individual households and also of the impact of the peasant economy on macro tendencies we can point out that peasants had agency, were industrious, and took decisions about their own economy. The household economy came together through incomes from all three economic sectors: agriculture, manufacturing, and service. Peasants did not rely only on agriculture for their subsistence, but their household economy was an integrated economy that combined agriculture with market-oriented activities. By far the most common non-agrarian activity on the farm in socialist Slovenia, according to our research, was wage labour in the industrial sector, most often with peasants being employed in the factory in the nearest town. This activity was time consuming for farmers but it provided them with a regular monthly salary. We can also understand wage labour in the industrial sector as an activity which took place at the expense of the development of other non-agricultural activities, such as rural tourism or managing a tavern or a shop which were barely perceptible in our study.

To compare the results of our study with the IPE concept, we are delivering the Integrated peasant economy activities checklist for empirical comparisons (Table 9.5).

To discuss the concept further we would like to focus our attention once again on the importance of the exchange of mutual services in socialism, which could be placed into all three sectors in the IPE features. Many products were not paid in the form of money, but by an exchange of another product or by creating a favour in the form of mutual work assistance. Especially common among relatives, friends, and neighbours, mutual favours as services served not only as a survival safety net, but, with its moral and social dimensions, also as a way for people to meet and connect while forging alliances.

Funding

This research was carried out within the project *Concepts of peasant economy: a theoretical and empirical comparative approach (15th-20th c.)*, financed by the Slovenian Research and Innovation Agency (ARIS).

Table 9.5. IPE checklist according to the interviews on socialist-era Slovenia

Activity	Check
Primary sector	
Agricultural specialization	✓
Intensification of cultivation (no fallow, mixed-cropping, …)	✓
Wage day-labour in agriculture and longer-term farmhands on larger farms	✓
Extension/intensification of animal husbandry	✓
Intensification of forest exploitation (in primary sector, but also secondary and tertiary)	✓
Extension of cultivated land (reclamation of commons and woods)	✓
Quarries	✓
Fishing	✓
Secondary sector	
Transformation of primary resources/products (e.g. wine, cheese, meat products; charcoal, lime)	✓
Rural crafts	✓
Domestic, putting-out system (proto-industry)	–
Work in 'centralized' industries and plants (manufactures, mining, etc.)	✓
Migrant/mobile craftsmen (e.g. bricklayers)	✓
Wage labour in the industrial sector	✓
Tertiary sector	
Services in the field of long and medium distance trade (draft animal lease, fodder, lodging, inns)	✓
Transport of other people's products and goods over short to medium distances	✓
Trade with own products and goods over short to medium distances	✓
Peddling	✓
Smuggling	✓
Migrant/mobile workers (dock-workers etc.)	✓
Works of trust (estimation of land value, testimonies, etc.)	✓
Household, agricultural machine repair service and car repair service	✓
Tourism	✓
Inn/tavern keeping	✓

Source: Findings from thirty-five interviews.

Bibliography

Archival sources

SI, Republika Slovenia, Arhiv Republike Slovenije, AS 1589/III, CK ZKS, šk. 43, a. e. 1454, Dnevne informacije organizacijsko inštruktorske uprave CK ZKS, 1950.

Published sources

Čoh Kladnik, M. (2012), *Kulaški procesi v Sloveniji med letoma 1949 in 1951*, Ljubljana, Študijski center za narodno spravo.

Drnovšek, D. (2000), *Zapisniki Politbiroja CK KPS/ZKS 1945-1954*, Ljubljana, Arhivsko društvo Slovenije.

Ilić, M. (1994), *Results of Surveys. Census of the Population, Households, Housings and Agricultural Holdings in the Republic of Slovenia in 1991. Results by municipalities*, Ljubljana, Zavod Republike Slovenije za statistiko.

Mikola, M. (ed.) (2006), *Dokumenti in pričevanja o povojnih delovnih taboriščih v Sloveniji*. Ljubljana, Ministrstvo za pravosodje Republike Slovenije.

Statistični letopis Republike Slovenije 1990 (29), Ljubljana, Zavod Republike Slovenije za statistiko.

Bibliography

Barbič, A. (1990), *Kmetov vsakdan: Položaj in prihodnost družinskih kmetij na slovenskem*, Ljubljana, Cankarjeva založba.

——— (2000). 'Kmetica in kmečka družina v tranziciji: teoretična razmišljanja in empirične ugotovitve', *Družboslovne razprave*, 16, 34/35, pp. 97-125.

Beguš, I. (2017), 'Peasant Income Integration in Early Modern Slovenia: A Historiographical Review', Panjek, A., Larsson, J. and Mocarelli, L. (eds), *Integrated Peasant Economy in a Comparative Perspective: Alps, Scandinavia and Beyond*, Koper, Faculty of Humanities, University of Primorska, pp. 51-83.

Bokovoy, M. K. (2014), 'Collectivization in Yugoslavia: Rethinking Regional and National Interests', Iordachi, C., Bauerkämper, A. (eds), *The Collectivization of Agriculture in Communist Eastern Europe: Comparison and Entanglements*, Budapest, New York, CEU Press, pp. 293-328.

Brandth, B. (2002), 'Gender Identity in European Family Farming: A Literature Review', *Sociologia Ruralis*, 42, 3, pp. 181-200.

——— (2006), 'Agricultural body-building: Incorporations of gender, body and work', *Journal of Rural Studies*, 22, 1, pp. 17-27.

——— and Haugen, M. (2010), 'Doing farm tourism: the intertwining practices of gender and work', *Signs*, 35, 2, pp. 425-446.

Centrih, L. (2020), 'Polkmetje in socialistična država: integrirana kmečka ekonomija v Sloveniji v letih 1957-1965', *Prispevki za novejšo zgodovino*, 60, 2, pp. 152-167.

Čepič, Z. (1991), 'Povojni beg z zemlje. Notranje migracije v Sloveniji 1945-1960', *Zgodovinski časopis*, 1, 45, pp. 85-106.

——— (1995), *Agrarna reforma in kolonizacija v Sloveniji 1945-1948*, Maribor, Obzorja.

——— (1999), 'Oris pojavnih oblik kmetijske politike v letih 1945-1960', Čepič, Z. (ed.), *Preteklost sodobnosti: izbrana poglavja slovenske novejše zgodovine*, Ljubljana, Inštitut za novejšo zgodovino, pp. 175-188.

——— (2005), 'Spremembe v socialni sestavi', Borak, N. et al. (eds), *Slovenska novejša zgodovina. Od programa Zedinjena Slovenija do mednarodnega priznanja Republike Slovenije, 1848-1992*, Ljubljana, Inštitut za novejšo zgodovino, Mladinska knjiga, pp. 1132-1133.

———, Guštin, D. and Troha, N. (2017), *Slovenija v vojni 1941-1945*, Ljubljana, Modrijan.

Destovnik, I. (2002), *Moč šibkih: ženske v času kmečkega gospodarjenja*, Celovec, Založba Drava.

Horvat, B. and M. Kramer (1974), 'The Postwar Evolution of Yugoslav Agricultural Organization: Interaction of Ideology, Practise and Results', *Eastern European Economics*, XII, pp. 1-106.

——— (1989), *ABC jugoslavenskog socijalizma*, Zagreb, Globus.

——— (2016), *The political Economy of Socialism. A Marxist Social Theory*, London and New York, Routledge.

Hrobat Virloget, K. (2017), 'Peasant "Economic Industriousness" in Slovenian Ethnology (19th-20th Centuries)', Panjek, A., Larsson, J. and Mocarelli, L. (eds), *Integrated Peasant Economy in a Comparative Perspective: Alps, Scandinavia and Beyond*, Koper, Faculty of Humanities, University of Primorska, pp. 333-350.

Kautsky, K. (1988), *The Agrarian Question*, London, Zwan Publications.

Klemenčič, M. (1974), 'Socialna in ekonomska struktura mešanih delavsko – kmečkih gospodinjstev na kmečkih gospodarstvih. Problemi mešanih gospodinjstev v Sloveniji', *Geografski vestnik*, XLVI, pp. 61-74.

Klemenčič, V. (1965), 'Regionalni procesi in kmetijstvo v Sloveniji', *Teorija in praksa*, 4, pp. 604-614.

——— (1968), 'Problemi mešane strukture gospodinjstev in kmečkih gospodarstev v Sloveniji', *Geografski vestnik*, XL, pp. 19-52.

——— (1991), 'Tendence spreminjanja slovenskega podeželja', *Geografski vestnik*, 63, pp. 25-40.

Kovačič, M. (1983), *Tipi kmetij v Sloveniji in njihove značilnosti*, Ljubljana, Kmetijski inštitut Slovenije.

Lazarević, Ž. (2017), 'Peasant Economy in Interwar Slovenia – Policies of Income Diversification', Panjek, A., Larsson, J. and Mocarelli, L. (eds), *Integrated Peasant Economy in a Comparative Perspective: Alps, Scandinavia and Beyond*, Koper, Faculty of Humanities, University of Primorska, pp. 351-375.

——— (2018a), 'Integriranje dohodkov v kmečki ekonomiji v dobi industrializacije', Panjek, A. and Lazarević, Ž. (eds), *Preživetje in podjetnost. Integrirana kmečka ekonomija na Slovenskem od srednjega veka do danes*, Koper, Fakulteta za humanistične študije, Univerza na Primorskem, pp. 189-215.

——— (2018b), 'Kmetje in zasebni gospodarski interes po letu 1945', Ajlec, K., Balkovec, B. and Repe, B. (eds), *Nečak's Edited volume: Processes, Themes and Events from the 19th and 20th centuries*, Ljubljana, Znanstvena založba Filozofske fakultete, pp. 399-418.

Levstik, J. (1964), *Ekonomska in družbena problematika polproletariata v SR Sloveniji. Poročilo Skladu Borisa Kidriča*, 4. parts (cited as 1964a, b, c, d), Ljubljana, Kmetijski inštitut Slovenije and Biotehniška fakulteta Univerze v Ljubljani.

Lorenčič, A. (2012), *Prelom s starim in začetek novega. Tranzicija slovenskega gospodarstva iz socializma v kapitalizem, 1990-2004*, Ljubljana, Inštitut za novejšo zgodovino.

Makarovič, G. (2002), 'O vsebinah sintagme "žensko delo"', *Etnolog (Nova vrsta)*, 12, pp. 63-80.

Novak, M. (1996), 'Periferna agrarna transformacija; slovenski primer', Borak, N. and Lazarević, Ž. (eds), *Prevrati in slovensko gospodarstvo v XX. stoletju: 1918-1945-1991*, Ljubljana, Cankarjeva založba, pp. 23-35.

O'Hara, P. (1998), *Partners in Production? Women, Farm and Family in Ireland*, Oxford, Berghahn Books.

Panjek, A. (2017), 'The Integrated Peasant Economy as a Concept in Progress', Panjek, A., Larsson, J. and Mocarelli, L. (eds), *Integrated Peasant Economy in a Comparative Perspective: Alps, Scandinavia and Beyond*, Koper, Faculty of Humanities, University of Primorska, pp. 11-49.

Portelli, A. (1981), 'The peculiarities of oral history', *History Workshop*, 12, pp. 96-107.

Prinčič, J. (1999), *V začaranem krogu. Slovensko gospodarstvo od nove ekonomske politike do velike reforme 1955-1970*, Ljubljana, Cankarjeva založba.

Ramšak, M. (2003), *Portret glasov: Raziskave življenjskih zgodb v etnologiji – na primeru koroških Slovencev*, Ljubljana, Društvo za proučevanje zgodovine, antropologije in književnosti.

Ritchie, D. A. (1995), *Doing Oral History*, New York, Twayne Publishers.

Thompson, P. (2000), *The Voice of the Past: Oral History*, Oxford, New York, Oxford University Press.

Sitar, P. (2020), 'Workers becoming tourists and consumers: social history of tourism in socialist Slovenia and Yugoslavia', *Journal of Tourism History*, 3, 12, pp. 254-274.

Swain, N. (2014), 'Eastern European Collectivization Campaigns Compared, 1945-1962', Iordachi, C., Bauerkämper, A. (eds), *The Collectivization of Agriculture in Communist Eastern Europe: Comparison and Entanglements*, Budapest, New York, CEU Press, pp. 497-534.

Thomson, A. (2005), 'Anzac Memories', Perks, R. and Thomson, A. (eds), *The Oral History Reader*, London, New York, Routledge, pp. 300-310.

Vadnal, K. (1979), 'Neki vidovi feminizacije slovenačke inokosne poljoprivrede', *Sociologija sela*, 63-64, pp. 35-48.

Varga, Z. (2013), 'Conflicts and compromises between the Hungarian socialist state and the peasantry: contextualising the "Hungarian agricultural miracle"', Moser, P., Varley, T. (eds), *Integration through Subordination: The Politics of Agricultural Modernisation in Industrial Europe*, Turnhout, Brepols, pp. 203-222.

Veselinov, D. (1987), *Sumrak seljaštva*, Beograd, Ekonomika.

Visković Razpotnik, N. and Serućnik, M. (2013), 'Ugled kmečkega poklica in polkmetov v slovenski družbi po drugi svetovni vojni', *Geografski vestnik*, 1, 85, pp. 25-36.